TRISHA BROWN : DANCE AND ART IN DIALOGUE , 1961–2001

TRISHA BROWN : DANCE AND ART
IN DIALOGUE , 1961–2001

1	2	3	4	5	6	7
start Place facing	facing	# of Travel steps	TRAVEL steps	Level	Beats TRAVEL	altered (BY)
1-15	1-8	1-5	skip Jump GALLOP Hop walk Run step Roll CRAWL SLide Leap turn	sit floor stand knees ABove stand 1-5	1-5 still slow med fast very fast	Add subtract multiply

DN stg.

1 2 3 4 5
6 7 8 9 10
11 12 13 14 15
DN stg.
proSc.   prosc

15	16	17	18	19	20
Plane	Plane Degree 1-5	Beats	altered (BY)	BY	Parts Relationship
sugital Sagital Lateral " vertical "	front Back Left Right Right left	1-5	1-5	+ − × ÷	0 ½ 1 2 3 4 5	simultaneous overlap separate

Looking DN on

vertial

lateral

sagital

FRONT Lateral

LEG 5

arm

vertical & SAGITAL

8	9	10	11	12	13	14
by	arriving	# of Actors	actions	# of Parts	Parts	which
0	1-15	1-5	Bend	1-5	Head	Right
1			straighten		Neck	Left
2			Hold		chest	Both
1			lower		shoulder	
2			raise		pelvis	
3			Turn/		torso	
4			rotate		upper arm	
5			swing		lwr. arm	
					whole arm	
					wrist	
					Hand	
					elbo	
					upper leg	
					lower leg	
					whole leg	
					knee	
					ankle	
					foot	
					whole Body	
					1-19	

PROSC

PROSC

1	2	3	4	5
6	7	8	9	10
11	12	13	14	15

21

DUSG

tional
relation
ship

ter face w/
ccompany
ide
Support
copy
Callide
Conceal

TRISHA BROWN : DANCE AND ART
IN DIALOGUE , 1961–2001 / ROLAND AESCHLIMANN /
NANCY GRAVES / DONALD JUDD / FUJIKO NAKAYA /
ROBERT RAUSCHENBERG / TERRY WINTERS /
EDITED BY HENDEL TEICHER /

ESSAYS BY MAURICE BERGER / GUILLAUME BERNARDI /
TRISHA BROWN / MARIANNE GOLDBERG / DEBORAH JOWITT/
KLAUS KERTESS / LAURENCE LOUPPE / STEVE PAXTON /
YVONNE RAINER / HENDEL TEICHER /

PUBLISHED BY THE ADDISON GALLERY OF AMERICAN ART,
PHILLIPS ACADEMY, ANDOVER, MASSACHUSETTS /
DISTRIBUTED BY THE MIT PRESS, CAMBRIDGE, MASSACHUSETTS,
AND LONDON, ENGLAND /

TRISHA BROWN : DANCE AND ART IN DIALOGUE, 1961–2001

Trisha Brown: Dance and Art in Dialogue, 1961–2001 is made possible by a major gift from Oscar Tang, in memory of Frances Young Tang (Abbot Academy, Class of 1957; Skidmore College, Class of 1961). Additional support has been generously provided by The Andy Warhol Foundation for the Visual Arts, Inc., the Fifth Floor Foundation, J. Mark Rudkin, and the Sun Hill Foundation. The recreation of *Opal Loop/Cloud Installation #72503* by Fujiko Nakaya is supported by the Asian Cultural Council.

EXHIBITION DATES

Addison Gallery of American Art, Phillips Academy,
Andover, Massachusetts
September 27–December 31, 2002

The Tang Teaching Museum and Art Gallery at
Skidmore College, Saratoga Springs, New York
April 5–June 22, 2003

Contemporary Arts Museum, Houston, Texas
July 12–September 14, 2003

New Museum of Contemporary Art,
New York, New York
October 10, 2003–February 10, 2004

Henry Art Gallery, University of Washington,
Seattle, Washington
March 25–July 18, 2004

Library of Congress Cataloging-in-Publication Data
Trisha Brown/Dance and Art in Dialogue, 1961–2001/
edited by Hendel Teicher.
   p. cm.
  Includes bibliographic references (p.).
  ISBN 0-262-20139-9 (hc : alk. paper)
  1. Brown, Trisha, 1936-—Criticism and interpretation.
  2. Choreographers—United States. 3. Dancers—United
  States. I. Title: Trisha Brown. II. Teicher, Hendel.

  GV1795.B76 T75 2003
  792.8′2′0973–dc21   2002016500

Cover: Trisha Brown, *Glacial Decoy,* 1979. Set and costumes by Robert Rauschenberg. Pictured: Trisha Brown, Nina Lundborg. Photograph by Babette Mangolte.
Frontispiece: Trisha Brown, Two pages from choreographic notebook, 1990–91. Pencil on paper, 11 3/4 x 16 1/2 in. (29.8 x 41.9 cm). Collection of Trisha Brown.

Note on the Illustrations: Unless otherwise noted, choreography and visual presentation of dances is by Trisha Brown. Date in caption is that of choreography. Persons shown are listed from left to right.

Editor: Joseph N. Newland, Q.E.D.
Designer: 2x4, New York City
Printed and bound in Singapore by Eurasia Press.

FOREWORD

IN THE LAST PARAGRAPH OF TRISHA BROWN'S ESSAY FOR THIS VOLUME, "How to Make a Modern Dance When the Sky's the Limit," she writes about a rehearsal of *L'Orfeo*, the Monteverdi opera she directed in 1998:

Opposite page: *Man Walking Down the Side of a Building*, 1970. Pictured: Joseph Schlichter. Photograph by Caroline Goodden.

> When I walked out into the center of my studio to improvise Orfeo's speech to Caronte in the monumental aria "Possente Spirito," I had sorted out my identity. I was both Orfeo asking for permission to enter Hades and the words he sang. I was primed with music, text, poetry systems, literature. I was the faithful shepherd (Guarini, Il Pastor fido), the Spirit was with me and, most of all, I also could arpeggiate my body in the clear place of a compositional mind that does operate on its own when Trisha is busy with a handful of other aesthetic concerns. I knew, at that moment, the long haul of my apprenticeship in choreography was over.

This is a remarkable admission for a choreographer/dancer of such extraordinary accomplishment who has plied her art for forty years, created more than eighty-five pieces, and presented them in thousands of performances in more than a dozen countries. For her to feel that she had just finished her apprenticeship reveals how Brown's attitude and approach is that of a perpetual learner, an individual who takes nothing for granted other than discovery itself. Brown has investigated the fundamental characteristics of movement—gravity, weightlessness, duration, sequence, and repetition. She has questioned the relationships among kinetic, aural, visual, and verbal experience. Her works have reconsidered the relationships between the audience and the performer, the viewer and the viewed, the everyday and the exceptional, the perceptual and the visceral, and, common to all of these, art and life.

Brown began her career presenting works in galleries, museums, and lofts as well as small theaters. In the 1960s the difference between the performative and the visual was less evident and perhaps less significant. Brown's concerns were allied to those of visual artists such as Robert Whitman and Robert Rauschenberg. While she largely identified herself as a dancer, her artistic practice at that time belonged to a unified field of artistic experimentation. Although it is not common for museums to present an exhibition devoted to dance, it is fitting that Brown's work now returns to the museum for consideration, appraisal, and enjoyment. It is also appropriate that the two museums that have instigated this examination are teaching museums set within academies of higher education. Just as examination, experimentation, and intuition are key to Brown's approach, so too are these means central to teaching museums. Our institutions do not exist simply to confer and confirm "greatness," but to question what makes something great, to test assumptions, received knowledge, and accepted attitudes. The Addison Gallery of American Art and The Tang Teaching Museum and Art Gallery are laboratories of visual culture. They are integral parts of a larger, multidisciplinary endeavor. Accordingly, the visual arts are not treated in isolation but in the context of other studies.

Trisha Brown is an exemplary teacher who has taught or influenced not only generations of dancers but also, through her collaborative process, visual artists, singers, composers, filmmakers, and writers. As alluded to at the beginning of this introduction, it is her attitude of learning—from others, from process, and from herself—that sets Brown apart: her powers of observation; her ability to challenge herself and simultaneously trust her own process; her desire to draw from remembered experience and to confront the challenges and possibilities of the present moment. She takes inherently problematic concepts such as ambiguity, contradiction, unpredictability, incompatibility, instability, disorder, and the peripheral and turns them into opportunities for invention and creation. Brown's approach is a lesson for us all, but it is particularly crucial for a younger generation that is increasingly confronted with a complex, global, electronically driven society. For them to experience the fundamental and essential simplicity of invention itself as well as the risks and rewards of collaboration is critical. These accomplishments are not achieved of course without tremendous commitment, sacrifice, and hard work. One might think because of the emphasis on experiment, intuition, and vernacular movement that "anything goes" in Trisha Brown's work. As she has said, "People think dancers are very free spirits up there, but they're not. They're perfectionists, they're disciplined." This too is her lesson.

This book and the exhibition it accompanies are themselves risks, improvisations, and contradictions in terms. How does one make Brown's collaborations with artists come alive minus dancers performing in real time? How is the ephemeral made perpetual? How does one convincingly reconstitute the past without historicizing, aggrandizing, and losing its spirit? This has been the challenge and long-time preoccupation of Hendel Teicher. Teicher—who began to formulate the concept for this project more than a decade ago—has thought, worked, collaborated, improvised, and now ultimately created a remarkable pair of parallel projects that each in its own way reveals the headiness, energy, determination, and ingenuity of Trisha Brown and her collaborators. As Brown has written, "If one is working with form and not formula, then the ideas take a visual presence in mind and one must find a method to decant that vision." We are grateful to Teicher for doing just that and, for her fortitude in bringing these projects to fruition. Teicher's search for form was greatly aided by the projects' designers, 2x4. Susan Sellers in association with Alex Ching and Alice Chung enthusiastically and deftly worked on the design for the book and exhibition under enormous constraints of time and budget. The visual spark of both is due to their efforts. We would also like to acknowledge the tireless commitment of two other individuals—Elizabeth Finch, research assistant to Hendel Teicher, whose exacting, patient, exhaustive research and confirmation of information have helped to make this the definitive volume on Brown's work; and Joseph N. Newland, whose guidance in the organization of the book and careful editing have given this complex volume a seamless dignity.

The realization of this project was handled with great energy and commitment by the staffs of both museums. We would like to recognize in particular from the Addison Gallery, BJ Larson, Director of Museum Resources, whose efforts coordinating the exhibition and book have been nothing short of herculean; Les Maloney, Chief Preparator, whose involvement with design, construction, and logistics was essential; Juliann McDonough, Curatorial

Associate, whose perseverance and focus on detail were critical to the realization of the book; Denise Johnson, Registrar and Financial Administrator, whose oversight and advice guided us in the complex relationship with our many partners; Jennifer Mergel, Curatorial Fellow, whose total immersion in and commitment to obtaining loans and assisting with all aspects of the installation was invaluable; John Sirois, who took the utmost care in the construction and reconstruction of exhibition sets and furnishings; Louann Boyd, who handled all the travel arrangements with alacrity and aplomb; and Elizabeth Kelton, who was cheerfully available to help assist with both the catalogue and the exhibition. From the Tang Museum we would like to acknowledge Chris Kobuskie, Preparator, who assisted with many of the nuts and bolts of the exhibition's technology; Gayle King, Assistant to the Dayton Director; Ian Berry, Curator; Barbara Rhoades, Registrar; and Helaina J. Blume, Designer and Special Projects Coordinator.

The administrative staff of the Trisha Brown Dance Company have made tremendous expenditures of time and effort to ensure realization of this project while simultaneously finding a new home for the company and keeping up its regular, already exhausting level of activity. We are deeply appreciative to LaRue Allen, Executive Director; Jodi White, Company Manager; and Laura Hymers, Director of Education and Outreach, for their help with research, loans, and involvement with the residencies that accompany the exhibition. They have been generous partners.

The early support of museum directors and curators who quickly and wholeheartedly signed on to participate in the tour of the exhibition cannot be underestimated. We are greatly indebted to Marti Mayo, Director, Contemporary Arts Museum, Houston; Richard Andrews, Director, and Robin Held, Assistant Curator of the Henry Art Gallery, University of Washington, Seattle; and Lisa Phillips, Director, New Museum of Contemporary Art, New York.

This exhibition and book could never have come to life without the vision, risk taking, and belief of an exceptional group of funders and friends of both the Addison and Tang museums. A project such as this is always satisfying—if not trying—yet it is made all the more gratifying by the confidence and enthusiasm of wonderful and thoughtful funders. We are especially indebted to Oscar and Argie Tang for their generous and major support; to Susan Malloy of the Sun Hill Foundation and Mark J. Rudkin for their substantial commitment to the project; and to the Andy Warhol Foundation for the Visual Arts, Inc., the Fifth Floor Foundation, and the Asian Cultural Council for their generosity.

Lastly, we would like to thank Trisha Brown, who, thank God, realized early on that "the modern choreographer has the right to make up the WAY that he/she makes a dance." We are grateful for her commitment, clarity, patience, and generosity of spirit.

Adam D. Weinberg
The Mary Stripp and R. Crosby Kemper Director,
Addison Gallery of American Art, Phillips Academy

Charles Stainback
Dayton Director,
The Tang Teaching Museum and Art Gallery
at Skidmore College

ACKNOWLEDGMENTS

TRISHA BROWN: DANCE AND ART IN DIALOGUE, 1961–2001 has been an enormous undertaking that could never have been accomplished without the help and good will of many people. First and foremost, I thank Trisha Brown for believing in this project and for sticking with me through all of the many details and demands it required. She has been astoundingly generous with her time and knowledge, and it is an understatement to say that she is a great collaborator. Closely following Trisha's choreography for many years has meant immersing myself in the work of the artists she admires. This exhibition features Trisha's main collaborators in the visual arts over the last twenty years: Nancy Graves, Donald Judd, Fujiko Nakaya, Robert Rauschenberg, and Terry Winters. I am profoundly grateful to all of the artists that comprise Trisha's artistic world, past and present. I also wish to acknowledge Roland Aeschlimann, an accomplished and innovative stage designer who has been Trisha Brown's primary collaborator in the world of opera. All of the projects they have worked on together are represented in this catalogue.

Documenting dance is an art in its own right, and there have been a few remarkable photographers and videographers who have vividly captured Trisha's practice and her collaborations. I wish in particular to acknowledge Burt Barr, Babette Mangolte, Joanne Savio, and the late Peter Moore. I am also indebted to Barbara Moore, who has nurtured an archive of documents and images that have been invaluable to this project. Keeping track of an artist's work is an essential link from the past to the present. At the Robert Rauschenberg studio, I thank David White and his staff for their diligence and generosity. At the Nancy Graves Foundation, I was happy to meet and work with Linda Kramer, who thoughtfully guides the foundation, and her helpful staff.

This book is intended as a collective portrait of the dancer, choreographer, and woman Trisha Brown, and it has been realized through a variety of approaches. I offer my thanks to the essayists: Maurice Berger, Guillaume Bernardi, Marianne Goldberg, Deborah Jowitt, Klaus Kertess, and Laurence Louppe. Working from different perspectives, all of these writers, either directly or indirectly, have been "collaborators" with Trisha Brown over the years in the degree to which their scholarship has shared her passions and pursuits. In addition, two of Trisha Brown's peers, Steve Paxton and Yvonne Rainer, have provided candid and personal reminiscences of the intense creative atmosphere out of which her work emerged. Trisha Brown has also joined this discussion by contributing an essay that knits together her collaborative experiences through the years. I sought the comments of many other people who have worked with and been close to Trisha over the last forty years. Although any such collage of voices remains by definition incomplete, I am grateful to the following people for speaking with me about Trisha, writing comments for this book, and/or contributing images: Louisa (Brown) Adams, Laurie Anderson, Robert Ashley, Burt Barr, Mikhail Baryshnikov, Mel Bochner, Gordon Brown, Spencer Brown, Alvin Curran, Dave Douglas, Merce Cunningham, Simone

Forti, Bryant Hayes, Simon Keenlyside, Susan Klein, Carolyn Lucas, Diane Madden, Elizabeth Murray, Graciela Oddone, Stephen Petronio, Salvatore Sciarrino, Judith Shea, Jane Sherman, Annette Stricker, Billy Sullivan, Ken Tabachnick, Jennifer Tipton, Coosje van Bruggen, Robert Whitman, and Peter Zummo. As such a collage suggests, the editor of this book had a monumental task, and I am deeply grateful to Joseph N. Newland, who has done a fantastic job. I thank Jeanine Herman for her translation of the Laurence Louppe essay.

Adam D. Weinberg, the Director of the Addison Gallery of American Art, was an early champion of the idea of bringing Trisha Brown's dance together with the art of her collaborators in an exhibition. I couldn't have wished for a better partner in this project. I am grateful to Adam for his enthusiasm, determination, and unfailing ability to see his work in a larger context. It has also been a great pleasure to work with the staff of the Addison Gallery of American Art. I am thankful for the contributions of each of its members and, in particular, wish to acknowledge BJ Larson, Director of Museum Resources, who guided and oversaw a complex project with a remarkable sense of efficiency and flexibility. Charles A. Stainback, the Dayton Director of The Tang Teaching Museum and Art Gallery, has been a crucial part of this endeavor. I am especially grateful for his keen ability to recognize the interdisciplinary potential of this exhibition and its related programs. I was extremely fortunate to work with a thoughtful and efficient research assistant, Elizabeth Finch, who helped me with many aspects of this project. Susan Sellers, with her team at 2x4, envisioned intelligent and sensitive designs for the book and the exhibition.

Finally, close to home, I am deeply grateful to my friend Trisha and her New York family, Burt Barr and Adam Brown. It has been an eventful and enriching journey, which could not have been completed without the support of Terry Winters, who shared with me all its surprises and gifts.

Hendel Teicher

Following spread: *Roof Piece*, 1971. 53 Wooster Street to 381 Lafayette Street, New York City. Photograph by Babette Mangolte.

GRAVITY'S RAINBOW
MAURICE BERGER

IN APRIL 1970, TRISHA BROWN STRAPPED A MALE DANCER into a mountaineering harness and sent him walking down the façade of a seven-story building at 80 Wooster Street in Manhattan. The now-legendary dance piece, *Man Walking Down the Side of a Building*, contained no tricks or illusions. As the man made his way down—arms at his sides, his straight legs moving perpendicular to the building, an assistant on the roof slowly letting out the rope that held him—the radically altered relationship of his body to gravity only served to draw attention to the simple mechanics of walking. His powerful body in motion, as Brown would later observe, illustrated the "paradox of one action working against another... gravity working one way on the body... a naturally walking person in another way."[1] More than just an analytical exercise, the work was also an awesomely beautiful and challenging performance. With each fantastic step, the man dared his audience on the ground to question their perceptions of a reality that seemed almost impossible.

To understand the radical nature of *Man Walking Down the Side of a Building*, we might consider a series of celebrated performances in which a man descended from the roof of a building: Yves Klein's *Leap Into the Void* (1960). On the surface, Klein's descent was far more audacious, for he did not simply march down buildings with the aid of ropes and equipment. He jumped off of them. Some of these "leaps" were faked, such as the famous photomontage of Klein's birdlike dive from the roof of a Paris apartment building. Others were brutally real, resulting in broken bones and other serious injuries. If Brown's work epitomized the innovations of postmodern dance—the concentration on simple tasks, props, and movements; the rejection of narratives, storytelling, and theatrical illusionism; the full acceptance of the complexity and limits of the human body in motion—Klein's performances merely reiterated modernism's long-standing fascination with symbolism, surreality, and metaphor. The *Leap Into the Void* exemplified Klein's multivalent aesthetic mission, reflecting both his desire for spiritual freedom and alchemical transformation (an idea rooted in his allegiance to the Rosicrucian teachings of Max Heindel) and his obsession with the interrelationship between sexuality, violence, and death. Unlike Brown's interest in the mechanics of the moving body, the physical act of the leap itself was less important to Klein than achieving the perfect, evocative moment—the metaphoric instant when the mind and eye would be fooled into believing the unbelievable or rudely awakened by the thud of his muscular body hitting the ground.

The most significant difference between *Leap Into the Void* and *Man Walking Down the Side of a Building* lay in their divergent relationship to gravity. While gravity was for Klein an earthly encumbrance to be transcended or a violent, transgressive force, it had become for Brown and many of her dance-world contemporaries a natural variable to be explored, analyzed, and challenged. Brown did not simply succumb to gravity's pull. She played with it, resisted it, only to accept its inevitability. In the duet *Lightfall* (1963), for example, Brown

Opposite page: Spectators in a courtyard at 80 Wooster Street, New York, attending the performance of *Man Walking Down the Side of a Building*, 1970. Photograph by Peter Moore.

1. Trisha Brown quoted in Anne Livet, ed., *Contemporary Dance* (New York: Abbeville Press, 1978), p. 51. I would like to thank Beth Finch for her assistance in tracking down information about this performance as well as other of Brown's works.

and Steve Paxton took turns leaping onto each other's backs and sliding off as their partner changed position. *La Chanteuse* (1963) called for Brown to assume ballet's fourth position only to fall out of it and slowly topple to the ground. *Falling Duet [I]* (1968) consisted of Brown and Barbara Lloyd repeatedly falling onto the stage until they were too tired to continue. In *Pamplona Stones* (1974) the dancer Sylvia Palacios (then Whitman) dropped a large rock onto the stage as Brown, in a forceful shout, vainly commanded it to stop in midair. *Set and Reset* (1983), a work with sets by Robert Rauschenberg and music by Laurie Anderson, called for dancers to repeatedly fall and get up in "slow motion, at odd angles, and in sweeping moves" while the dancer Diane Madden "walked" on a brick wall, held aloft by four strong dancers. Even the elegant allusion to skydiving in *Planes* (1968)—achieved by projecting aerial footage onto a wall being scaled by dancers (their strenuous labor assisted by foot holds)—was broken at the work's end, when the exhausted dancers rapidly climbed down to the stage.

Brown's embrace of gravity was part of a broader cultural zeitgeist both in dance and in the visual arts, disciplines that over the past half-century have looked to each other for ideas and inspiration.[2] When Jackson Pollock placed the canvas on the floor to create his first drip painting in 1947, he presaged a major reorientation of the art object and its production from the vertical to the horizontal axis. Pollock's active, almost choreographic painting process—his expressive body dancing around and onto the horizontal canvas surface, his gesticulating arms dripping and splashing paint—worked along with the natural pull of gravity. Several years later, Robert Rauschenberg challenged the traditional, vertical orientation of painting when he splattered paint onto his quilt-covered bed, which he upended and transformed into a work of art (*Bed*, 1955). In the early 1960s, the paintings of Andy Warhol and Roy Lichtenstein referenced pop imagery taken directly from the printed page, thus associating the vertical plane of the canvas surface with the horizontal coordinates of the magazine layout or the comic book. The minimal and installation art and the earthworks of the 1960s and '70s intensified this shift from the vertical to the horizontal axis, from sculptures composed of liquid latex, molten lead, or soil poured or tossed onto the gallery floor to land-reclamation projects that called for passageways and paths to be cut directly into the earth.

Brown's analytical conception of gravity extended, as well, to her understanding of the human body. She treated the body as she treated gravity, as something to be respected, challenged, and explored. In *Leap Into the Void*, as in modernist dance and performance in general, Yves Klein took authority over the body, subjecting it to the preemptive (and, in his case, self-destructive) process of representing other things or sensibilities in the world. Brown, on the other hand, allowed her dancers—and herself—to analyze and celebrate the strength, logic, and endurance of the body in its own right and in relationship to the natural forces around it. From at least the time she studied with Robert Dunn, in the legendary class he taught at the Cunningham studio in 1961, she has been committed to freeing the dancer from the "restrictions and rules of what [she] perceived as an older, more rigid generation" of dancing.[3] Dunn opened up the analysis of choreographic form and movement to the individual needs, tastes, and limitations of his students. Rather than looking for correct answers to the problems he set, he was interested in the "individual solutions his students discovered for themselves and helping them to understand what they created."[4] As Brown later recalled:

After presenting a dance, each choreographer was asked, "How did you make that dance?" The students were inventing form rather than using the traditional theme and development or narrative, and the discussion that followed applied non-evaluative criticism to the movement itself.... The procedure illuminated the interworkings of the dances and minimized value judgments of the choreographer, which for me meant permission, permission to go ahead and do what I wanted to do or had to do.[5]

Whether performing a duet with a skateboard in an Ann Arbor, Michigan, parking lot (*Motor*, 1965) or asking performers to dress in a horizontal position while suspended from a lattice-work of pipes and hanging clothes (*Floor of the Forest*, 1970), Brown gave the dancer permission to explore the considerable possibilities of invention, instinct, and self-expression. In her able hands, the symbolic or metaphoric body of modernism was replaced with an active, democratized conception of the body, one that regarded dancers as full "players" in the choreographic process "rather than tools or robots."[6]

While Brown's conception of the active, emancipated body never quite extended to the politically activist body—she has consistently avoided overt social content in her work—it was, to a certain degree, commensurate with the liberationist politics of its day, the politics of equality, civil and worker rights, and sexual liberation. A more recent work, *Another Story as in Falling* (1993), offers important insight into this relationship. The work called for repetitive, somber dancing that was nearly devoid of the "springy vocabulary" and fluidity of movement that have exemplified Brown's style. Dancers in baggy suits marched flatly across a spare, gray set, their uniformity and deflated postures meant to personify the "Little Man," as Brown would say, the millions of "everyday Joes plodding quietly through their separate lives."[7] An aura of sadness permeated the work, a pathos intensified by the underlying tension between proximity and isolation, between the sterile interaction of worker drones and the reality that they will always remain emotionally alienated from one another. In retrospect, *Another Story as in Falling* reads both as a defiant, heartbreaking picture of a world of youthful, vital bodies beaten down by the interests of the state or the corporation and a testament to how far Brown had come in her then thirty-year struggle to liberate the body from the oppressive forces of art and life.

This struggle, joined by many of Brown's dance-world contemporaries, was embraced as well by visual artists. But if the choreographer wished to unshackle the dancer, visual artists of the 1960s and '70s placed much of their emphasis on the viewer. Their work—in the form of Minimalist sculpture, earthworks, and conceptual, installation, and video art—actively challenged the traditional relationship between a fixed and static art object and a fixated and static spectator. In a kind of parallel to Brown's gravity-bound, antisymbolic approach to the dancer's body, they relieved the art object of the task of representing other objects or things in the world, thus avoiding psychological or narrative references that would get in the way of the spectator's phenomenological exploration. The shifting aesthetic terrain of the period offered many such experiences: viewers stepped through a mirrored doorway that reflected their every move (Robert Morris, *Passageway*, 1961), or followed a spiral path onto the Great Salt Lake in Utah (Robert Smithson's *Spiral Jetty*, 1970), or tracked their own progress on a video monitor as they walked down a narrow, claustrophobic passageway (Bruce Nauman, *Live Taped Video Corridor*, 1969–70).[8] In the context of these

Opposite page from top: Robert Rauschenberg, *Bed*, 1955. Combine painting: oil and pencil on pillow, quilt, and sheet, supports on wood, 75 1/4 x 31 1/2 x 6 1/2 in. (191.1 x 80.0 x 16.5 cm). The Museum of Modern Art, New York, Gift of Leo Castelli in honor of Alfred H. Barr, Jr., 1989.

Yves Klein's *Leap Into the Void* pictured on the front page of his *Dimanche, le journal d'un seul jour* (Sunday, the one-day newspaper), 27 November 1960. Four pages, 21 5/8 x 15 in. (55 x 38 cm). Collection of Robert Pincus-Witten.

2. Brown's long-standing collaboration with visual artists underscores the extent to which the aesthetic, philosophical, and ideological imperatives of progressive art, dance, and performance have been intertwined over the past half-century, from the Happenings of Allan Kaprow and the street performances of Adrian Piper to the films of Shirin Neshat and Matthew Barney. The work of the Judson Dance Theater in New York, an early and seminal home to Brown and other groundbreaking choreographers of the mid-1960s, proved particularly generative and influential to visual artists who looked to the new dance as a source of ideas, both formal and ideological. Robert Morris and Carolee Schneemann, for example, though known primarily as visual artists, choreographed dance pieces for the Judson that greatly influenced the sensibility and direction of their oeuvre. For more on their relationship to the new dance, see Sally Banes, *Democracy's Body: Judson Dance Theater, 1962–1964* (Durham, N.C.: Duke University Press, 1995), pp. 147–49, 172–74, 177–78, 197–98, 213, and 209; and Maurice Berger, *Labyrinths: Robert Morris, Minimalism, and the 1960s* (New York: Harper & Row, 1989).
3. Banes, *Democracy's Body*, p. 20.
4. Ibid.
5. Brown quoted in Livet, *Contemporary Dance*, p. 45.
6. Steve Paxton in his "Brown in the New Body," in this volume.
7. My description and analysis of Brown's *Another Story as in Falling* is indebted to Deborah Jowitt's "Redefining Virtuosity: Trisha Brown in the Eighties and Nineties," in this volume.

works, spectators behaved more like performers engaged in odd, somewhat decentering aesthetic tasks. The perceptual experience of walking down Nauman's corridor, for example, allowed viewers to see themselves in an entirely outer-directed and unnatural way: videotaped from behind as they moved forward in space. In each case, the eye and mind were momentarily set free from the deeply rooted preconceptions, habits, and expectations that normally prescribe one's interaction with the world.

Brown's dances similarly counterpoised the basic forces of their craft—the body and gravity—in ways that tested viewers' perceptions about their own physical and psychic bearing relative to what they were seeing and experiencing. The convoluted relationship of the dancer's body to gravity in *Man Walking Down the Side of a Building*, for example, was also destabilizing to the viewer. The unnatural angle through which viewers observed a man walking toward them—their heads tilted sharply backward, their eyes gazing seven stories upward—underscored the distance between the conventional orientation and functioning of their bodies in the world and the absurdity of the experience at hand. Ultimately, only by understanding the mechanics and limitations of their own bodies—the give and take of the muscles in relationship to gravity, the psychology of fear, the potential of physical strength and endurance—could viewers grasp the relatively simple, but no less extraordinary, mechanics of the dancer's feat and of Brown's art.

Brown has always encouraged this empathic relationship, eschewing the kind of stylized, theatrical movement that distances dancer from audience. She breathed new life and meaning into ordinary movements, turning simple actions like sitting, running, or putting on one's clothes into fluid, exuberant variations on a theme. In an early dance improvisation from 1960 she pushed a broom with such force that she lifted herself energetically into the air. In *Walking on the Wall*, a work performed at the Whitney Museum of American Art in 1971, she suspended dancers from cables attached to the ceiling and sent them walking and running parallel to the floor. And in *If you couldn't see me* (1994), she turned her back to the audience and danced a breathless ten-minute solo of twists, darts, and jumps. To watch one of Brown's dances is to learn much about one's own body, to understand its energy, its expressive potential, and its limits. If the choreographer has created an aesthetic that allows her to explore and "further access her [own] physicality," she has done so with the full intention of inviting her audience along for the ride.[9]

And what a ride it has been. If Brown's work is about any one thing, as the choreographer herself suggests, it is about change: the change that inhabits the body as it moves from one place to another, the change demanded by gravity as the body adjusts to its force, the change that occurs in the body over time. Brown's conception of the body in flux could not be more different from that of Yves Klein. The *Leap Into the Void* imagined change that was impossible or regressive, a leap into immortality or into pain and suffering. Klein never found peace in the mortal world. Depressed and ailing, the 34-year-old artist died of a heart attack just two years after his first leap. Brown's work celebrates the body's changes and momentum while also accepting its mortality. Faced with the task of naming the first dance of her own she would perform solo in public, Brown chose "trillium," a wildflower that wilts and fades almost as soon as it is picked. "That's how she saw movement," observes Steve Paxton about her choice of the word. "It was wild, it was something that lived in the air."[10]

Another image comes to mind when thinking about Brown's work—gravity's rainbow, the seemingly oxymoronic title of Thomas Pynchon's groundbreaking 1973 novel. Gravity's rainbow is, literally, the term scientists use to describe the arc of gas that is left in the wake of a rocket after takeoff, a vapor trail that lasts for only the short time it takes the air and gravity to disperse it. Brown's work reverberates with such images: the exuberant leaps followed by the deflating falls of *Trillium*, the words "my father died in between the making of this move and this move" blurted out by Brown while performing the solo *Accumulation* (in 1973), the allusion to the Japanese notion of the passage of life contained in the ever-changing landscape of fog created by the sculptor Fujiko Nakaya for the dance *Opal Loop/Cloud Installation #72503* (1980). The powerful humanity of Brown's dances is born of her deeply humanistic understanding of life and art. In the end, it is this humanism that allows her to dance as energetically and rigorously as ever, a humanism bounded by an unwavering respect for the human body and for the limits and changes imposed on it by gravity.

Previous spread: *Floor of the Forest*, 1970. Pictured: Trisha Brown. Photograph by Peter Moore.

Opposite page: *Motor*, 1965. Pictured: Trisha Brown. Photograph by Peter Moore.

Following two spreads: *Planes*, 1968. Pictured: Simone Forti, Trisha Brown, Michelle Stowell. Photograph by Peter Moore.

Yves Klein, *Un homme dans l'espace! Le peintre de l'espace se jette dans le vide* (A Man in Space! The Painter of Space Leaps into the Void). Photomontage by Harry Shunk and Paul Kender from a photograph taken in front of number 3, rue Gentil-Bernard at Fontenay-aux-Roses on 19 October 1960.

Flyer for performance at the Whitney Museum of American Art, New York, picturing *Man Walking Down the Side of a Building*. Photocopy on paper, 11 x 8 1/2 in. (27.9 x 21.6 cm). Collection of Trisha Brown.

8. The imperative to emancipate viewers—to make them active, self-conscious players in the aesthetic experience—went so far as to engage them in one of democracy's most sacred practices: voting. In *MOMA-Poll* (1970), the artist Hans Haacke asked visitors to the *Information* exhibition at the Museum of Modern Art to deposit ballots into Plexiglas boxes indicating whether they could support New York Governor Nelson Rockefeller's reelection bid given his refusal to denounce President Nixon's hawkish Indochina policy.
9. See Marianne Goldberg, "Trisha Brown, U.S. Dance, and Visual Arts: Composing Structure," in this volume.
10. Steve Paxton quoted in Banes, *Democracy's Body*, p. 121.

Trisha Brown

photograph by Caroline Goodden

another fearless dance concert

Tuesday, March 30 & Wednesday, March 31, 1971
at 8:30 P.M.

Whitney Museum of American Art
945 Madison Avenue at 75th Street
New York, New York 10021

Tickets are available on a first-come basis
beginning Wednesday, March 24. There is no
charge other than the usual $1.00 admission
to the Museum. Cushion seating.

IF IN ONE'S MIND'S EYE IT WERE POSSIBLE TO FOCUS A CAMERA on Trisha Brown's choreography and keep its aperture open for forty years, one would witness a world of immense creativity. Her formal training in modern dance began in 1954, when she enrolled at Mills College in California. As her choreography has evolved over such a substantial span of time, it has coalesced into distinctive phases of work, each with similar compositional pursuits. The first phase involved her introduction to culturally venerable forms of American modern dance. She struggled with these forms at Mills, since they were unfamiliar to her, coming as she did from the vernacular childhood dance recitals, the high school water ballets, and the hopeful training for the Olympics in her backyard in Aberdeen, Washington. Throughout her young life, she had explored "environmental athletics," experiencing the intense beauty of the Pacific Northwest's terrain. While this physical immersion in wilderness would provide a foundation for many years of future choreography, Brown's formal training at Mills in a top art technique—that of Martha Graham and Graham's choreographic mentor, Louis Horst— led her initially to compose in that tradition. As Brown understood her classes at Mills, they were focused not on Graham's deep emotional, psychological intensity, nor on her extraordinary narrative structures, but on her innovative, breath-infused physicality. From Horst's method studied at Mills, and later with Horst himself at the American Dance Festival, she learned compositional tools that, along with Doris Humphrey's teachings, defined an entire era. Brown could not find sustaining catalysts in these studies for her own developing work, but when she turned to different sources in the sixties, she knew her history.

On the West Coast and in New York City, dancers were searching for new physical and conceptual inspiration. Brown began a second, highly experimental phase of her work after graduating from Mills. From 1958 to 1960, at Reed College in Portland, Oregon, she taught dance improvisation and invented movement structures. Some were precursors to forms she encountered at Ann (later Anna) Halprin's studio in California in the summer of 1960 and others to ideas she would subsequently be drawn to in New York City. Halprin's workshop took place north of San Francisco, in Marin County, on an outdoor dance deck. Even while being introduced to radical, challenging ways of constructing movement, Brown felt at home in the environment, which reminded her of the gullied surfaces of her childhood improvisations. Halprin was turning away from previous modern dance in her philosophical and physical inquiry, as were Merce Cunningham and John Cage, and as Robert Dunn would at the workshop that led to the Judson Dance Theater.

Throughout the twentieth century, a series of choreographic innovators had created a tradition out of rebellion: they learned from their predecessors, then ventured away, experimenting anew. Isadora Duncan and Denishawn (the company of Ruth St. Denis and Ted Shawn) were highly influential early in the century, giving Graham, Humphrey, and Charles Weidman aesthetic forms to consider and then challenge. A lineage extends from

Opposite page: *Skunk Cabbage, Salt Grass, and Waders*, 1967. Pictured: Trisha Brown. Photograph by Peter Moore.

these choreographers to Brown: Cunningham performed in Graham's company; Graham was a student of Denishawn; and Brown also owes much to Duncan, whose work gave Americans a sense of homegrown dance as "serious" art, not entertainment. Denishawn's exotic subjects would today be considered stereotyped, with their use of Asian cultures, yet this lent their work an aura of high art at the time.

Graham and Humphrey-Weidman rejected exoticism in favor of American themes. They developed an early abstraction, but did not go as far as separating dance from any other medium. Their inclusion of drama and narrative would later be considered a compromise of abstraction as "pure" dance. Yet they did focus on what writer John Martin called "metakinesis," the conception of the *kinesthetic*—rather than theatrical or literary themes—as the overriding source for meaning in abstract modern dance. In the fifties, Cunningham, unlike his teachers, envisioned abstraction as clearing choreography of anything outside its own medium of movement. Cage and Cunningham developed a philosophy inspired by chance and the *I Ching* as anti-narrative strategies. They pursued pared-down, moment-to-moment kinetics and the actual, non-illusory environment, as would Brown in the seventies through the mid-eighties.

Halprin's workshop offered Brown her initial exposure to Cage, who would become a major aesthetic influence throughout her life. What Halprin called "task" was similar to Cage's confluence of art and daily life, bringing the dancer to a kinesthetic confrontation with the present instant. As her daily task form, Brown chose to sweep a broom across the deck. Pedestrian in origin, this became anything but mundane in inner experience. Sweeping and sweeping, she found herself at the far edges of imagination. She pushed the broom with just the right amount of momentum until it swept her up, as if levitating, "flying" straight out, parallel to the deck.

At Halprin's Brown met several dancers whom she would join in New York City—Simone Forti, Yvonne Rainer, and June Eckman among them. Forti's improvisational brilliance on the dance deck formed indelible images for Brown, and she considered Forti her mentor in this form. Rainer gave Brown many performing opportunities in the City, which included choosing movements live on stage and the highly influential experience of speaking while dancing. Halprin had encouraged vocal improvisation with tones and words in her workshop. This verbal experimentation reconnected Brown to her lifelong love of language, first inspired by word games with her mother, who was very knowledgeable about Shakespeare. Eckman became a teacher of Alexander movement training, and with her Brown began initial studies to let go of traditional techniques and to *re-train* her body for task and improvisational work.

Brown released the dancer's "set," a particular tensile way of holding the body in the forties and fifties, which she had learned through studies at Mills and at the Merce Cunningham Studio after she arrived in New York in 1961. Through Alexander and also intensive, long-term study of another emerging form, Kinetic Awareness, founded by the Judson choreographer and filmmaker Elaine Summers, Brown began to initiate movement from very different kinesthetic knowledge. These newly surfacing somatic ideas offered alternatives to how to hone her body for dancing. She shed the stylized use of her muscles and the tensile alertness through the spine and skin. Focusing instead on subtleties of elegant, relaxed alignment of her spine and limbs, she moved with ease and a spatial clarity that stemmed from innovative inner imagery. Brown looks at home physically in these moves, and a different virtuosity and creativity emerged, grounded in anatomically clear and efficient action. New sensations, perceptions, and energy developed within her body and between body, space, time, and geometry. These changes became a technical breakthrough for dance in America. They separated many in the sixties and seventies generations from others who stayed with Cunningham or Graham techniques. Brown's in-depth new studies did become major catalysts for creating her own movement. When she formed her company in the early seventies, she chose performers who also reconceived the human structure and the meaning of physical skill.

Just as Brown was defining herself physically, she participated in the Judson Dance Theater, one of the most important performance groups of the 1960s. At Judson she found a path to further access her own physicality and to perform within a community of artists. Judson began as a composition class sponsored by Cunningham and taught by Robert Dunn, who had trained with Cage in composition. Brown knew some of the participants from Halprin's workshop and had met others after coming to New York. Dunn introduced Cage's aesthetics and his own studies of eastern philosophy, Bauhaus theory, and existentialism. He gave students assignments that stymied them inspirationally.

It was mostly the *physical* effect of Dunn's teachings that initially held great meaning for Brown, although he emphasized the conceptual in compositional structures. In the collective memory of today's art and dance audiences, what actually happened in the monumental sixties, is often confused with what did not occur until the early seventies. Brown did not develop extensive conceptual work herself until the later decade. By "conceptual" I refer to work that focused almost entirely on the compositional idea, not the visceral. In the sixties, Brown experimented with non-formal movement and instinctive physical responses to Dunn's assignments, as well as a blend of the conceptual and the physical, in her *Rulegame 5* (1964), with its structured rules for vigorous games composed of basic moves. This "pedestrian" approach followed from Cage's belief in the everyday in art. Here again Brown altered the superhuman technical set of the dancer. *Rulegame 5* allowed even non-trained dancers, including visual artists such as Robert Rauschenberg, to perform.

During the sixties, in addition to Judson, Brown joined in events with other groups of experimental artists from various fields: music, poetry, the visual arts, and dance. She participated in Fluxus events, and in Happenings composed by Robert Whitman; Whitman created a film for Brown's *Homemade* (1966). Ironically, in a "professional" context, *Homemade* played on the everyday, with Brown articulating a list of mimetic domestic gestures, during which she wore a film projector strapped to her back. The film playing across surfaces of the performing space behind her showed the same dance, previously filmed by Whitman. Filmic and live realities overlaid, as they did in a number of "intermedia" artworks of the time. *Homemade* connected Brown to visual artists creating Happenings, early makers of "film-dance" who used cameras in innovative ways, and—through the domestic actions and the baby backpack holding the projector—to early performance artists who blended art and daily life.

In a third phase of artistic work during the late sixties, Brown momentarily turned away from the group whose aesthetics embraced "objective" dance. She became one of the few dancers to create autobiographical work in the performance art medium. Visual artists came to this new form from the opposite direction, one in which static objects became animated. Brown's *Homemade* brought animated movement into performance art with the use of non-dance gestures and an objectlike performer. Brown created several works in this phase. Looking back to her youth in Aberdeen in *Skunk Cabbage, Salt Grass, and Waders* (1967), she

explored memories of hunting with her father when she was a teenager. An intensely personal work, *Salt Grass* also brought Brown closer to Rauschenberg, who christened the piece.

Rauschenberg and Brown had met at Cunningham's, and began what has become a life-long friendship and collaboration. Their works have fascinating correspondences, more from unspoken affinity than consciously related explorations. Brown moved mattresses around in her 1974 piece *Pamplona Stones*; Rauschenberg had applied paint to a bed and hung it on the wall (*Bed*, 1955). Both used ordinary objects completely out of context, for example, chairs, the quintessential object of the sixties and seventies (Rauschenberg, *Pilgrim*, 1960; Brown, *Nuclei for Simone Forti,* 1963). Brown's work also shows thematic similarity—sometimes by synchronicity, sometimes by direct mutual influence—with that of other visual artists and dancers in a developing New York community.

As the sixties drew to a close, Judson Memorial Church was handed down to a second generation. Many original members stepped out in one of two directions: some defined their work individually rather than communally; others joined Yvonne Rainer's outrageous improvisational troupe Grand Union. Brown did both. In Rainer's improvisations, this time it was Brown who emphasized language as part of the mix. She also showed a great deadpan, ironic humor and invented absurd tasks that demanded what seemed to be aesthetically point-less physical risk. She would open paper grocery bags, place them in a line, and then jump from one to another at near-impossible distances. The ordinary led to the tongue-in-cheek display of extraordinary skill when she would succeed in such a task.

Simultaneous to performances with Grand Union, in the early seventies Brown began a fourth artistic phase when she organized the Trisha Brown Dance Company, as well as initiat-ing an intense involvement with dance scores. As they did for many visual artists of the sixties and seventies, scores offered Brown a means to compose structure. She used mathematical scores, imaginative "instructions" to dancers, or the visual phenomena of performers geometrically positioned within a loft or museum space as ways of structuring her works. In this she shared an aesthetic with such artists as Sol LeWitt, Donald Judd, Carl Andre, and Richard Serra. She thought both as a visual artist and as a choreographer, as she has throughout the decades.

Before Cunningham, it had been customary in modern dance to create analogies between a work's structure and its musical score. Brown instead founded each work on its own independent movement score. She also left instructions given in the scores open to interpretation, as did Sol LeWitt in the programs for his early wall drawings. Now she fully culled conceptual ideas from Dunn's and Halprin's workshops, from improvisations with Forti, and from structures she had invented when she taught at Reed College and later in New York City. At first she designed simple scores that audiences could easily perceive as the central "content" of a piece. Later her structures became so complex that often they could not be grasped visually. In her emphasis on the conceptual through the mid-seventies, Brown continued to bridge the dance and art worlds and to provide leadership in both.

The Trisha Brown Dance Company toured the United States and Europe, often performing in galleries, with works such as the Structured Pieces and Accumulations. The Structured Pieces (numbered I through IV, 1973–76) were loosely strung together sequences of tasks, games, and manipulations of pedestrian objects. They were related to works Brown had choreographed at Reed and in New York in the late sixties and early seventies, such as *Planes* (1968), *Leaning Duets [I]* (1970), or *Floor of the Forest* (1970), exploring relationships between movement, special rigging, and environmental space.

The Accumulations became a signature form for Brown. The first, *Accumulation* (1971), is a solo in which she articulates movements in a list, as in *Homemade*, but abstract gestures rather than mimetic ones. Structured as simply "one thing after another" (as Donald Judd would say), this strategy differs entirely from that of early modern dance, which stressed emotive reason as crucial to well-conceived choreographic sequence. As it was so foreign to this rationale, so-called objective conceptual art such as Brown's was at first not taken seriously by some, who considered her and her colleagues to be irreverent renegades.

Yet a piece like *Accumulation*, as performed by Brown in an early film, holds great mystery and presence. Unlike her silky, seamless performance of the same gestures in the eighties, in this early version Brown parses out poignantly awkward and eccentric gestures with great precision, each distinct and inscrutable. The question emerges: do Brown's moves mean anything? Lacking modern dance codes of expression, they could be considered devoid of emotion. Brown appears to simply *be* there, over and over, intentionally empty of anything—except the profoundly existential. Because of the great intention she presses into each gesture, and her idiosyncratic way of moving, *Accumulation* actually communicates great subjectivity of a new kind: being there in intense presence. Brown's gestures did not look like anything seen before. She traveled beyond the known lexicon of modern dance.

In the visual arts, the type of composition used in the Accumulations and Structured Pieces was variously labeled "primary structure," "Minimalism," or "ABC art" to indicate a bare-bones compositional strategy. The philosopher and artist Henry Flynt applied the term "concept art" to these kinds of pieces; Brown's *Walking on the Wall* (1971) is uncannily close

Previous spread: *Pamplona Stones*, 1974. Pictured: Trisha Brown and Sylvia Palacios. Photograph by Babette Mangolte.

Opposite page: *Leaning Duets*, 1970. Pictured: Trisha Brown and unknown. George Maciunas is among the spectators (third from left). Photograph by Peter Moore.

to Flynt's "imagined actions," such as the performance of walking through walls or defying gravity. When Brown's dancers "walked" on the walls of the Whitney Museum of American Art (supported by harnesses), the only movements were variations on walking, but in extraterrestrial ways. Performers stepped and leapt parallel to the floor until it seemed that the audience was looking down on them. The piece's trompe l'oeil extended to other Brown works. Sometimes she created ironies or puns between language and movement, at other times between environmental space and dance. For instance, in *Group Primary Accumulation* (1973), Brown instructed one group of performers to keep performing an Accumulation phrase no matter what, but asked another group to stack the first set of performers on top of one another against walls. This environmental directive made it nearly impossible for group one to continue inexorably with their phrase.

Scores and instructions took Brown to a new realm of creating illusion with gravity. Whether expressed in a specific gesture or in a broad action of the group, this resulted in quixotic, phenomenological works. Brown used intelligent physical humor to inquire about gravity, language, and objects: she had a performer drop a stone, and in midair told it, "Stop." Another time she laid a chair on its side and sat in it like that, playing with spatial expectations by holding her posture to complement the illusion. Previous generations of modern dancers, through the forties, had not used objects in this way: "props" had been employed as part of the story, for the expression of feeling, or as metaphors for the interiority of the human being. Brown, like many visual artists of her generation, worked with objects as external items that maintained their own presence, equal to, rather than dominated by, the person in the determination of their "meaning."

During this period, Brown pointedly performed outside of theaters to rid her conceptual works of baggage from conventions established as far back as the Renaissance construction of perspectival space and still utilized by traditional ballet masters—and often subliminally by modern dancers, particularly on proscenium stages. She chose lofts, galleries, outdoor locations, and what were called "found" places never before used for dance, such as rooftops, parking lots, or plazas. In 1972, outside the Walker Art Center in Minneapolis, her company performed a group version of *Primary Accumulation* with each supine performer on a raft, drifting across a lake in the rain, maintaining synchronization despite changes in placement and orientation due to the wind. Traditionally, the further dancers move to the margins of a stage, the lower they are in the visual hierarchy. But by performing on a lake, unpredictable currents carried some dancers to central places in the spectators' vision and others to more peripheral ones. Brown completely avoided the way the proscenium emphasizes centerstage as the most important place to be. The audience, walking along the banks, literally followed the dance where the wind carried it. Also, with bicyclists, pedestrians, and various people carrying out daily activities within the performance frame, Brown established an entirely new context for viewing dance.

These experiments fed directly into Brown's complex dance works of the late seventies forward. In 1975, with *Locus*, skills from scores and alternate movement techniques came together to lead Brown back to her first movement that looks rudimentarily like "dance." This marks a fifth artistic phase. In *Locus*'s complex score, she integrated language with the three-dimensional kinesphere of space that surrounds a dancer's body. She designed an imaginary cube for each performer to inhabit, with points on it labeled with numbers corresponding to letters of the alphabet. Dancers' gestures literally spelled out sentences from a statement written by Brown as a professional autobiography, which would never be decipherable to the spectator without viewing corresponding choreographic drawings. The sketches graphed for the first time multilayered, multidirectional movements that Brown had experienced before only in ephemeral, unrepeatable improvisations. She built up moves simultaneously, forming multipoint gestures, and the drawings gave Brown a new tool—a way to memorize even more complex, spontaneous movements and teach them to her company members. The score for *Locus* brought together many elements of Brown's stance from her "anti-dance" years: the belief in "pure" movement without connotation; cross-media experimentation with linguistics; invented but simple geometric shapes; a focus on compositional structure rather than movement "content"; and the integration of dancer and environment (here, the imaginary cubes). Yet, paradoxically, *Locus* was also a pathway *back* to technical dance for Brown: its moves, although still relatively basic, could not be performed by non-dancers; and its graphing system provided a way for Brown to transfer her own highly complex, technically advanced and innovative improvisational moves to other trained dancers.

Locus next led Brown to a breakthrough in non-scored intuitive work, with her 1978 bounding solo *Watermotor*. She let go of scores into highly instinctive movement. What she had learned through *Locus* went into her body, and she was able to spontaneously create far more complex multipart moves through improvisation—a major accomplishment, a sixth artistic phase. When next she spliced together the fluid, traveling, and revved-up *Watermotor* with the sculptured, stationary, and stoic *Accumulation*, she brought two movement "voices" into counterpoint. The piece ricochets between differing geometries and approaches to architectural space. Brown spliced *Watermotor* into *Accumulation with talking* after she had begun switching back and forth between telling two stories. In her virtuosic play she improvised with all four alternating linguistic and physical tracks, remixing at each performance.

Following *Watermotor*, Brown began a three-year process of teaching her company to memorize complex improvisational moves, so the intricate movement would not evaporate. She laboriously searched for ways to capture spontaneity in repertory. The result is an entire oeuvre that functions as a retrospective of Brown's history as an artist to date. By the late seventies and eighties, she had created an entirely new compositional strategy from her juxtaposition of scores with improvisation, a seventh artistic phase extended from the sixth. Added onto these new compositional and physical virtuosities were advanced studies of Kinetic Awareness and Alexander Technique, which by then had blossomed in dancers' bodies into a highly articulate aesthetic and athletic grace. From 1979 on, with *Glacial Decoy* (1979), *Opal Loop/Cloud Installation #72503* (1980), and *Set and Reset* (1983), Brown developed even further this ability to memorize spontaneity. Beginning in the early eighties, she and many of her dancers began an extensive study of the Susan Klein Technique, another alternate training, which, when combined with the others, has allowed the Trisha Brown company to acquire skills that bring her dance works to the heights of human physical capability.

Brown began an eighth artistic phase when she brought her choreography to the proscenium stage and grappled with its historical conventions of theatricality. In the pieces first sited on stages, Brown often quoted from her vintage works of the sixties and seventies in order to bring radical ideas into these traditional spaces. If one follows these echoes, it is possible to see just how divergent her theatrical works are from previous modern dance conceived for

Previous spread: *Walking on the Wall*, 1971. Performance at the Whitney Museum of American Art. New York, March 30, 1971. Pictured (left): Douglas Dunn. Photograph by Caroline Goodden.

Opposite page: Trisha Brown and Richard Nonas preparing the equipment for *Walking on the Wall* at the Whitney Museum of American Art, March 1971. Photograph by Peter Moore.

prosceniums. Just because *Set and Rest* and *Opal Loop* may be placed in traditional theaters does not mean they sit comfortably within their frames, as do conventional images centered within a pictorial painting. Instead, Brown plays with the edge of the stage, finding innumerable ways to undermine it as a frame. She has even gone so far as to hire a marching band to accompany *Foray Forêt* (1990) and have it circle *outside* the theater, barely audible, linking stage space to urban streets. In a more intimate commentary, a dancer actually holds in her mouth the hallowed velvet drapes that define the stage borders. Shockingly irreverent, because dancers traditionally do not even graze the drapes, yet at the same time endearing and humorous, this moment points to Brown's contradictory artistic position of inhabiting the proscenium as her home while continually going beyond its frame.

Brown also changed the organization of staged space. In this she initially built upon Cunningham's reinvention of hierarchies of stage and body. He decentralized the spatial field inside the frame so that all parts are equal, periphery as important as center. Brown often places crucial choreography at the stage margins. Or she faces dancers backstage, away from viewers, so it is as if she had rotated the theater: the audience sees the expressive "back" of the piece, usually hidden from view. Her approach to an individual's body is also decentralized. Isadora revered the solar plexus, Graham the pelvis, as body centers. Graham created the pelvic contraction to express a dancer's subjective experience of intense emotion. Brown reinvents the body as a field of equal places, with varying centers. Action can be initiated from any place at any time.

Previous spread: *Skunk Cabbage, Salt Grass, and Waders*, 1967. Pictured: Trisha Brown.

Opposite page: *Group Accumulation*, 1973. Pictured: Trisha Brown. Photograph by Babette Mangolte.

This page: *Group Accumulation*, 1973. Pictured: Caroline Goodden, Carmen Beuchat, Sylvia Palacios, Penelope. Photograph by Babette Mangolte.

Following spread: Trisha Brown, Untitled, 1975. Pencil and ballpoint pen on paper, 12 1/6 x 9 in. (30.8 x 22.9 cm). Collection of Trisha Brown.

Brown's equalization of gesture within an individual body is analogous to the way she architecturally designs groups in counterpoint or partnering. Works such as *Son of Gone Fishin'* (1981) or *Set and Reset* are composed with an allover, fieldlike composition and no single stage focus. Duos, trios, or the entire group initiate phrases that others pick up across stage, then echo or alter unexpectedly, none more central than the other. In later pieces such as *Lateral Pass* (1985) or *Newark (Niweweorce)* (1987), Brown places separate movement voices in juxtaposition. They buck off one another, as when she combined *Accumulation* with *Watermotor*. Opposite voices are not hierarchical but rather add meaning to one another as they occupy a single temporal and visual space.

Also as part of this eighth phase, Brown began to focus on artistic collaboration, adding sound/music, visual presentation/installation, and theatrical costumes and lighting. As in a Cunningham-Cage piece, various arts coexist, with no one determining the meaning of the other. But in Brown's dances, the different arts are more closely tied. In rehearsal she extensively develops intriguingly rich interrelationships between media, even as she maintains the self-determination of each art. Although each stands on its own, Brown carefully considers its conceptual and sensual interplay with the others.

Continual innovation has characterized Brown's repertory over the years. Her initial entry into the theater as an "outsider" choreographer has given her the distance, wit, and versatility to foreground modern dance conventions even as she consciously utilizes them in new ways. Her ongoing challenge is to find fresh perceptual approaches to dance. Beginning with *Newark* and the opera *Carmen*, both in process during 1986 and cross-fertilizing each other, she has reconsidered character, narrative, emotion, and historical music. In her dances of the nineties, Brown continued to include traditional components of modern dance theatricality, but in ways that encompass what she learned while composing her early work. In the seventies, when she believed in the possibility of "pure" movement, she constantly deflected connotation. Yet later Brown acknowledged the intently "subjective" experience of performing even those pure works. Since then she has explored relationships between "expressive" psychology and "pure" geometry, or between intimations of narrative meanings and seemingly abstract durations. These are heightened compositional endeavors, the results of decades of choreographic questioning. Trisha Brown is still branching along unique pathways, continuing to find catalysts for recreating that kinetic, three-dimensional experience called dance.

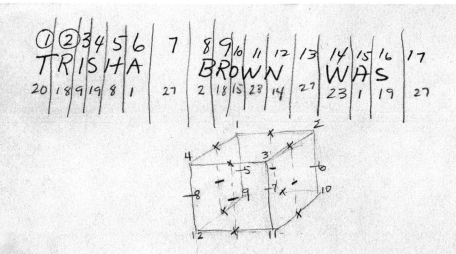

①	②	3	4	5	6		7		8	9	10	11		12		13		14	15	16		17
T	R	I	S	H	A				B	R	O	W	N			W		A	S			
20	18	9	19	8	1		27		2	18	15	23	14		27		23	1	19		27	

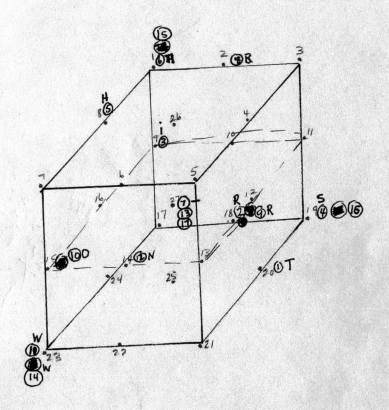

• **27 points on cube/~~bodies~~**

points numbered 1 — 26,
center = 27 = space between words

numbers correlating to alphabet. A — Z

current biographical data —

I FIRST MET TRISHA BROWN IN 1960 AT ANN HALPRIN'S SUMMER WORKSHOP in Kentfield, California. Several years younger than I, she had already been exposed to the standard academic modern dance education then offered by Mills College, where she had obtained a degree. Chafing at my own physical limitations, I marveled at the amazing elasticity of her body. Sitting on Ann's outdoor dance deck, she could stretch her torso forward, belly flat on the floor, long legs stretched apart at 180 degrees.

I cherish another memory of Trisha's physical prowess from this period: in response to an assignment to work with everyday objects, she pushed a long-handled brush-broom with such force that her body was catapulted into the air parallel to the ground. Two years later Trisha would duplicate that move without the broom in her solo *Trillium*, in which she gave herself the tasks of sitting, standing, and lying down while in the air, again demonstrating her innate kinetic humor and fearlessness.

In a group photo of the Halprin workshop participants Trisha is nowhere to be found, unless one remembers, as I do, where to look. She is the standing figure whose hair is pulled over her face and tied around her neck. Such self-effacement is hard to imagine in one who was to become one of the West's most famous postmodern choreographers. Yet now I can recognize even then, and with this photo as evidence, the signs of her ambition and waggish reserve.

Trisha was a consummate daredevil. I remember her hurling herself against a column and crashing to the floor in somebody's—it may have been Bob Rauschenberg's—loft. Her duet, *Lightfall*, performed in the early sixties at Judson Church, although more delicate in tone, still projected an element of danger as she and Steve Paxton perched precariously on each other's bodies, waiting for the other to shift position and send the partner sliding to the floor. The ropes, pulleys, tracks, and walls of her subsequent Equipment Pieces (influenced—as I was in entirely different ways—by Simone Forti's 1961 *An Evening of Dance Constructions*) were utilized not only for the defying of gravity but to produce an effect of utmost ordinariness. In a gravitational field seemingly turned 90 degrees, her performers were instructed to maneuver as though they were in the street. The spectacle of the death-defying feat (*Man Walking Down the Side of a Building*) and the restraint of the so-called pedestrian task (*Walking on the Wall* and *Floor of the Forest*) made for a terrific tension in her work of this period. *Planes* was unusual for its use of 16mm aerial footage that was projected onto the wall-clambering performers to create an illusion of skydivers floating in the air.

In later years Trisha sometimes talked as though the Judson ethos forbade personal movement invention, thus delaying explorations and elaborations of her own physical gifts. I myself was unaware of this. Coming to dance relatively late, I was absorbing and making the most of everything I encountered in dance technique and ideas floating around the Cunningham/Cage/Rauschenberg nexus. My early dances would contain both demanding

Opposite page: *Woman Walking Down a Ladder*, 1973. Pictured: Trisha Brown. Photograph by Babette Mangolte.

one-legged balances (*Three Satie Spoons*, 1961) and "ordinary" movement (*We Shall Run*, 1963).
Truer to the grand tradition of twentieth-century avant-garde "refusals," Trisha and Steve, both
blessed with extraordinary virtuosic capability—Steve was already dancing with Merce—
absolutely refused to exploit these gifts which—whether articulated as such or not—were
associated with previous modern dance. But I always thought such refusal was more a matter
of choice than a response to any proscription emanating from the Judson workshop.

Then came what I'll call, for want of a better term, her "structural" dances of the early to
mid-seventies: *Accumulation*, *Locus*, *Sololos*, *Line Up*. A geometric or mathematical system
usually characterized, either overtly or subliminally, these austere and witty works. They
retained a connection to the Equipment Pieces insofar as they now explored cubic space
rather than two-dimensional vertical or horizontal surfaces. Then in 1978 Trisha made a sharp
departure with a solo called *Watermotor*, followed shortly by the group piece *Glacial Decoy*.
These were the dances in which she began to explore the full range and dynamic possibilities
of her unique physical apparatus and, in the process, create a personal style that would
shape her future work.

These two dances knocked me out. (I had stopped dancing in 1975, but still followed
Trisha's career closely.) The unpredictable rhythms, about-faces, counterpointing gestures
rippling across extremities, the lightning-quick images that coalesced and evaporated in the
fluid movement—I felt she was truly coming into her own. And then she upped the ante:
she superimposed extemporaneous storytelling on *Accumulation*, and later added *Watermotor* to produce *Accumulation with talking plus Watermotor*. And she succeeded in teaching
her movement to others. I was awestruck. It seemed the eleventh hour. But she was on a roll.

Opposite page: "Play," part four of
Yvonne Rainer's *Terrain*, 1963.
Pictured: Yvonne Rainer, Trisha
Brown. Photograph by Al Giese.

This page: *Glacial Decoy*, 1979.
Sets and costumes by Robert
Rauschenberg. Pictured:
Trisha Brown. Photograph by
Babette Mangolte.

Following spread: *Watermotor*,
1978. Pictured: Trisha Brown.
Photograph by Babette Mangolte.

1. Yvonne Rainer and Trisha Brown,
"A Conversation about Glacial
Decoy," *October* 10 (Fall 1979); 30.
2. Ibid., p. 32.

The teaching had already begun to take place with *Locus*. She was finding ways to articulate and communicate her movement. As she so eloquently expressed in a 1979 conversation:

> My work is about change—of direction, shape, velocity, mood, state. There are total, instantaneous shifts from one physical state to another. This is tumultuous to perform, but if the momentum is just right, there is an ease.[1]

Trisha was creating, as I asserted in the same conversation, "a new dance grammar," a slowly evolving grammar—idiosyncratic but not eccentric—that included an investigation of, as she put it, "public and private gestures": "I perform both, but you are not supposed to see the private ones. I am telling you this because it accounts for coloration or nuance and the appearance of universal eccentricity."[2] Ha! She contradicts me. Of course "universal eccentricity," while a contradiction, is also a typically Trisha provocation. Let me examine her relation to gesture (as distinct from dance "steps") in terms of emotional affect and unconventionality, both of which were visible in the dances of 1978–79, and reached an apogee in her staging of the opera *Luci mie traditrici* in 2001.

A little digression into pre-Brown history: Martha Graham created a whole new lexicon of movement, but by the 1950s it was a language that had become codified and "normalized" to the point that her audiences required no program notes to digest its meanings. The kinetic signifiers of emotive state and narrative trajectory had become perfectly clear, having shifted over time from startling innovation to a kind of pantomimic populism. The critics who supported Graham complained of Merce Cunningham's "coldness," mistaking his non-narrative classicism for "lack of emotion." They could not see that the performing human

body is in and of itself an emotion-conveying instrument, something that we who had studied with Merce intuitively absorbed and accepted. The emotionality in Merce's choreography, however, in being kept immanent, a given, and not brought to the surface, remained an unarticulated assumption.

By this stage of her development, in the mid- to late seventies, Trisha had passed through the crucibles of these two titans and heaved herself out the back doors of Judson Church and Simone Forti. She would now focus down hard on developing, if not a cohesive language (which could later be codified, canonized, writ in stone), then a new way of thinking about body articulation, gesture, and feeling.

> The first time I talked while doing the *Accumulation* I said, "My father died in between the making of this move and this move." Which knocked me out. I was amazed that my body had stored this memory in the movement pattern…I became silent and composed myself. I was devastated that I had said that.[3]

Memory stored in the body. Here Trisha is referring to something other than the commonly understood kinetic memory that allows dancers to remember and execute, once learned, complicated sequences of movement without "thinking," just as native speakers spontaneously enunciate language without having consciously to think about the act of speaking. To the contrary, she is talking about emotion stored in the muscles and the process of accessing it through gesture and movement. This is a very different idea from "expressing" emotion through gesture, a more conventional method for finding an appropriate movement to match a known emotional state. In conversation Trisha once told me that hers was a very dangerous process: "All of a sudden you find yourself saluting the flag," she said (without knowing it or wanting it, she might have added). Another provocative Trishaism, the quote is indicative of a highly selective and critical consciousness that treads a narrow path between the familiar and the ambiguous, the recognizable and the hard-to-recognize. Back then, when her work was still so novel, for some it was disconcerting to see Trisha's combination of loping leggy fluidity and gestural upper body moves, the emotional affect of which might come and go in lambent waves. (I must remind my reader that these are my words, not hers.) Her dancing from now on, in its rootedness in idiosyncratic personal/physical history, detachment from musical and narrative cues, and refusal to conflate emotional expressivity with recognizable mimesis, would push her toward nothing less than rewriting the terms of choreographic expression and its previous manifestations.

Twenty-three years later, when I saw *Luci mie traditrici*,[4] something clicked. It was as though Trisha had returned to the newness and wonder of her late-seventies dancing. This is not to say that I have not followed everything she's done in the intervening years with great interest and pleasure. It was more that what she is about, or has been about, was suddenly illuminated all over again. I had become a somewhat jaded, though still faithful, lover of her work, but now, seeing this opera, I could respond with renewed clarity and enthusiasm.

I've seen it only once, unfortunately, in contrast to the numerous opportunities afforded over the years for viewing most of the dances. As a melodrama the libretto mines all of those tropes of excessive feeling and act that are so familiar in operatic and Hollywood genres: desire, jealousy, rage, remorse, murder. As she started to work on it, Trisha expressed reservations about being able to deal so directly with sex and murder. It was true, in her previous stagings of *Carmen* and Monteverdi's *L'Orfeo*, the "old chestnut" aura of the one and the classic trappings of the other, plus the use of her own company, imparted a formal distance that was more choreographic than dramatic. But now she was faced with a modern opera involving the passions of two characters. I couldn't imagine what she was going to do.

There had never been any sex in Trisha's work. Sensuality, maybe, but in a very oblique form, always modulated or overshadowed by other concerns. Unlike Cunningham's male/female partnering, Trisha's gender relationships never settled into any pattern that lent itself to sexual interpretation. Specific emotions, implied in the gestures, were fleeting, evanescent, never underlined or made much of. You had to be quick in your attention to catch them on the wing, which was their strength and beauty, and innovativeness.

The Russian formalist Viktor Shklovsky's notion of "making strange" is not easily brought to bear on dance, an art form that, for reasons too complex to elaborate in this essay, so readily succumbs to re-inventing every wheel in its solipsistic universe without apparent historical or self-reflection. In the early seventies when I began to deal with some specifics of emotional life in theater pieces and films, I resorted to cliché as a time-honored arena which I thought I might revitalize by reworking and "making strange"—through tableaux vivants, projected texts, displacement of voice, melodramatic props, etc.—beginning with Leo Bersani's observation:

> Cliché is, in a sense, the purest art of intelligibility; it tempts us with the possibility of enclosing life within beautifully inalterable formulas, of obscuring the arbitrary nature of imagination with the appearance of necessity.[5]

The high melodrama of *Luci mie traditrici* seemed like a trap ready to spring, luring and leering with every cliché in the book. But in Trisha's hands the opera was indeed "made strange" through the workings of that same rare sensibility that had placed the moment of her father's death "between the making of this move and this move."

It begins with looking. The man and the woman stand at opposite sides of the sloping stage and look toward and away from each other. They do this for what seems like a very long time (while singing, of course, for after all, this is an opera). By the end of the opera Trisha has had the two large, unstreamlined bodies engage in the most astonishingly unconventional—and unclichéd—partnering I have ever seen. It is not at all flashy; there are successions of delicately awkward poses that register regret, longing, or dread; there are maneuvers whereby the man brings the woman, in several variations, inexorably to the floor and up again, finally laying her out in the ultimate murder (I can't remember the actual act; it must have been very minimal). The movement is not erotic, though the text is rife with desire and passion. If I recall correctly, after the opening exchanges of looks, as they move closer and closer they look at each other less and less. When entwined in an oddly shaped embrace they look away from each other, as though not daring to look, or perhaps looking for release from this diabolical entanglement. The sadism of the man is palpable, though not graphically pantomimed. Of course the super-titled translations and the very peculiar sawtooth-marked decor and the eerie, sparsely dissonant score support these interpretations, but I was surprised to find myself, uncharacteristically, reading ruthlessness and doom into the bending of torsos and reaching of arms. And perhaps strangest of all, I could see the same tension between excess and restraint that I had seen in Trisha's Equipment Pieces. The death-defying feat on the side of the building had metamorphosed into doomed love, the pedestrian walk into gazes, exchanged and averted.

October 11, 2001

Following spread from left: Trisha Brown, *I want to give my eye a rest...*, c. 1973. Typewritten ink on paper, 11 x 8 1/2 in. (27.9 x 21.6 cm). Collection of Trisha Brown.

Trisha Brown, *I want to give my eye a rest...*, c. 1973. Pencil on paper, 11 x 8 1/2 in. (27.9 x 21.6 cm). Collection of Trisha Brown.

3. Ibid., p. 34.
4. Music by Salvatore Sciarrino, scenic design and lighting by Roland Aeschlimann.
5. Leo Bersani, introduction to *Madame Bovary* (New York: Bantam Books, 1972), p. xviii.

I want to give my eye a rest that man will never forget.

I want to give my eye a rest that men will
never forget.

↓ the life of him — get.

I
I want
I want to
I want to give
I want to give my
I want to give my eye
I want to give my eye a
I want to give my eye a rest
I want to give my eye a rest that
I want to give my eye a rest that won
I want to give my eye a rest that won
   will
I want to give my eye a rest that won
   will never
I want to give my eye a rest that won
   will never forget.

BROWN IN THE NEW BODY

STEVE PAXTON

Opposite page *Lightfall*, 1963.
Judson Memorial Church
gymnasium. Pictured:
Trisha Brown, Steve Paxton.
Photograph by Peter Moore.

IN WRITING ABOUT TRISHA BROWN, IT HAS BEEN SUGGESTED THAT I WRITE SOMETHING along the lines of "why and how New York was a hotbed for interdisciplinary explorations between dance, performance, music, and visual arts."

I think that was true of New York in the early sixties, but not of Trisha.

Trisha foregrounded the body: her body with all its neuronal liveliness, and the various bodies of those who worked with her. It might be assumed that because dance is a medium employing the human body, foregrounding the body would be essential and inevitable. But in reviews of Judson Dance Theater it has been seen that the bodies and movements of the non-dancers (who were actually painters, musicians, and composers) are mentioned more than those of the dancers. It is as though the term *dancer* suggested a generic body type, already known all too well. A dancer's job was to dance in work by a choreographer. What was seen was not their body, but the movements their body made, their technique, perhaps their interpretation.

But Trisha resisted this assumption. In her own work, private images are responded to with movement improvisation in performance; it was her particular body that was performing, and no one else's could do her work.

In *Lightfall* (1963), a duet created (there seems to be no exact word for what she did) for one of the early Judson performances, she provided some ideas, the title, some images, some nudging, and a lot of trust in me, her partner.

This is a now familiar armamentarium of choreographic method used to provoke a general understanding of what is to come, yet leave the new performer a lot of space to adapt. The desired result is to make the performer take enough initiative to eliminate the look of "learned movement." It is like sketching a scenario, which the performer fleshes out. That is, the performer's improvising body fleshes out the sketch, while their mind must inhabit but not inhibit the body in real time. This process is seen as part of the creation.

That is perhaps true in choreography, too; yet in set works there is the possibility that any role could be taken by another dancer. In Trisha's work, the body of the dancer was often seen as unique, and to substitute another person would completely change the work.

Even in her works described as "rulegames," where the casting was not so sensitive, during performance the dancers made choices based on Trisha's rules. This was a relatively new level of improvisational control, leaving the dancers looking like players, rather than tools or robots.

Escaping the devalued image of the "dancer" caused Trisha to disguise the fact that her feet are remarkable ergonomic events, a definitive pair of remarks on the idea of "arch." In her creations her feet were not displayed; they were fully used but not often presented fully contracted or flexed, not foregrounded. We were, in other words, not shown the decisive feet of the dance technician, but their relaxed connection to the body doing the dance.

I don't want to write about how I can tell the difference between those two words, body and dance, or the single action they present. Just to point out that I could understand even less how the event (dancer dances) occurs, and had to look at her body with all possible focus to grasp the new unity she presented.

Trisha and her friends Simone Forti and Yvonne Rainer were some of the few dancers I knew in those days who improvised. The rest of us tended to create structures in which our rigid legs and pointy toes were accepted as the natural way for a dancer to exist. Perhaps the rare mention of the nature of the dancers' bodies in those days had to do with a sort of paralysis learned in dance class, and perhaps we looked so much alike in our efforts to transmute the dross of human movement into art that we could be taken for granted.

In these women's improvisations, however, it was clear that something special was offered. I have found myself using the word "magic" to describe their effect, for which I apologize, yet perhaps with qualification it will be useful. Magic, I understand, is often about transformation. Performance is too. When the transformation of performance is again transformed by improvisational minds in action, it can make me breathless, as though I can't watch fast enough to see the dance. Choreography rarely rouses this feeling.

Actually, improvisation seldom does, either. But without these examples, good examples, I doubt improvisation would ever have interested me, and the last thirty-three years would have been very different. They were hot moments, and I was made curious. What were they doing? They were constructing milliseconds with their sensations and their ideas in a heady mix which swirled through time catalyzed by our complicity, our viewing. We saw anew. What a relief.

The other issue I was asked to address is "the contemporary moment in relation to one of the richest periods in the history of American dance. How does the past exist and/or how has it been transformed within Trisha's and [my] own work as well as in the practice of emerging choreographers, artists, and performers?"

Such large woozy questions usually leave me wordless, but with a little adjustment, this question becomes one of my big woozy speculations these days, and I will give it a whirl. I would like to open the question to the whole century. I think the 1960s, the time which I assume is referred to by "one of the richest periods in the history of American dance," was not by itself particularly rich. It is part of a much larger period in which the whole idea of modern dance was developed; became in conservative America after World War II, entrenched; and in the fifties created its very own anti-particle, Merce Cunningham. The Judson work, though undeniably pretty rich, was small potatoes compared to the uptown work of Graham, Balanchine, Limón, and the Henry Street work of Nikolais and Louis—and many others; the mature and entrenched Modern Dance.

What an accomplishment. The history usually starts with one name, Isadora, setting out some new parameters, then it appends Nijinsky's ballets, moves on to St. Denis and Shawn. It splits then into Graham, and Humphrey-Weidman. Due to the wars fought in Europe, the United States gained a number of dancers and choreographers, while Modern Dance in Europe and especially Germany was curtailed for the duration.

Ostensibly, this artistic wave was seen as being in opposition to Classic Ballet, which was viewed as decadent and illogical, and dependent upon an old repertory. However, ballet pulled itself together, and by mid-century had created new repertory and revamped and furthered the technique.

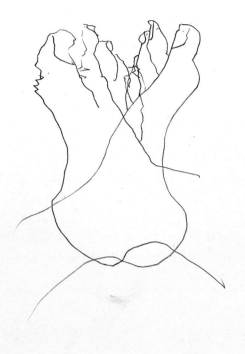

Trisha Brown
I

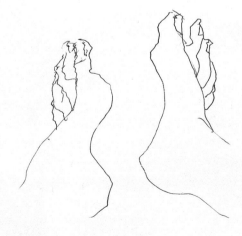

Trisha Brown
2

By this point, a certain critical mass and certain patterns had been established. The major choreographers established new techniques and new material for repertory. Women, men, and people of color were represented, making dance as they wished, an extremely democratic arena. They were mostly tied to balletic forms, in the way that one has a firm relationship to the enemy, yet also had elements of anthropological research: ethnic dances on the New York art stages. In a way, all this was presaged by the ballet, but it was taken to a new and optimistically modern level.

By the 1950s the battle against ballet was rather old news. And yet hypocritically, young students such as myself and, I assume, Trisha, were still being indoctrinated, while Cunningham, who was starting his own company, was busy synthesizing a modern/ballet technique. He also rewrote the aesthetic of Modern Dance, as though resisting the pressure to continue what was an already well-charted direction into story-dance (shades of *Giselle*) and psychology, history, Greek myth, social commentary, or the Nikolais experiments in art, costume, and technology.

I think by this point, Modern Dance was historically unprecedented. In only fifty years, dance thinking had been enormously expanded and confirmed.

To some extent under the critical radar, the physical education departments of our country had been laced with the many dancers produced by the various new techniques, outposts in the hinterlands preparing new audiences and appreciators. And the nation was paying attention. Cunningham made the cover of a national magazine in his *Nocturnes* makeup, and Graham was considered famous enough to be a mystery voice on national radio. Nikolais's work was shown on the Perry Como TV show many times. Modern Dance had currency at home.

Again beneath the radar of the press however was a development produced by Mabel Elsworth Todd, Lulu Schweigard, and Barbara Clark et al., called Ideokinesis ("The image or thought as facilitator of the movement." —Andre Bernard). Perhaps more to the point is the title of Todd's book, which circulated among dancers, *The Thinking Body*. Where dance history concentrates our attention on the performance accomplishments of a relatively few people, this work concentrates upon the nature of the body, and as the title suggests, gives that nature a mind, or rational component, apart from the aesthetic accomplishments of the choreographers.

Choreographers don't, of course, ignore for long the health of the physical systems (bodies) they employ, but in a swiftly moving aesthetic period, mistakes can be made, perhaps not to be seen for many years. Dancers preparing and repairing themselves began to turn to ideokinetic thinking, and it began to inflect their thoughts and aesthetics as it, too, gained currency in the dance subculture.

So as the 1960s approached, the palette of young dancers, technically, aesthetically, anatomically, plus ideokinetically, was rich. At about the same time, the movement arts of the Near and Far East became available to the West. Each of these many systems define the body's movement in different ways. So, by the advent of the Judson Dance Theater in 1962, a multitude of ways and thoughts about the body were in the air, which had not been incorporated directly into the art-dance performance idiom. Whether Trisha directly studied any of this (as I had not), the thought of a natural body, or working with nature when moving, was around to be noticed.

The Body had currency. The Cartesian split, pitting the mind versus the body, was not an issue for us. Trisha's work began on this ground, and evolved into a particularly vital and

This page: *Primary Accumulation*, 1972. Photograph by Babette Mangolte.

Following spread: *Primary Accumulation on Rafts*, 1972. Performance on a lake in Loring Park, Minneapolis. Pictured: Trisha Brown, Carmen Beuchat, Sylvia Palacios, Caroline Goodden. Photograph by Michael Glen.

rich modern dance form as she took the direction of the stage/large company. She did not change her aesthetic, I think, but rather adapted to the rigor of stage presentation, took the challenge of that tradition, while preserving essential early visions as references and guides; and in her choreographies, as revelations in performance.

One job the arts accomplish in our culture is to refresh our thoughts; the arts provide direction, new or renewed perceptions of our time. This stimulation is not only necessary, but is probably unavoidable, particularly in the dance, because while one can get through a life never picking up a brush, camera, violin or laptop, the bodymind is us. We seem to require reminding of this basic idea.

At this moment, on the centennial (sort of) of modern dance, the amount of movement study and dance presentation available is extraordinary. I have to say, it might not last. The teaching might fade into history, the repertories degenerate, the political situation might isolate us again, major achievements might be revised, discredited, discarded. You know what we're like.

Nonetheless, at this moment it is difficult to envision a more prolific and profound dance/movement culture ever existing.

At the same time, in the United States, it is hard to imagine a funding system which would impoverish, infantalize, and retard the work of dance to a greater degree. Trisha Brown's accomplishment is to express the new body, surmount the system, and beat the dictates of those who have no idea of their own body, or anyone's.

Vermont, November 10, 2001

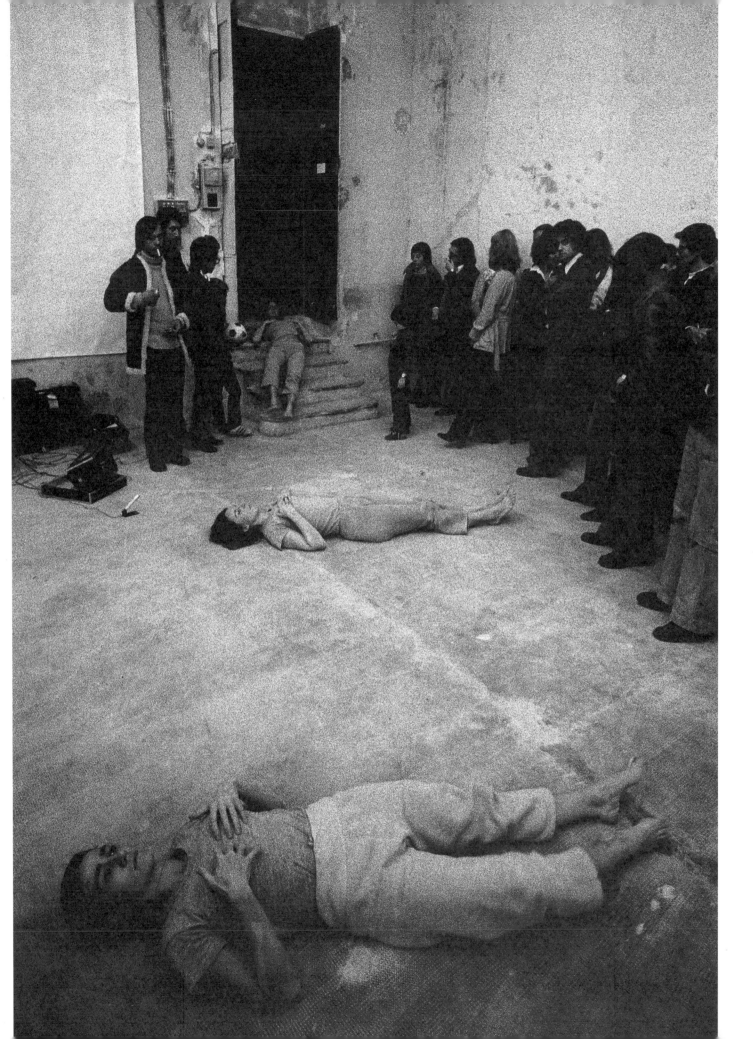

BROWNIAN MOTION AND FRANCE: CARTOGRAPHY OF AN IMPRESSION

LAURENCE LOUPPE

TRISHA BROWN'S INFLUENCE HAS RADIATED THROUGHOUT EUROPE. Her works have been included in the most prestigious programs. Institutions and festivals have been eager to contribute to their production. It was the Festival d'Automne, that great revealer of the American avant-garde, which brought Trisha Brown to Paris in 1973. Not to a performance hall, but to a museum. Which was in keeping with the site-specific nature of her work till then, particularly the Accumulations, a group of serial, though not repetitive, works, executed on the floor, from which the viewer could draw different perceptions depending on where he stood. Then, invitations followed from the experimental space of Sainte Baume at the Théâtre de la Ville in Paris, with stops at the Avignon Festival. We might note here that the passing away of its founder and the inspiration of the Festival d'Automne, Michel Guy, would be evoked with melancholy by Trisha Brown in her renaming of the piece now called *For M.G.: The Movie* (1991), a dialogue between stasis and acceleration, between the single and the multiple, each reversible, like time and memory. Other curators took the baton. And to the present day, Trisha Brown's creations continue to be received with the greatest of interest.

A CIRCLE OF ADMIRERS

Increasingly, Trisha Brown's work has commanded attention in the cultural arena. Her work first became known among an elite involved in the visual arts. The performances of 1969–71, generally referred to as Equipment Pieces, deeply struck the artistic world in Europe. The work, both political and corporal, dealt with urban space as well as the flouting of its laws and those of gravity (in the famous *Man Walking Down the Side of a Building*), and these living sculptures connected to the corporal art being developed on both sides of the Atlantic at the time. The dance critic Lise Brunel, who also collaborated on art reviews, belonged to this world. It was she who would edit a monograph on Trisha Brown, with images by the important photographers Babette Mangolte and Guy Delahaye, published in Paris by Editions Bougé in 1987.[1] Around that time, given her reinvigoration of theatrical space, Brown's audience broadened well beyond the circle of initiates. Simultaneously, her collaborations with great artists (Rauschenberg, Judd) reignited the art world's interest. In addition, almost secretly, the visual artist in her endured, particularly through the most intimate practice there is: drawing. An exhibition was organized in 1998 at the Musées de Marseille, gathering drawings and filmed images (performances, art videos). Julia Kristeva wrote about the drawing that "there is no distance between the thought and the hand; their instantaneous unity captures the most concentrated interiority in visible bodies."[2]

The relationships between Trisha Brown and France are multiple and variable—in keeping with her activities, her audience, her admirers, witnesses to her art.

Opposite page: *Group Primary Accumulation*, 1973. Pictured: Carmen Beuchat, Caroline Goodden, Trisha Brown. Photograph by Giorgio Colombo.

1. Lise Brunel, Babette Mangolte, and Guy Delahaye, *Trisha Brown* (Paris: Editions Bougé, 1987).
2. Julia Kristeva, "Visions capîtales," in *Trisha Brown: Danse, précis de liberté* (Marseille and Paris: Musées de Marseille and Réunion des musées nationaux, 1998), p. 12.

CRITICAL THOUGHT AND BROWNIAN MOTION

In 1979, the essayist, art critic, and philosopher Guy Scarpetta applied to her dances the notion of "Brownian motion" (*le mouvement brownien*) through an evocative, anachronistic shift, upon seeing *Glacial Decoy*: there was the turbulence and intensity of a body that placed no limits on the possibilities of its movement and that all of a sudden gave shape to the notion of "expenditure," formulated much earlier by Georges Bataille.[3] Later, in his *L'impureté*, Scarpetta attributed to Trisha Brown an important role in the renewal of art through an "incessant variation of frameworks...a series of acts inciting an art of maximally heterogeneous rhythms, at once unleashed and shattered, as though paroxysmally propelled." If the radical performances of the seventies and eighties offered important examples of subversion, Scarpetta then saw in them a greater, "supercoded" impact. Her move in the eighties to the traditional proscenium "did not constitute a sobering up but on the contrary a growing insolence, an increase in exuberance."[4] It was with Scarpetta that the figure of Trisha Brown as paradigm of corporal freedom was born in France, as the rebelliousness of an infinite movement that nothing could contain.

TRISHA AMONG DANCERS IN EUROPE

But there were other influences, still more profound. And this is perhaps where Trisha Brown's passage through Europe has left the most traces on both bodies and imaginations: on the community of dancers, in France as well as in Belgium and the Netherlands, places where European dance has long integrated the messages of modernity. There they also have dealt with the legacy of the sixties and seventies, which is more alive today than ever in terms of creation, certainly, but even more so in terms of teaching, reflection, and practice. The first encounter took place in 1978 on the stages of Sainte Baume, where the choreographer Stéphanie Aubin, among others, would find the source of a movement forever liberated. Today the head of a national artistic program, Aubin favors experimentation and inquiry based on important works of the twentieth and twenty-first centuries—and the work of Trisha Brown figures prominently.

From Amsterdam to Arnhem, as well as in Brussels, there are dancers who teach, sometimes former fellow travelers of Trisha Brown, that share her aesthetic positions and ideas and have developed creative methods and ways of working that are very similar to her own. New schools have been born that have made Brown's oeuvre a point of reference, a framework of excellence, such as the graduate school in Brussels, P.A.R.T.S. (Performing Arts Research and Training Studios, directed by Anne Teresa De Keersmaeker). In France, over several decades, Trisha Brown has been invited to different places to present not only performances but master classes in composition and improvisation, as well as lectures. Confidence in the power of her work and her artistic vision led the choreographer Dominique Bagouet to invite Brown to create for and to work with his company in 1991. The result, a masterpiece, is a corporal poem, *One Story as in Falling*, all diffuse shadows of falling, held in check by slowness. The collaborators on this project, members of the company of this French choreographer (since deceased), are among the most forward thinking today in terms of experimentation and inventiveness.

The 1990s saw great transformations in European dance, particularly in France. Several things might explain this: first, a deeper reflection and historical knowledge that recalled the experiments of the Judson Dance Theater—and thus the interest in a certain radicality in experimental behaviors too easily forgotten. Then a more extensive practice of various methods of bodily awareness: of the technique of "release" with a renewed approach to the Alexander Technique, or "Body Mind Centering." This unleashed approaches to the body that are particularly in sync with Trisha Brown's aesthetic. The education of the audience in kinesiology, animated by Hubert Godard, a kinesiologist and academic who was very influential among dancers in France, foregrounded these same new values. Trisha Brown's important and continuing research on the body and movement invited viewers to traverse an "interior geography."[5] Godard notes: "In her work, one sees an extraordinary quality of undulation, what I call 'motility,' a way of authorizing movement without restriction.... This kind of dance is bewildering because it is located at a point of extreme radicality which eliminates all tensions and all forces." And that "to locate oneself on the scales of tonicity is also to constitute oneself as a body in history" and raises the stakes for Trisha Brown's "profoundly disarmed body."[6] At issue here is an aesthetic and theoretical reflection on dance and movement that is less attached to the external aspect of narrative and the motifs developed in modes of representation than to the forces that flood the movement and underlie a bodily ideology that creates meaning, on the political level, too. In this regard, Godard developed a metaphor inspired by Burt Barr's superb video *Trisha and Carmen*.[7] In the prelude of the third act, we see Diane Madden move about in an undulating fashion. Then the dancer Lance Gries enters the field. He places his hand on her body—and each time he does so, the touched part is blocked. Beyond the relationship of male authority/woman, police state/anarchist that the theme of *Carmen* compels, there is the repeated halting of a movement that is segmented, petrified, and which designates the place of its expiration. Trisha Brown's art, to our sense much more than to any other, illuminates the places affected by what Michel Foucault calls bio-power (or somato-power), which may penetrate "the thickness, the depth, of bodies without having been relayed by the representation of subjects."[8] Without involving a specific arena of identity, violence, a constant for Foucault, is exerted at every instant on every body. The network of processes is brought to light through the microstrategies of power relations. Such preoccupations are not unrelated to the work of young Europeans such as Boris Charmatz, Jérôme Bel, Emmanuelle Huynh, Alain Buffard, and Rachid Ouramdane, among others.

Which is to say that Trisha Brown's impact on the renewal of choreographic creation and ways of thinking about dance in France has become an obvious fact. Not only through her practice of a body breaking its chains but also through her incessant quest for creative processes. Through her explorations in multiple fields, from drawing to opera. Through her unquenched thirst for the unknown. As evidence: Emmanuelle Huynh, justly considered a major new figure on the choreographic scene, conducted a series of fascinating interviews with Trisha Brown between 1992 and 1999 (as yet unpublished).[9]

In a reexamination of Brown's work, one can see the possible or ambiguous dialogues between several experiences, between two different generations of artists—each obsessed with surpassing limits. One can see, above all, the expectation of answers that are always pushed toward their irresolution. Thought and vision here find their source at the open threshold of the possible.

Translated by Jeanine Herman

Previous spread: *Group Primary Accumulation*, 1973. Pictured: Carmen Beuchat, Caroline Goodden, Trisha Brown, Sylvia Palacios. Photograph by Giorgio Colombo.

3. Guy Scarpetta, "Trisha Brown, le mouvement brownien," *Art Press* [Paris] (1979): 34.
4. Guy Scarpetta, *L'impureté* (Paris: Grasset, 1986), p. 196.
5. Hubert Godard, "The Missing Gesture," trans. David Williams, *Writings on Dance* 15 (Winter 1996): 44.
6. Hubert Godard, "Le déséquilibre fondateur," trans. David Williams, *Writings on Dance* 15 (Winter 1996): 19.
7. Based on the production of Bizet's *Carmen* by Lina Wertmüller, Teatro di San Carlo, Naples, 1986.
8. Michel Foucault, *Dits et écrits* (Paris: Gallimard, 1984), 3:231.
9. Emanuelle Huynh, "Face à dos: Entretien avec Trisha Brown," *Nouvelles de danse*, no. 23 (1995): 5–12.

NEITHER PRADA, NOR ARMANI, NOR HERMÈS, NOR MIYAKE, NOR HELMUT LANG had yet dreamed of invading the lower Manhattan neighborhood, still not named SoHo, that bristled with the stern beauty and cavernous spaces of cast-iron loft buildings, when Trisha Brown moved there in 1965. If any shoppers were to be seen, they were carrying only aesthetic currency and most likely scavenging choice pieces of detritus left in containers or on the sidewalk by the light industries gradually vacating the neighborhood and inadvertently making way for the enterprise of art.

In 1966 Brown created a work in collaboration with Robert Whitman, who had lyrically conjured up some of the first mixed-media performance works in the late 1950s. Titled *Homemade*, this piece comprised units of remembered movements such as Brown's father cocking and releasing his forearm to cast his fishing line into the water. The dance told neither the story of her father nor of fishing but strung together heterogeneous movements transferring their physical meaning one onto another onto another—creating a seamlessly meandering metaphor of the body's making of metaphor. Via sight, touch, and the movements of the body we first perceive the world; our perception is not fully automatic but layered from disparate data into a whole. We do not instantly perceive distance or local color or scale but create them. We understand the world through the construction of metaphor. Brown re-embodied physical consciousness, not verbal consciousness; she celebrated the marvel of totally ordinary movements.

And Robert Whitman filmed her as Brown danced this dance of ordinariness. When *Homemade* was then performed, Brown had a projector strapped to her back that projected Whitman's film of the dance she was dancing. Dance and the reflection of dance; consciousness and self-consciousness. A duet of projection and reality moving around that moment where the quest of self-consciousness to perceive itself slips into a blind spot.

In their construction of complex simplicities, Brown and Whitman were not alone but part of a dynamically anarchic community that included dancers, painters, sculptors, filmmakers, and composers all wildly bent on reinventing and making porous the boundaries of their making. Radical innovation and brilliance were located in low-tech improvisations and jubilant combinative play. While communities of shared intentions dot the terrain of modernist painting and sculpture, from Post-Impressionism to Abstract Expressionism, the inclusion of dance in the shared intentions of the visual arts community may be singular to the 1960s and early 1970s.

Nineteen sixty-six does not mark the beginning of this new community's achievement, but rather a high point. So, where to begin? During the 1950s, in various locations, the frame (of the proscenium arch in the case of dance) that separated the viewer and the viewed illusion, hierarchical composition, and virtuoso technical execution that had long since been rejected by modernist painters and sculptors began to be undermined by various choreographers and

Opposite page: Still from the video *Aeros* (1990) by Burt Barr. Includes footage from Robert Whitman's film for *Homemade*, 1966.

performers. In California, Ann Halprin conducted dance workshops that opposed narcissistic performance; she encouraged her students to explore the body's unpredictability and imposed ordinary tasks as arbitrarily chosen restraints on dance movement. The dancer-soon-to-become-sculptor Robert Morris and his dancer-choreographer wife Simone Forti attended Halprin's workshop as did the composers Terry Riley and La Monte Young. In that hotbed of artistic dialogue in North Carolina, Black Mountain College, Robert Rauschenberg first met John Cage and Merce Cunningham in 1949; and there, in the summer of 1952, what has often been cited as the first "Happening" (a term disdained by Rauschenberg), John Cage's *Theater Piece No. 1*, unfolded. This work simultaneously included Cunningham improvising dance around and through the audience, Cage reading a lecture, and Rauschenberg projecting slides of his paintings while playing old records on a hand-wound Victrola. Cage with his seer's voice, immersion in Buddhism, trust in the *I Ching* and consequent elevation of chance, improvisation, and indeterminacy was soon to become all things to all people avant-garde. And Cunningham would, in the course of the late 1950s and early 1960s, become the avatar of a new kind of dance, with Rauschenberg providing the sets and costumes for his company. In 1962, the influence of the various protagonists of this long paragraph coalesced in downtown New York in a church called Judson, which gave its name to the beginning of such new dance as Trisha Brown's *Homemade*. After the initial concert organized by Robert Dunn at the Judson Memorial Church, a remarkable group including Brown, Yvonne Rainer, Steve Paxton, Cage, Rauschenberg, Morris, and Forti, singularly and in collaboration with each other, turned Judson Church into a laboratory of dance. The return to everyday issues pervading the post–World War II culture of the 1950s and visible in the elevation of the ordinary objects in Jasper Johns's enigmatic paintings of flags and targets and the joyously subversive disjunctiveness of Rauschenberg's combines of found detritus, created in the mid-1950s, mixed and mingled with the improvisatory structures built on the teachings of Halprin and Cage. The anarchic utopianism that marked so much of the 1960s found one of its many havens at the Judson Church. Just as Cage rejected conventional musical composition in favor of found sounds, randomness, and silence, the Judson dancers threw out scenery, music, conventional expertise, and the constrictions of the proscenium arch. Ordinary sounds. Ordinary movements. Ordinary spaces.

Already, in 1961, Brown had collaborated with Simone Forti to create a structured improvisation in which three dancers pointed at various parts of a wood-burning stove and discussed, in front of the audience, how they would improvise based on the architecture of the stove. Freewheeling collaboration and improvisation pervaded Judson and countless other locations. Brown and Rainer could as readily jump onto a chicken coop and let loose, at the sculptor George Segal's farm in New Jersey, while Rauschenberg and a male dancer donned skates and sailed around a roller rink, each with a parachutelike wing attached to his back, while Carolyn Brown, a stunning member of Cunningham's troupe, danced on point (*Pelican*, 1963).

Rauschenberg reveled in the same kind of enigmatic combinative play figuring his paintings. *Spring Training* (1965) began with him mopping up eggs dropped from the rafters and continued with his son Christopher, in darkness, taking lit flashlights from a laundry hamper and placing them on the floor. As the lights began to move and the ambient light increased, the audience slowly apprehended that the flashlights were strapped on the backs of turtles.

Trisha Brown, who performed in this piece, and the other younger dancers preferred sparer, more purely body-generated activities. While Cunningham's improvisations were based on invented movements, Brown, Rainer, and the younger dancers structured seamless non-sequiturs made up of recognizable, task-oriented movements—walking, running, falling, etc. They created non-narrative fields of energy engaging each viewer directly in her physical space.

In an essay written in 1966, Rainer succinctly recounted the many correspondences between Minimalist objects and contemporary dance and presented a list of strategies both eliminated or minimized, followed by a list of their replacements.[1] Evidence of the artist's hand in the making of objects and phrasing in dance were replaced by factory fabrication and energy equality, respectively; hierarchical relationships of parts and development and climax were replaced by unitary forms or modules and equality of parts; illusionism and performance were replaced by literalness and task or tasklike activity; monumentality and virtuosic movement were replaced in both practices by human scale, and so forth. Much of Rainer's account parallels Robert Morris's two treatises on contemporary sculpture published in *Artforum* the same year as the publication of Rainer's essay.[2] However, while the Minimalists were continuing in modernist art's tradition of constant reinvention, the dancers were suddenly and unexpectedly jumping off the stage into the audience's space.

Together with these correspondences between dance and the visual arts developed a blurring of the boundaries between sculpture and dance. Abetted by the introduction, in 1965, of affordable and portable video cameras and projectors and by already active underground filmmakers such as Michael Snow, Hollis Frampton, and Paul Sharits, the performative entered the realm of sculpture. Similar task orientations were to be found in both endeavors. The English artist Richard Long made sculpture by simply walking, variously recording his activity with a camera or arranging traces of his walk (stones, leaves, etc.). A straight line erratically configured by the tracks of his feet walking on grass constitutes *A Line Made by Walking* (1967). In California, Bruce Nauman, impressed by Man Ray's 1926 movie *Emak Bakia*, in which the movie camera was the main protagonist and generator of zany action, began making work in film, video, and holography. His sixty-minute video *Lip Sync* (1969) features a close-up of part of his upside-down head wearing headphones and repeating the title over and over, his lips in and out of sync with his voice. Ordinary non-narrative activity stretched into the extraordinary by ceaseless repetition—not too distant from dance activity. And lest we forget where this essay started, Brown's co-conspirator Robert Whitman had already in 1964 created a work in which a 16mm film loop of a nude bather was projected into an actual shower stall with running water and more (*Shower*).

In SoHo again, activities subverting notions of sculpture's fixed objecthood proliferated—sometimes faster than they could be witnessed—and often might as readily have been called dance as sculpture. By the late 1960s, Minimalism turned into Anti-Form or Process art, Body art, and Earth art. The more pronounced emphasis placed on sculpture as a record of the acts of process that often atomized the sculptural object and the more visible confrontation with gravity so often responsible for configuring the new sculpture drew sculpture and dance and performance art ever closer.

In 1972, Brown's friend Gordon Matta-Clark, who a year earlier had begun carving into abandoned and unoccupied buildings to transform a place into a state of mind, created *Open*

1. Yvonne Rainer, "A Quasi Survey of Some 'Minimalist' Tendencies in the Quantitatively Minimal Dance Activity Midst the Plethora, or an Analysis of Trio A," in *Minimal Art*, ed. Gregory Battcock (E.P. Dutton & Co., New York, 1968), pp. 263–73, chart on p. 263.
2. Robert Morris, "Notes on Sculpture," Parts 1 and 2, *Artforum* (February and November 1966) reprinted in ibid., pp. 222–35.

House. With found wood and abandoned doors he turned a container into a house and hosted a barbecue in the front yard that was the street. There he also hosted a dance performance featuring Tina Girouard, Susan Harris, and others. In 1971, he and his partner Caroline Goodden, who danced with Brown, started a restaurant called Food where artists were invited to cook. In Düsseldorf, food art had already been practiced by Joseph Beuys and such Fluxus artists as Daniel Spoerri who opened Food's precursor in 1970 and asked artists to make limited editions out of food (chocolate sculptures, mayonnaise drawings, ground-lamb reliefs, etc.). Daily, it seemed, new boundaries were erased.

Brown, meanwhile, had begun a series of works exploring the dynamics of body weight and mass that made viscerally visible the role of gravity and/or the defiance of gravity. She called them Equipment Pieces, but they could as readily fall under the category of Extreme Dance. In 1968, she turned the wall into the floor, putting foot- and hand-holds in a wall, down which dancers spiraled as though in a slow-motion free fall. *Leaning Duets [I]* (1970) featured pairs of dancers, each attached by rope, the partners of each pair leaning and swiveling against the restraint of the rope that joined them. The most radical, most anti-balletic, most anti-gravitational, and, perhaps, the most emblematic work of the downtown dance scene was created by Brown in 1970 with the assistance of the artists Richard Nonas and Jed Bark and the employment of standard mountain climbing gear. Called *Man Walking Down the Side of a Building*, it was just that. No story, no literary narrative. If there was a story, the body alone told it.

During these same years, sculptors such as Barry Le Va and Richard Serra were similarly engaging and defying gravity. With such works as *Within the Series of Layered Acts (Glass Thrown from 3 Feet, 6 Feet, 12 Feet)*, created in 1968, Le Va literally shattered sculpture's conventional objecthood and entered the realm of the performative. Richard Serra's *Splashing* (1968) extended Pollock's flung paint into three-dimensional site-specificity by his hurling of molten lead into the space where the wall meets the floor. And his *One Ton Prop (House of Cards)* (1969), in which four plates of lead each four feet square prop each other up, without benefit of conventional sculptural joints or soldering, relates very closely to Brown's *Leaning Duets.* Serra, indeed, professed great admiration for the idea of Brown's *Man Walking Down the Side of a Building.*[3]

There is no end to this story about no story; but the community of high adventure and collaboration, in which Brown was such a vital participant, had ultimately to give way to consolidation, more individual creativity, and the full bloom of maturity. Brown formed her own dance company in 1970 and began to build on the new vocabulary she had formed with her co-adventurers. In 1971, in the first of a group of Accumulations, she extended the dancers' anti-compositional liberation from literary narrative into full body independence by turning each part of the individual dancer's body into a unit of interdependent movements; and those movements, in turn, became a unit of the dance with each dancer's body becoming a unit of the dance, mirroring and permuting the interdependent movements of the other dancers—unfurling a stunning ripple like a molecular chain reaction. These Accumulations have continued to erupt joyously throughout her subsequent making. Athletic grace and precision, humor, and improvisation still fuel Brown's choreography, just as have collaborations with other artists, most frequently Rauschenberg. And, when Brown moved to the frame of the proscenium arch, she eschewed the hierarchical structures associated with the

Previous spread: *Homemade*, 1966. Pictured: Trisha Brown. Photograph by Peter Moore.

This page: *Group Accumulation*, 1973. Pictured: Judith Ragir, Trisha Brown, Elizabeth Garren, Mona Sulzman, Wendy Perron. Photograph by Christiane Robin.

Following two spreads: Trisha Brown, Untitled, 1976. Pencil on paper, 13 3/4 x 9 3/8 in. (34.9 x 23.7 cm). Collection of Trisha Brown.

Trisha Brown, *Defense*, 1980. Pencil on paper, 15 1/4 x 12 1/8 in. (38.7 x 30.8 cm). Collection of Trisha Brown.

Trisha Brown, *Sololos*, 1980. Pencil on paper, 15 3/4 x 11 1/2 in. (40.0 x 29.2 cm). Collection of Trisha Brown.

3. Trisha Brown in conversation with Klaus Kertess, 29 October 2001.

stage and gave as much emphasis to activating the wings of the stage as the center. Flying we have witnessed on the stage and walking on walls. Brown even re-engaged music in her dance, and has studied, in succession, the structure of Bach, Webern, Monteverdi, and the contemporary composers Dave Douglas and Salvatore Sciarrino, not letting the music determine the dance but creating parallel structures in collaboration with the music. But this is a story to be elaborated elsewhere in this book and exhibition. For now, we can only look back again and marvel at the pioneering beginnings.

Pure movement is a movement that has no other connotations. It is not functional or pantomimic. Mechanical body actions like bending, straightening or rotating would qualify as pure movement providing the context was neutral. I use pure movements, a kind of breakdown of the bodies capabilities. I also use quirky personal gestures, things that have specific meaning to me but probably appear absurd to others + they perform an everyday gesture so that the audience does not know whether I am setting out dancing or not and, carrying this irony further, I seek to disrupt their expectations further I I set up an action to travel left and then cut right or, at the last moment realize I imagine they have caught onto me, in which case I might stand still. I make people uncomfortable. Use a pure or echolaic arm motion gesture in another part

Oct 76   Trisha Brown

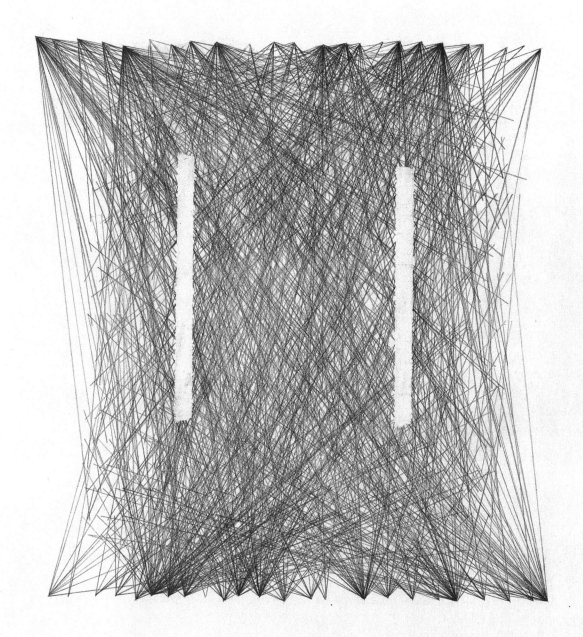

defense   Trisha Brown
                                           april 80

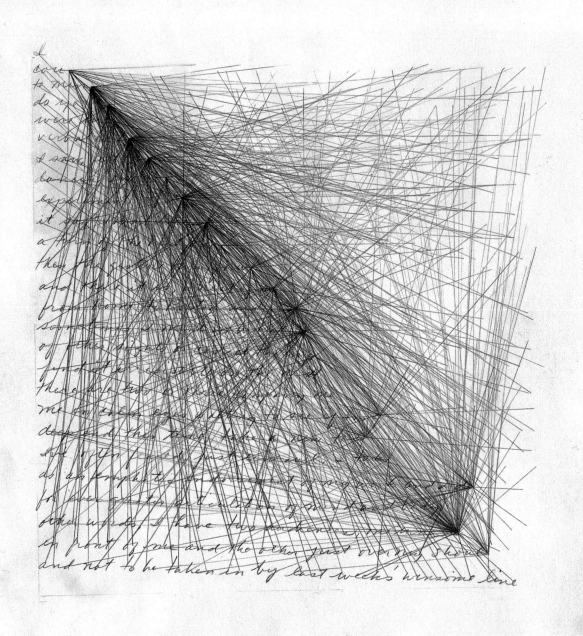

Sololas
Oct 80

Trisha Brown

THE WORDS THAT I AM SPEAKING ARE COMING UP THROUGH A SMALL HOLE in the floor of the auditorium and following each other one by one around the room, eventually tracing out a map of the Unites States, including Aberdeen, Chicago, Oakland, and San Antonio. Those words having difficulty keeping up with the others are being helped by invisible gnomes. Those words who refuse to participate will be forced to write "I AM SORRY" in capital letters over and over again on the side panels. Those words representing animals have been asked to fashion their movements after the gait of the animal mentioned. So if you hear "horse," know that H-O-R-S-E-S are trotting out to take their places as border, valley, and capital.

Skymaps are not new. Astronomy has been around for years and years. So relax. If a letter or two or whole word (God forbid) should fall in your vicinity, please function as a gnome assistant and toss it back up. Already lakes are beginning to form. I didn't realize that L-A-K-E-S, when they got together, could turn blue. I do know and must warn you that clichés, especially "sorry about that," have been known to nest in the pockets of people in the area. If this happens to you, try shouting "fumigator" in an original way. Stutters and uh's unavoidably used by the speaker have been asked to take the position of dotted lines representing unfinished highways and dirt roads. People unable to control coughing or sneezing should be chastised by those people in the audience who care about state lines. All audience members who are unable to visualize the map overhead will get lost on the way home.

Now I have to give you some words, so that you can carry out the project of making a map. Don't get lost in the content. Stick to your task and be kind to the Midwest.

Ourfatherwhoartinheavenhallowedbethynamethykingdomcomethywillbedoneon-earthasitisinheavengiveusthisdayyourdailybreadandforgiveusourdebtsaswe-forgiveourdebtorsandleadusnotintotemptationbutdeliverusfromevilforthineisthe-kingdomthepowerandthegloryforever. I'm sorry to do that to you, but—we have a lot of mountains to place. From time to time I will pause, so you can hear the words working. Snoqualmie Pass...Don't forget Alabama...Yellowstone... Willamette River...Skyline Boulevard...Boise...Tahoe...Wyoming...Devil's Hopyard... Mount Rushmore...Black Lick...West Virginia...Bismarck...Texarkana...Eunice, New Mexico...Pleasington...Salina...Centralia...Delaware...Hutchinson...

I'd like to get into something now that's a little sticky. Do you remember saying prayers? Saying them so often you couldn't remember what they

meant to save your soul? "Our Father Who art in Heaven" always confused me.
I had an uncle Art. I mean for a flash I thought Art was Our Father Who Lived
in Heaven. It means that God lives up in heaven it does not mean that
my uncle Art did anything up there and it doesn't mean that God makes art in
heaven. "Give us this bread"—my mother always bought an extralong loaf of
white bread called Wonderbread. "Surely goodness and her sister mercy mild"—
no matter how good I was all day I always failed because I couldn't remain
alert while I said my prayers to know that I was saying my prayers right.
And then "Amen" at the end. I mean—for a little girl to say "Ah men"—uh—I
know this is very weighty stuff, but—I told you about the mountains.

Now that I'm into it I thought I might as well tell you about Reverend
Shangler. Shangler should go directly to Philadelphia because I understand
that's where he lives now. He turned me on to religion in the beginning.
I must have been—two. A great guy, skinny and glasses and they ran him out
of town. They said he visited the lame instead of the halt or something like
that and out he went. I shouldn't be talking about all this because it was
a small town and very gossipy and I used his real name and for all I know
he's in the audience. Maybe he's all around us. Fort Oglethorpe...
Connellsville...Wishkaw, Quinault, Quillute River, Adirondacks...Alaska...
Woonsocket, Buffalo, Hazelhurst, Willacoochee, Vaughan, Jetmore, Oh Lord, save
the day and all the people using it...Wolf...Frostproof, Florida...Wetumpka,
Back Bay, Molokai...I... am...sorry...Flagstaff, Oklahoma, Brooklyn, Port Arthur,
L.A., Erie, Kodak, Seattle, Green River, Bivalve, Washington, D.C.

The beaches are good. One way I considered training the words was to have
them pile up on the Pacific Coast and then spread them like peanut butter
across the continent. But the words function better as individuals, going
along one after another. Then of course we could have added raspberry jam for
highlights like the mountains and rivers.

Patriiicia! Goooooordon! Louiiiiisa! Diiiiiner!

South Carolina, Oklahoma City, Fort Lauderdale, Hartford, Amazonia,
Wheeling, Hinckley, Monterey, Kalamazoo, Smith-Corona, Saturday night,
Sarasota Springs, Vista View, spring chicken, answering service, Golden City,
prairie dog, Sea Girt, Sitka.

B as in Boise. You begin to notice the individual personalities of the
letters as they move out to do their work. B's all right, a little slow-
witted. Actually, I'm quite fond of B, it's on all my mother's silver. I
find it hard to believe that O is fifty years old. Z I believe but O. Z is
not in Boise anyway. It is not clear to me. I can't really put my finger
on who I is. S is pregnant. S and W got married. They have a nice house out
on the Island. Windows, curtains, cockroaches. E is not blond. E is a good,
solid, ordinary working letter.

Lake Awosting, Oyehut, West Point, Phoebe, Monrovia, Plain Dealing, New
Braunfels, Orange, Mount Desert Ferry, Muleshoe, Yakima, Noxen, Eldoro. Call
weather bureau, botanic gardens, order meat, get photos, tax, Rome meeting,

get forsythia, Debbie rehearsal, Shawn. Dinner Steve and Susan, summer
flowers, Debbie here, film. Deb and David's, bring slides, set up wall,
Alex's opening, get money. View eight millimeter, chicken noodle, tuna fish.
Deb ten to eleven, Ann Burton. Four Walter Gutman, one whole chicken. Four
pounds chopped meat, nine to eleven Newark State. Animal Hospital. Dentist.
Nine to one Trish, Adam to Ann's, nine to one Trish, eleven Deb, Martha and
Bill. Bob's opening, call animal doctor, Peter Poole, wildflowers, Justin
here, call Don Boice, white paper, staplegun. Number 202 tape. Ten Deb here,
one Christopher and Jason, 4:30 Julia, seven Joan, Judy, Keith's concert,
get two bartenders, order ice, clean Cinematheque.

I had quite a hassle with their union. Words are not supposed to get up
off their page. But since this project is of a patriotic nature, permission
was granted. Deserts are easy, so why don't we stick a few cities out in
the desert, to speed things up. And while we're taking liberties, let's make
a rolling hill in the shape of a big chair. Let's make it a very soft chair.
There should be a super-soft chair hill.

Red Desert, Hobgood, Benson Junction, Zortman, Wynona Oklahoma, Lame
Deer, Oakely, Dawsonville New Hampshire, Dover, Jolly, Berkeley, Yakatat,
Lydia, DeQueen, Lava Field, Julesburg, Sierra Blanca, Birdsboro Pennsylvania,
Manchester, Rumford, Biddleford, Carbondale, Lynchburg, Raleigh, Bemidgi,
Enders Reservoir, Red Hills, Eureka, Parsnip Park.

SOS, garbage liners, paper towels, dishwash soap, Borax, suntan lotion,
cigarettes, beans tomatoes brownrice mushrooms greens fruit milk bread juice
cheese and frozen vegetables.

Those spiderwebby things spreading out from Chicago are railroads. Took a
lot of rehearsal.

That should be enough material now. There's really nothing to be done.
Except for those who are not finished, go ahead and finish up. And the rest
of you can sit back and enjoy it.

ACCUMULATION WITH TALKING PLUS WATERMOTOR, 1979

THE FOLLOWING TRANSCRIPT IS FROM A PERFORMANCE of *Accumulation with talking plus Watermotor* at Maison de la Culture de Woluwe in Brussels on November 1, 1979. I annotated lengths of silences between words by the number of seconds, and the circled numbers represent minutes of actual performance. The entire dance was twelve minutes and fifty-four seconds long.

.**11**   the first time **9**   I performed this dance **20**
it was four and a half minutes long **9**   to the Grateful Dead's **5**
Uncle John's Band ① **16**   the next time **4½** I performed this dance **8**
   it was fifty five minutes long **6**   and in silence **33**   ②
        following that **24**   I began talking while doing
this dance **5**   as a lecture form **13**   ③ I found that **3** I liked the fact
that I could not keep track of my dancing while talking **4** and vice versa **4**
I am not**2**however**2**quite so sure about that tonight **53** ④
                   in that first lecture **4**   in Paris **4**   I said **4**   that
my father died**2**in between the making**2**of this move**2**and that move **4**   I was
amazed **5**   that⑤ my body had stored a memory in a movement pattern **49**
                  in Boston a member of my⑥ audience **6**
   told me **4** that this dance**2**reminded him**2**of a cat **2½** drinking milk**2**in a
rural district **20**   it was **3** at that moment **6**   that I
realized **4**   just how vast **3** are the liberties**2**with which**2**my audience takes
my⑦ work **13**   as time would have it **7**   the doing of this dance
became less difficult **4**   flat **4**   and I set about **3** looking for **3** another
element **21** ⑧   in New York **45** ⑨
     that paragon of verbal activity⑨ **6**   I attempted telling two
stories at once **13**   woops **11**   this has happened before **5**   it
is called losing one's place **17**   there **4½** found it **7** ⑩ A **3**
Mr. Preble called from Aberdeen B Corky met me at the airport and on the way
into town A asked me if I would accept the distinguished alumnus award at my
High School B forewarned me that I might not have an audience **4**   at my
lecture **3** A I accepted **4**   B on the contrary **4½** the house was filled to
overflowing A I asked my friends what can I say to these graduating seniors B
4 I came out and began this dance A two people said tell them to join⑪
the Navy B **6**   following that performance **3** a noted art historian **5** A I
decided to do this dance B **16**   told me that most of the moves in
this dance occur on the right hand side of my body **4** and that an event like
this generally precedes an era of great chaos **5** A **15** ⑫   my problem
was I did not want to receive an award in my bare feet **7**   and so **5**   I
did this dance in four inch wedgies **22**   .

Accumulation with talking plus Watermotor is the performance of two dances
and the telling of two stories at once. I shift back and forth between these
four elements according to impulse in performance. I never stop dancing. I do
stop talking. The one dance, *Accumulation,* is stationary and consists of the
methodical build-up of carefully chosen gestures. I begin with one gesture,
repeat it about six times, add gesture 2 to 1 and repeat them about (*Watermotor*
would cut in here) six times, add 3 to 2 and 1, et cetera. *Accumulation* had its
own life as a dance prior to *Talking* and it was monumental in its simplicity.
Watermotor, on the other hand, is the most reckless, ricocheting, high-driving
piece of never-ending now you see it now you what is going on, although precise
and sometimes poignant dance to date. It is erratic, emotional, unpredictable,
and the opposite of *Accumulation.* Soon after doubling the stories, I knew I
had to double the dancing to balance things. *Watermotor* was the inevitable
inclusion. It was sitting there, new, only five performances on its own and
those back-to-back with *Accumulation.*

The procedure for organizing the movement, accumulating, permeated the
structure and changed it. The first addition was *Talking. Talking* while dancing
is a ventilation system for my mind. It is explicit expression in a field of
muted abstraction, a format in which to assemble some of the peculiarities of
my experience.

Initially, the houselights were turned on so that I could see my
audience, and I said whatever came to mind following a pause in which I asked
myself, do you really want to say this. The audience and I were informed at
approximately the same moment of the verbal content of the piece. I talked about
what I saw, felt, thought, about them, about me, about dancing, and about making
this dance. It was an experiment. If a muscle could talk, what would it say.
Possibilities were strewn all over the place. A turn of the head provides a
momentary view offstage then the gesture turns forward again to the audience.
And there it is, a nest of memories of stage-right views from Rome to Boston
and from 1972 to the present. Sometimes I mention what I see or what I remember
of other sights or cancel the impetus altogether only to find it irresistible on
the next revolution. Always there are two or three company members backstage
holding me in calm eyes, waiting to see if I'm going to go off the deep end
this time, take a new tack, or perhaps, as I've often feared, just unravel. I
take their presence as an emphatic endorsement of my work and a demand for ever
greater articulation of mind and body. In other words, I have two audiences, one
innocent and in front of me and the other just over my shoulder and not to be
taken in by last week's winsome line. Around Tokyo, 1976, the houselights were
turned off, by accident, and I liked it. I liked the isolation; working in a
cup of light in the theatrical void from the inside out.

In each performance, there are gaps of silence, times when I am taking
inventory of my project. The silence suspends my intentions while the audience
continues with theirs. I re-enter, claim the narrative, carry it for a distance,
then drop out again, probably silenced by a flurry of actions or the ring of an
enigmatic verb. With the addition of the second story (after ten minutes on the
transcript), my mind spreads out to encompass all four elements, the dance
whirs, details and nuance compound. The end comes at me, I race, we meet.

Quadrilemna creates an overload which subverts or re-invents the selection
process. The form is imposed by the difficulty of the task and mediated by the
pluck of the performer.

LOCUS, 1975

PURE MOVEMENT IS MOVEMENT THAT HAS NO OTHER CONNOTATIONS. It is not
functional or pantomimic. Mechanical body actions like bending, straightening, or rotating would qualify as pure movement providing the context was
neutral. I use pure movements, a kind of breakdown of the body's capabilities. I also use quirky personal gestures, things that have specific meaning
to me but probably appear abstract to others. I may perform an everyday
gesture so that the audience does not know whether I have stopped dancing or
not and, carrying that irony further, I seek to disrupt their expectations
by setting up an action to travel left and then cut right at the last moment
unless I imagine they have caught on to me, in which case I might stand
still. I make plays on movement, like rhyming or echoing an earlier gesture
in another part of the body at a later time and perhaps out of kilter.
I turn phrases upside down, reverse them, or suggest an action and then not
complete it, or else overstate it altogether. I make radical changes in a
mundane way. I use weight, balance, momentum, and physical actions like
falling, pushing, etc. I say things to my company like, Toss your knees over
there, or Start the phrase and then on the second count start it again, or
Do it and get off it. I put all these movements together without transitions. I do not promote the next movement with a preceding transition and,
therefore, I do not build up to something. If I do build up, I might end
it with another build up. I often return to a neutral standing position
between moves; it is for me a way of measuring where I have been and where
I am going.

Opposite page: *Locus*, 1975.
Pictured: Mona Sulzman, Judith
Ragir, Trisha Brown, Elizabeth
Garren. Photograph by Babette
Mangolte.

Following spread: *Line Up*, 1976.
Pictured: Mona Sulzman, Wendy
Perron, Elizabeth Garren, Trisha
Brown, Judith Ragir.
Photograph by Babette Mangolte.

In 1979, the Trisha Brown Dance Company premiered *Glacial Decoy* on the proscenium stage at the Walker Art Center, Minneapolis. This new work was quickly acknowledged as a major change of direction, as almost all of Brown's previous dances had been showcased in more or less untraditional performance spaces such as lofts, galleries, museums, rooftops, streets, churches, and parks. For Brown, embarking on choreography for the stage was an urgent new challenge: how to take the lessons learned from movement experiments undertaken outside the theater and its particular formal demands and apply them to the very environment these same experiments were in opposition to. Brown has continued to ask this question in different ways for the more than twenty-two years she has been making works for the stage. With the same collaborative spirit that marked her work from the moment of her arrival in New York in 1961, Brown has embraced the theater as an interdisciplinary environment. In the sixties and seventies, Brown made dances that allowed, and even required, her dancers to talk; she unceremoniously broke the silence of the technicians of modern dance. Beginning in 1979, Brown's creative sensibility for dialogue expanded in a new way to the visual arts when she invited Robert Rauschenberg to design the set and costumes for *Glacial Decoy*. Brown herself had an affinity for visual art, making not only drawings but also choreographies that included sculptural props (for instance, *Ballet*, 1968) and even dancers that acted like sculpture (such as *Primary Accumulation*, 1972). Inviting Rauschenberg and, later, other painters, sculptors, and stage designers—Fujiko Nakaya, Donald Judd, Nancy Graves, Roland Aeschlimann, and Terry Winters—to join her in the collaborative creation of a work for the stage became a central feature of her practice. Rauschenberg had already worked extensively with Merce Cunningham and, on occasion, with other choreographers such as Viola Farber, Yvonne Rainer, and Paul Taylor. But none of the other artists Brown chose to work with had prior experience in theater design. Each collaboration has been a different, individual mix—this, in fact, has been the only constant.

Brown sees her own career evolving as a "traveling focus," where the core is continual movement. Some of the foci have brought about groups of works, which Brown has designated as "cycles," such as Equipment Pieces, Unstable Molecular Structure, Valiant, and Music. The development of the cycles is not strictly linear.

Rather, the transition to a new cycle always retains vestiges of the past. Brown has been aware during the choreographic process that she is grappling with a particular issue or set of problems, and she has named the cycles either retrospectively or concurrently to provide herself and others a framework for considering the work over time. In an art as potentially fluid as dance, no cycle, even once named, can remain entirely distinct. Brown's designations of cycles can be used as guides to the works, but other approaches are likewise worthy and welcome.

Just as Brown collaborated with visual artists, she began to do the same with composers, including Laurie Anderson, Alvin Curran, Robert Ashley, Peter Zummo, and, most recently, Dave Douglas and Salvatore Sciarrino. Early on she recognized lighting design as an art in its own right, entrusting its envisioning for a particular choreography either to the artist in charge of the overall visual presentation or to a specialist such as Beverly Emmons, Jennifer Tipton, Ken Tabachnick, or Spencer Brown. As her practice has developed, Brown has, on occasion, created her own sets and costumes (as for *For M.G.: The Movie*). She has also increasingly immersed herself in music and, in recent years, opera, which has required intensive study and brought new complexities to her creative process.

In the following chronology, factual information for each of Brown's pieces from 1979 to 2001 is presented along with commentaries — particularly the choreographer's own words and those of her collaborators. One change since 1979 is the length of Brown's works. When she moved her practice to the proscenium stage, her choreographies became significantly longer as she began to shape evening-length programs for audiences the world over rather than present brief pieces primarily for small audiences of dancers, artists, and others "in the know" in downtown New York. (See the chronology of works before 1979 in the Appendix.) Most of Brown's works for the stage have been commissioned by institutions outside of New York, the company's home base. France, in particular, has been supportive of her practice, and, to a lesser degree, other countries in Europe and sites in the United States. The first performances listed here are organized chronologically and according to three geographic distinctions: Europe, New York City, and the greater United States. With characteristic vision, Brown has found ways to explore the theater as a specific, tradition-laden environment, stripping away its conventions while also celebrating its capacity for the magical.

GLACIAL DECOY, 1979

TITLE / DATE
GLACIAL DECOY, 1979
LENGTH
18 MINUTES

SOUND
AMBIENT
VISUAL PRESENTATION
ROBERT RAUSCHENBERG
SETS
ROBERT RAUSCHENBERG
COSTUMES
ROBERT RAUSCHENBERG
LIGHTING
BEVERLY EMMONS WITH
ROBERT RAUSCHENBERG

DANCERS
TRISHA BROWN, ELIZABETH
GARREN, LISA KRAUS,
NINA LUNDBORG
FIRST PERFORMANCES
WALKER ART CENTER,
MINNEAPOLIS, MINNESOTA,
MAY 7, 1979
MARYMOUNT MANHATTAN COLLEGE
THEATER, NEW YORK CITY, [BEFORE
JUNE 30,] 1979
ESPACE FORBIN, AIX-EN-PROVENCE,
FRANCE, JULY 30, 1979

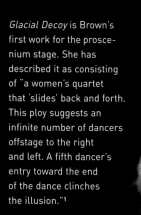

Glacial Decoy is Brown's first work for the proscenium stage. She has described it as consisting of "a women's quartet that 'slides' back and forth. This ploy suggests an infinite number of dancers offstage to the right and left. A fifth dancer's entry toward the end of the dance clinches the illusion."[1]

[In her early work Trisha] was using the world as it was for her sets and lighting, and as her theater.... I guess she went to the house [the theater] when she realized she didn't have that and missed it.[2]
ROBERT RAUSCHENBERG

VISUAL PRESENTATION

In 1954, Rauschenberg began to design sets, costumes, and lighting for performances by the Merce Cunningham, Paul Taylor, and Viola Farber dance companies. He became Cunningham's main designer in 1961, traveling with the company through 1964. In the early 1960s, Rauschenberg began to create and perform his own works, and Trisha Brown participated in some of these events in 1965, initiating a long-standing collaboration. *Glacial Decoy* is the first set he designed for her.

I've always been envious
of dance in the sense
that it's so immediate....
[Collaboration] involves
the minds and talents of
other people.... Everybody
is the material [and] I try
to indulge in processes that
are uncontrollable.[3] RR

SETS
I should design something
weightless you can carry
in your pocket and install in
a minute.[4] RR

[He made] 620 slides of
black-and-white photo-
graphs to be projected
on twelve-by-nine-foot
screens spanning the
back of the stage. The slide
images appear at four-
second intervals, progress-
ing from screen to screen,
creating an inexorable
passage of images.[5]
TRISHA BROWN

I didn't want to do a fixed-
image stage and so I
avoided that with continuous photographs...which
I took specifically for that
collaboration.[6] RR

Notes for this section
begin on page 319.

GLACIAL DECOY

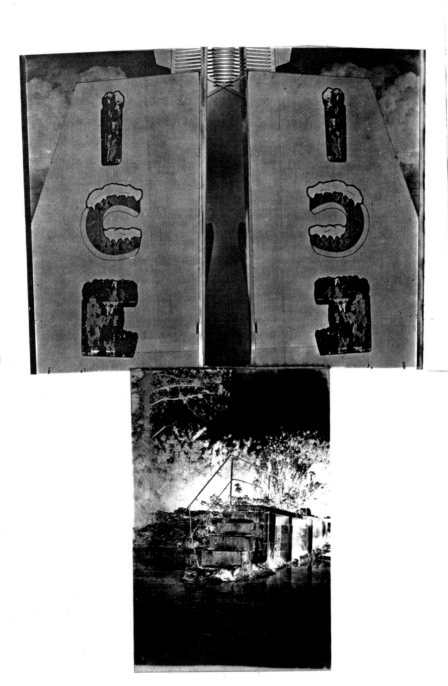

PAGES 94–95
Selections from the
photographs taken
by Robert Rauschenberg
for projection in
Glacial Decoy, 1979.

OPPOSITE PAGE
Robert Rauschenberg,
**Glacial Decoy Series:
Lithograph I**, 1979.
Color lithograph on paper,
$31^5/8$ x $47^3/4$ in.
(80.2 x 121.1 cm).
Published in an edition
of 28 by Universal
Limited Art Editions,
West Islip, New York.

THIS PAGE
Robert Rauschenberg,
**Glacial Decoy Series:
Etching III**, 1979. Color
etching on paper,
$24^4/8$ x $16^7/8$ in.
(62.5 x 43.0 cm).
Published in an edition
of 22 by Universal Limited
Art Editions, West Islip,
New York.

RAUSCHENBERG AP 1/5 79

OPPOSITE PAGE
Robert Rauschenberg,
**Glacial Decoy Series:
Etching II**, 1979. Color
etching on paper,
24 3/4 x 16 3/4 in.
(63.0 x 42.5 cm).
Published in an edition of
22 by Universal Limited Art
Editions, West Islip,
New York.

THIS PAGE
Robert Rauschenberg,
**Glacial Decoy Series:
Lithograph II**, 1980. Color
lithograph on paper,
66 x 40 1/8 in.
(167.7 x 101.9 cm).
Published in an edition
of 25 by Universal Limited
Art Editions, West Islip,
New York.

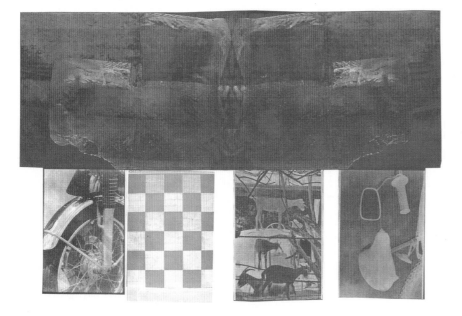

COSTUMES

White A-shaped dresses, with one-inch vertical pleats from collarbone to ankle. Short sleeves, made from the same fabric and with the same shape and pleats, were attached to the dancers' upper arms, their shoulders bare. These dresses were made of a transparent fabric used for silkscreens, which during the course of the dance bent in angular lines in keeping with the glacial metaphor.[7]

TRISHA BROWN

LIGHTING

Lighting is the strongest element because if you can't see the performance or if the light influences you so emotionally and dramatically, well then it doesn't matter what the person is doing.... A color can influence what you hear. So it even goes right off the stage right into the music.[8]

ROBERT RAUSCHENBERG

TITLE / DATE
*OPAL LOOP/CLOUD INSTALLATION
#72503*, 1980
CYCLE
UNSTABLE MOLECULAR STRUCTURE
LENGTH
15 MINUTES

SOUND
SOUND OF WATER PASSING
THROUGH HIGH-PRESSURE
NOZZLES
VISUAL PRESENTATION
FUJIKO NAKAYA
SETS
FUJIKO NAKAYA
140 FOG NOZZLES, 3 NOZZLE UNITS
WITH 3-CHANNEL CONTROL, 7 FANS,
AND HEATERS
COSTUMES
JUDITH SHEA

LIGHTING
BEVERLY EMMONS
DANCERS
TRISHA BROWN, EVA KARCZAG,
LISA KRAUS, STEPHEN PETRONIO
FIRST PERFORMANCE
55 CROSBY STREET, NEW YORK CITY,
JUNE 10, 1980

CYCLE

The Unstable Molecular Structure cycle is composed of a movement vocabulary that Brown describes as "about words that begin with 'S': sexy, sequential, seamless, silky, sensual. I compare the compositional form to the fluid chaos of microscopic motion."[9]

VISUAL PRESENTATION

Fujiko Nakaya created an ever-changing landscape of water fog that pursues its own maneuvers, at turns enveloping or receding from the dance/dancers.[10]

TRISHA BROWN

During the first half of *Opal Loop*, a cloud generated by fog nozzles gradually builds up like a backdrop, its form changing constantly. At times, small clouds drift off, travel forward across the stage, and envelop the dancers. When the dance becomes quiet, the cloud flattens and rolls forward across the stage like an ocean fog. Dancers disappear in fog. Upon reaching the audience, the fog is taken back almost instantaneously, clearing the stage and unveiling the dancers.[11]

ORIGINAL PRESS RELEASE FOR *OPAL LOOP*

This is the first and only set design to date that Nakaya has created using techniques she developed for making sculptures solely out of fog. Fujiko Nakaya met Trisha Brown in Japan in 1976.

The following comments were taken from an interview of Nakaya that took place in 1990:

Trisha spoke of the fog that rolls in waves towards the shore in Washington and its place in her childhood. I spoke of the images of fog in Japan. Trisha's description was so beautiful that trying to retell it would destroy it. Trisha and I decided we'd work separately on the image of fog. When after many experiments I succeeded in rolling fog forward and back on stage like ocean fog, I was very happy. Technically it was a big challenge for me because I had never worked with fog indoors. With the support of Billy Klüver and EAT [Experiments in Art and Technology], I conducted experiments and developed methods to control airflow using nozzles, fans, and pumps cycling on and off. I also invented a technique to move fog forward and back by reversing convection currents.

   After a week of testing, we invited dancers to come and try out dancing in fog. The first thing they said was, "the floor is wet. We can't dance." Programming fog was one thing, but keeping the floor dry posed a real problem. Billy Klüver calculated the amount of heat needed to keep the temperature of the floor higher than that of the air. A differential of 1 to 2

degrees Celsius is enough to keep fog from condensing on the floor. At the Crosby Street performance, we managed the heating with infrared heaters hung from above. At BAM, we had three big kerosene heaters burning underneath the stage.

When the piece was performed, the cloud configuration changed from night to night. I tried to be as precise as possible, but fog doesn't always respond in the way I expect. You are dealing with a delicate balance of air. It's a live process, an improvisation each time with the atmospheric conditions.

Fog sculpture can be defined as "articulated" nature. All the movements are there and, by controlling it, you reveal a larger structure. Seen from nature's side, it is completely natural, and seen from this side, it is completely artificial. Fog, like dance, is tangible and concrete, but it is also entirely abstract. I feel there is some affinity to Trisha's dance.[12]

FUJIKO NAKAYA

COSTUMES

Trisha had a new opal ring, if I remember. It was the flashing, the shifting, of colors that she related to movement. So I took this as a cue for the costumes.... Each one has a different reflective quality (satin crepe, shimmer Spandex, iridescent silk, matte canvas) as well as a different color. The order of the dance, to my eye, was four characters that start in a square, or box. Each begins a phrase later than the next. Soon, what began with such neat arithmetic order becomes a completely chaotic storm of angles and swirls of elbows and knees, and each dancer seems to be punching their way out of an isolated world. So, the different forms of the costumes exaggerate the amount of movement (square, draped, puffed, skintight). After watching *Opal Loop* develop in rehearsal, the shape of each costume was a response to the particular physical imprint of each dancer on the movements of the piece. I love this work. It is a gem, like a small dictionary of Trisha Brown moves.[13]

JUDITH SHEA

[Trisha's] costume, made out of an iridescent "faux" taffeta with an elastic waistband and elastic at the ankles, represented "postmodern dance"; Eva was "Isadora Duncan," and Stephen was "Jose Limón."[14] Lisa wore a unitard as close as we could get to her skin color. Her costume was about anatomy.[15] JS

TITLE / DATE
SON OF GONE FISHIN', 1981
CYCLE
UNSTABLE MOLECULAR STRUCTURE
LENGTH
25 MINUTES

MUSIC
ROBERT ASHLEY, "ATALANTA"
MUSIC PERFORMANCE
ROBERT ASHLEY WITH KURT
MUNKACSI; LIVE ONLY AT FIRST
PERFORMANCE
VISUAL PRESENTATION
DONALD JUDD
THIS WAS JUDD'S FIRST STAGE
COLLABORATION. HIS SECOND
AND LAST WAS BROWN'S *NEWARK
(NIWEWEORCE)* OF 1987.

SETS
DONALD JUDD
A SERIES OF FIVE DROPS UPSTAGE,
MOVING THROUGH A VARIETY OF
POSITIONS
COSTUMES
JUDITH SHEA
SHEA BASED THE FINAL COLOR
SCHEME OF COSTUMES ON DONALD
JUDD'S GREEN AND BLUE SET.
LIGHTING
BEVERLY EMMONS

DANCERS
EVA KARCZAG, LISA KRAUS,
DIANE MADDEN, STEPHEN
PETRONIO, VICKY SHICK,
RANDY WARSHAW
FIRST PERFORMANCES
BAM OPERA HOUSE, BROOKLYN
ACADEMY OF MUSIC, BROOKLYN,
NEW YORK, OCTOBER 16, 1981
FESTIVAL D'AUTOMNE À PARIS,
THÉÂTRE DE PARIS, FRANCE,
NOVEMBER 13, 1983

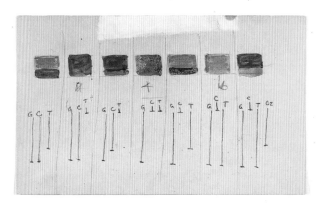

OPPOSITE PAGE FROM TOP
Judith Shea, **Costume study for Son of Gone Fishin'**, 1981. Watercolor on tracing paper, 8 7/8 x 17 in. (22.4 x 43.2 cm). Collection of Judith Shea.

Donald Judd, **Untitled**, 1981. Watercolor and pencil on card, 3 x 5 in. (7.6 x 12.7 cm). Collection of Trisha Brown.

THIS PAGE FROM TOP
Donald Judd, **Untitled**, 1981. Study for *Son of Gone Fishin'*, watercolor on paper, 24 1/2 x 32 1/2 in. (62.2 x 82.6 cm). Collection of the Judd Foundation.

Donald Judd, **Untitled**, 1981. Study for *Son of Gone Fishin'*, watercolor on paper, 24 1/2 x 32 1/2 in. (62.2 x 82.6 cm). Collection of the Judd Foundation.

This choreography was a "doosey." In it I reached the apogee of complexity in my work. The infrastructure of the piece was related to the cross-section of a tree trunk. ABC center CBA. Complex group-forms of six dancers were performed first in the normal direction and then in retrograde. Bob Ashley gave us a little library of different tapes to carry with us on tour. The dancers randomly chose which music we would use each performance. Something like having the band along with us.[16]
TRISHA BROWN

MUSIC
Ashley and Bob Shorr mixed three tapes, titled Willard, Max, and Bud, from orchestral parts of the three operas in *Atalanta (Acts of God)*. At the premiere only, Ashley played the organ and Kurt Munkacsi mixed and processed the combination of live and recorded music.[17] TB

I have admired Trisha Brown's work since I first saw it with the Judson Dance Theater in 1965. I have also admired the way she generally sticks with contemporary music, even in these cautious times. I hope she keeps it up. A few years ago I was on a panel discussion with her, when somebody asked wasn't she getting too old to dance. Trisha said she was going to dance until she dropped. Perfect.[18]
ROBERT ASHLEY

FIRST PERFORMANCES
PREVIEW OF PARTIAL VERSION
AT THE FESTIVAL D'AVIGNON,
LA CHARTREUSE, FRANCE,
JULY 20, 1982
NEXT WAVE FESTIVAL, BAM OPERA
HOUSE, BROOKLYN ACADEMY OF
MUSIC, BROOKLYN, NEW YORK,
OCTOBER 20, 1983

COSTUMES
ROBERT RAUSCHENBERG
WHITE TRANSPARENT COSTUMES,
SILKSCREENED IN PALE-GRAY-TO-
BLACK URBAN INDUSTRIAL IMAGES.
LIGHTING
BEVERLY EMMONS WITH
ROBERT RAUSCHENBERG
DANCERS
TRISHA BROWN, IRÉNE HULTMAN,
EVA KARCZAG, DIANE MADDEN,
STEPHEN PETRONIO, VICKY SHICK,
RANDY WARSHAW

MUSIC
LAURIE ANDERSON,
"LONG TIME, NO SEE"
MUSIC PERFORMANCE
LAURIE ANDERSON, VIOLIN,
AND RICHARD LANDRY, SAXOPHONE;
LIVE ONLY AT FIRST
PERFORMANCE
VISUAL PRESENTATION
ROBERT RAUSCHENBERG
SETS
ROBERT RAUSCHENBERG

TITLE / DATE
SET AND RESET, 1983
CYCLE
UNSTABLE MOLECULAR
STRUCTURE
SET AND RESET IS THE CULMINA-
TION OF THE UNSTABLE
MOLECULAR STRUCTURE CYCLE.
LENGTH
28 MINUTES

OPPOSITE PAGE
Robert Rauschenberg,
Untitled, 1985. Acrylic and
collage on fabric-laminated
paper, 59 7/8 x 36 in.
(152.0 x 91.4 cm).
Collection of Mr. and
Mrs. Roy S. O'Connor.

THIS PAGE
Robert Rauschenberg,
Untitled, 1985. Acrylic on
fabric-laminated paper,
41 7/8 x 64 1/2 in.
(104.5 x 163.8 cm).
Collection of Trisha Brown.

OPPOSITE PAGE
Robert Rauschenberg,
Set and Reset, 1983.
Collage, acrylic, and pencil
on illustrated board,
16 x 16 in. (40.6 x 40.6 cm).
Collection of the artist.

THIS PAGE CLOCKWISE
FROM TOP LEFT
Robert Rauschenberg,
Untitled, 1985. Acrylic and
collage on laminated paper,
24 x 24 in. (61.0 x 61.0 cm).
Private Collection.

Robert Rauschenberg,
Untitled, 1985. Acrylic and
collage on laminated
paper, 24 x 23 7/8 in.
(61.0 x 60.6 cm). Collection
of Vicky Schick.

Robert Rauschenberg,
Untitled, 1985. Acrylic and
collage on laminated paper,
24 x 24 in. (61.0 x 61.0 cm).
Collection of Iréne
Hultman.

Robert Rauschenberg,
Untitled, 1985. Acrylic and
collage on laminated paper,
24 x 24 in. (61.0 x 61.0 cm).
Collection of Randy
Warshaw.

Robert Rauschenberg,
Untitled, 1985. Acrylic and
collage on laminated
paper, 23 3/4 x 24 in.
(60.3 x 61.0 cm). Collection
of Diane Madden.

Robert Rauschenberg,
Untitled, 1985. Acrylic and
collage on laminated paper,
24 x 24 in. (61.0 x 61.0 cm).
Private Collection.

I started work on *Set and Reset* knowing only that Laurie Anderson would compose the music and that I would reconstruct a solo version of *Walking on the Wall* (1971) as part of the new piece. An amber light picks up Diane "Walking on the (back-stage) Wall," handheld by four dancers with out-stretched arms, her feet to the brick, the crown of her head to the audience. It looks like the radical 1971 equipment piece, but the dancers are now wearing gorgeous cos-tumes. All of the cross-overs were revealed using a transparent black scrim, which displayed our offstage behavior.[19]

TRISHA BROWN

MUSIC

Working with Trisha on *Set and Reset* was an amazing experience for me as a composer. I came to rehearsals to watch the early versions of the piece and everybody was falling — fast, slow motion, at odd angles, in sweep-ing moves. Falling has always interested me on many levels, but I had never tried to make music that fell. As I experimented with this Trisha gave me constant feedback but not in words, but through her body language. I had never communicated quite like that before, and it was exhilarating.[20]

LAURIE ANDERSON

SETS

Bob designed an overhead structure named *Elastic Carrier (Shiner)*. The central form is a large rectangular box made of a transparent white fabric stretched over an alminum frame with two slanted internal panels. At either side of the box, a pyra-midal form made of the identical materials is attached. Four films of black-and-white stock footage with sound — each film edited by Bob — are projected simultaneously onto the structure, their images refracting as they pass through the planes of gauze on their way to a state of what Bob called "tonal vagueries." The set, with its collaged film and accompanying sound fragments — pieces of text, instruction, music, and industrial noise — is, said Bob, "a translucent traveler luminated by four internal movies. Hopefully, to defract and register changing distortions of images in a mix to provide a hovering environment for the dance."

This "hovering environ-ment" is first seen resting on the stage floor…. Liftoff is one minute twenty seconds after curtain, the set rising (in tandem with the projectors) to its overhead position, where it remains for twenty-five minutes until the end of the dance. The stage's velour legs [the curtains at the sides] have been reconsti-tuted as see-through black scrim edged with a vertical stripe of ice-white satin, which demarcates the difference between onstage behavior and off. Our sanctuary is gone, invisibility dashed, down-time on display.[21] TB

COSTUMES

[I wished that the costumes would] provoke your looking *past* the costumes and back to the dance.[22]

ROBERT RAUSCHENBERG

LATERAL PASS, 1985

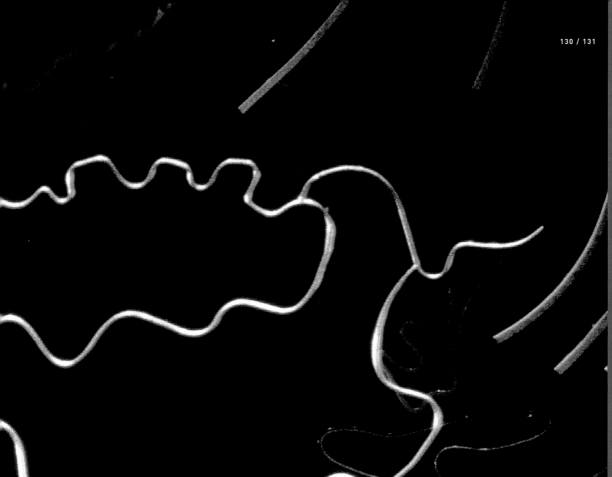

TITLE / DATE
LATERAL PASS, 1985

CYCLE
VALIANT
THE VALIANT CYCLE EXPLORES
WHAT IT MEANS FOR
DANCERS TO APPROACH THEIR
PHYSICAL LIMITS.

LENGTH
28 MINUTES

MUSIC
PETER ZUMMO
SELECTIONS FROM THE SUITE *SIX
SONGS:* "SCI-FI," "SLOW HEART,"
"SONG VI," "SONG IV"

MUSIC PERFORMANCE
THE PETER ZUMMO ORCHESTRA:
PETER ZUMMO, TROMBONE;
GUY KLUCEVSEK, ACCORDION;
ARTHUR RUSSELL, CELLO;
BILL RUYLE, MARIMBA;
MUSTAFA AHMED, PERCUSSION

VISUAL PRESENTATION
NANCY GRAVES

SETS
NANCY GRAVES

COSTUMES
NANCY GRAVES

LIGHTING
BEVERLY EMMONS

DANCERS
TRISHA BROWN, IRÉNE HULTMAN,
CAROLYN LUCAS, DIANE MADDEN,
STEPHEN PETRONIO, LISA
SCHMIDT, VICKY SHICK, RANDY
WARSHAW

FIRST PERFORMANCES
WALKER ART CENTER,
MINNEAPOLIS, MINNESOTA.
SEPTEMBER 5, 1985
CITY CENTER, NEW YORK CITY,
SEPTEMBER 17, 1985
MINZHU WENHUA GONG
THEATER, BEIJING, CHINA,
NOVEMBER 17, 1985
AKADEMIE DER KÜNSTE, BERLIN,
GERMANY, MAY 7, 1986

In this performance Brown resumes her long-time interest in flying by hoisting a dancer matter-of-factly into the air with the aid of a harness. He was lifted to a fixed height, about the head level of the dancers, and was able to drift from one side of the stage to the other, causing inevitable interactions with the dancing ensemble.

[Lateral Pass] went on to be a resource for years... broken patterns, making a traveling phrase.... I was thinking about my childhood [when I ran through the forest over] moss and mud and hardwood and rotten wood. If you're going fast, you just have to pick where you place your feet. It is a child's first experience of running fast. But it is not going to be your basic one-two-three, two-two-three, three-two-three. It was totally asymmetrical and unpredictable travelling patterns. It's an example of something I went on to explore later. It became a subject for me.[23]

Lateral Pass was Graves's first and only stage collaboration with Brown, a longtime friend.

When Trisha and I had our first meeting, I basically proposed some general ideas that had to do with light versus dark as the body moves. One of the ideas I considered was having the dancers holding flashlights as they moved and, in certain passages, wearing headlights such as those you might find in a sports catalogue. Another proposal was to have a man sit on top of a scaffold sawing steel that would throw out sparks onto the stage and that would move from left to right in the deep background. Another idea, and at this point everybody really raised their eyebrows, was a fire onstage. As Trisha and I began to share ideas, my attitudes about both sets and costumes became more concrete. New ideas evolved: for instance, the costumes had specific colors and forms according to whether they were intended for a solo, a duet, a trio, or a quartet.

[When developing the costumes], I had someone who would bring me swatches. And it was fantastic. It was better than Christmas. I would get these pages and books of fifty blues in all kinds of kooky textures. Things that you've never heard of before. And then I tried to consider the reality of using them.

Trisha's collaborations with artists represented a range of styles: from minimalist work to something as flamboyant and colorful and out-reaching as mine, to something as sophisticated and sensual as [Rauschenberg's] work.[24]

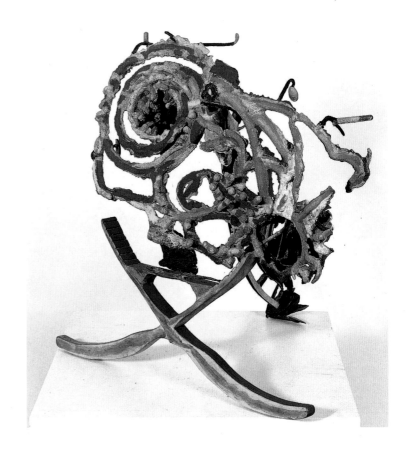

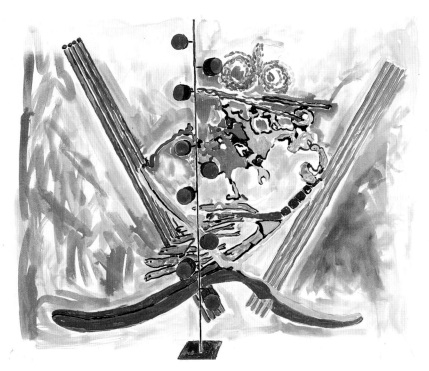

OPPOSITE PAGE FROM TOP
Nancy Graves, **Visage**, 1982.
Bronze with polychrome
patina, 19 x 17 1/2 x 19 in.
(48.3 x 44.5 x 48.3 cm).
Nancy Graves Founda-
tion, Inc., NY.

Nancy Graves, **Stay (Glass
Series)**, 1983. Enameled
bronze, 15 1/4 x 17 7/8 x 9 1/4 in.
(38.7 x 45.3 x 23.5 cm).
Nancy Graves Founda-
tion, Inc., NY.

THIS PAGE FROM TOP
Nancy Graves,
**Untitled #62 (T. Brown
"Lateral Pass") Poster
Study**, c. 1985.
Pastel, pencil, and
oil stick on synthetic
paper, 30 x 40 in.
(76.2 x 101.6 cm).
Nancy Graves Founda-
tion, Inc., NY.

Nancy Graves, **Lateral Pass
(Set Design for Trisha
Brown Co.)**, 1985. Gouache,
pencil, and acrylic on
paper, 30 x 40 in.
(76.2 x 101.6 cm).
Nancy Graves Founda-
tion, Inc., NY.

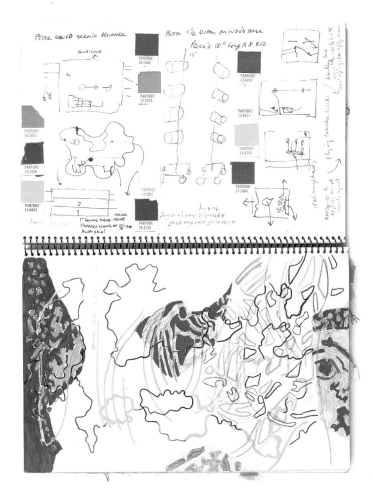

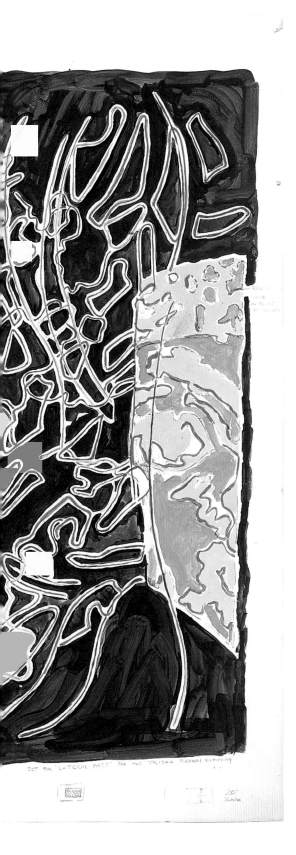

ON LEFT
Nancy Graves,
**Set for Lateral Pass
(Trisha Brown Co.)**, 1985.
Gouache on paper,
30 x 40 in. (76.2 x 101.6 cm).
Nancy Graves Founda-
tion, Inc., NY.

ON RIGHT
Nancy Graves, **Lateral Pass
Notebook**, 1985. Gouache,
graphite, ink, and fabric
samples, 30 x 40 in.
(76.2 x 101.6 cm).
Nancy Graves Founda-
tion, Inc., NY.

SETS

The choreography was precisely designed to permit seven huge set pieces — which we called "land forms" — drop down into its midst. Not only is the set within the choreography, but the parts move up and down on cues, permitting or blocking passage for the dancers.[25]
TRISHA BROWN

COSTUMES

I asked [Graves] to make sculptural costumes and that she did. She also made the funniest piece I ever saw in my life. She had panels of things hanging off people.... And she said they could change all the time. Well, people think dancers are very free spirits up there, but they're not. They're perfectionists, they're disciplined, and they don't want stuff flying around all over their bodies that might come off...while they're performing.[26] TB

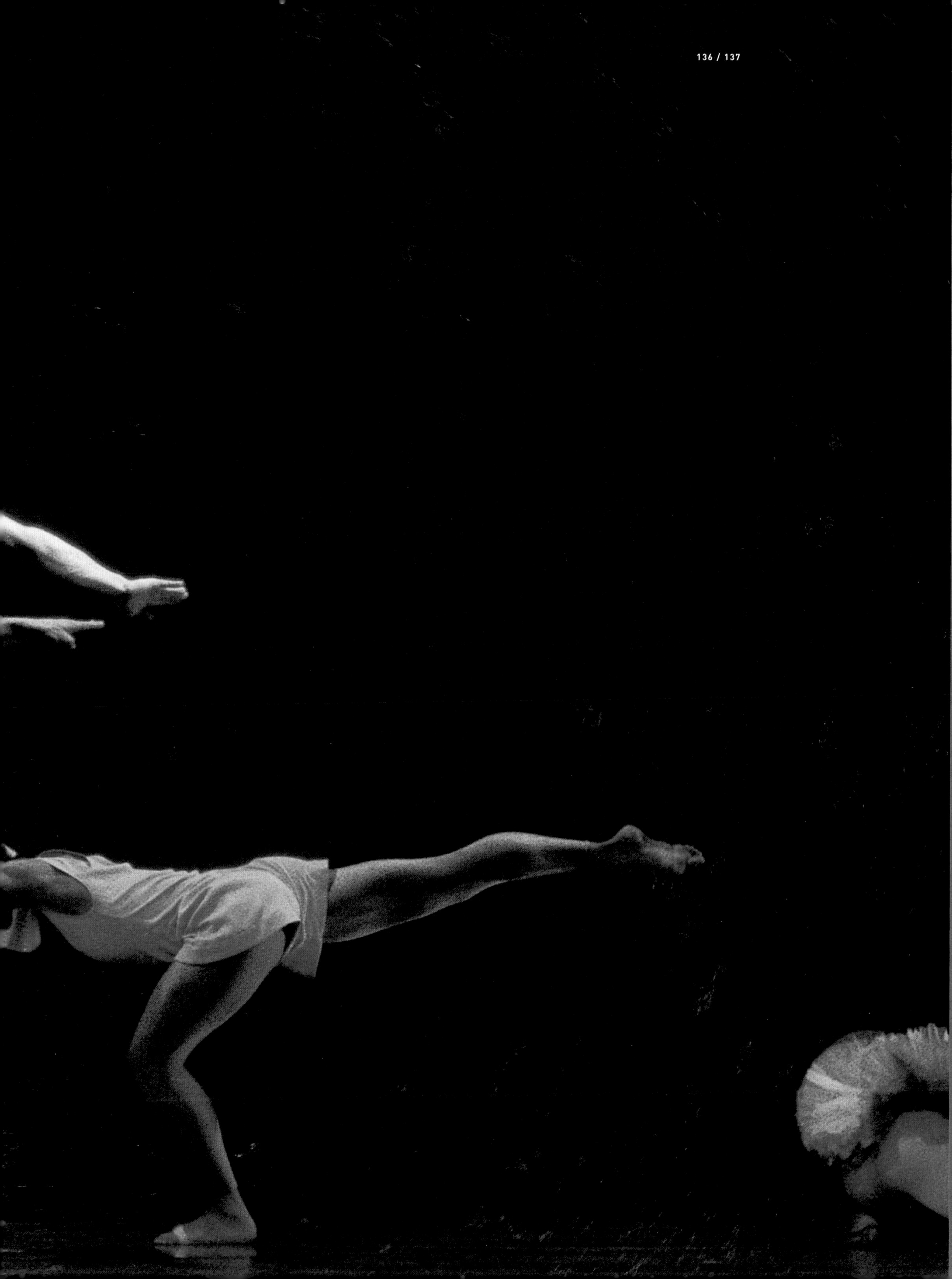

In January 1987 at the Teatro di San Carlo, Naples, the Graves set did not arrive, so Robert Rauschenberg created a replacement set and costumes in less than two days by driving around to junk shops as well as finding objects on the street. The found objects ultimately became autonomous sculptures.

Rauschenberg's substitute costumes were "black unitards...hand-cut with scissors...in jagged strokes at the sleeve and the leg. To these somber suits, ravaged at the edges, were added three-by-five foot polyester scarves, red, green, white, and beyond in color, in commemoration of some Italian soccer team. The dancers were instructed to tie their scarves onto their bodies or uni-tards in whatever way they chose."[27]

I like those kind of emergencies.... I think she [Nancy Graves] would have both been pleased that somebody could step in (and possibly that it might be me) but horrified at the results.[28]
ROBERT RAUSCHENBERG

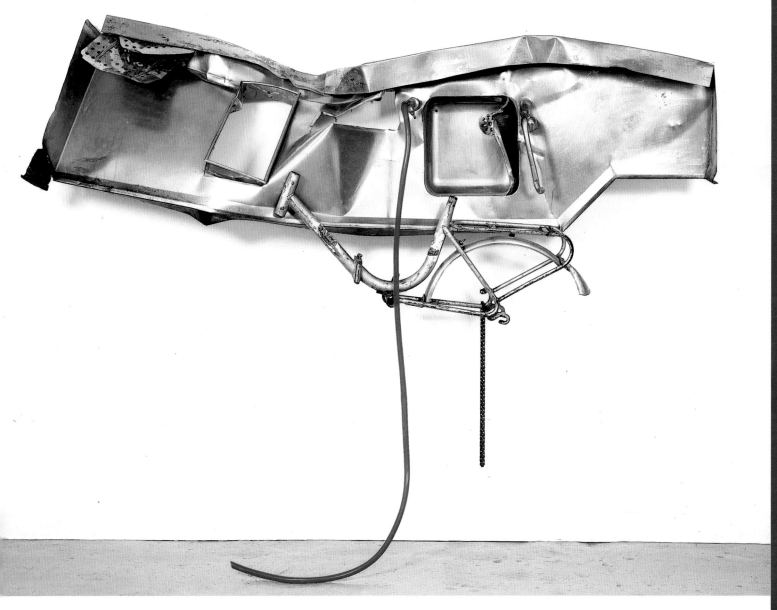

OPPOSITE PAGE
Robert Rauschenberg,
**Blind Rosso Porpora Glut
(Neapolitan)**, 1987.
Assembled objects,
51 1/4 x 76 x 15 3/8 in.
(130.2 x 193.0 x 39.1 cm).
Collection of the artist.

THIS PAGE
Robert Rauschenberg,
**Mobile Cluster Glut
(Neapolitan)**, 1987.
Assembled metal parts
with plastic hose,
41 1/4 x 94 1/2 x 18 1/2 in.
(104.8 x 240.0 x 47.0 cm).
Collection of the artist.

TITLE / DATE
NEWARK [N]WEWEORCE], 1987

CYCLE
VALIANT

LENGTH
30 MINUTES

MUSIC
PETER ZUMMO, FROM SOUND
CONCEPT BY DONALD JUDD

VISUAL PRESENTATION
DONALD JUDD

SETS
DONALD JUDD

COSTUMES
DONALD JUDD
GRAY UNITARDS

LIGHTING
KEN TABACHNICK, WITH JUDD'S
DIRECTIVE TO BE "PLOTLESS"

DANCERS
JEFFREY AXELROD, LANCE GRIES,
IRÈNE HULTMAN, CAROLYN LUCAS,
DIANE MADDEN, LISA SCHMIDT,
SHELLEY SABINA SENTER

FIRST PERFORMANCES
CENTRE NATIONAL DE DANSE
CONTEMPORAINE (CNDC)/NOUVEAU
THÉÂTRE D'ANGERS, FRANCE,
JUNE 10, 1987
CITY CENTER, NEW YORK CITY,
SEPTEMBER 14, 1987

During the making of this dance, one of Trisha Brown's production assistants would yell out "new work!" to announce on-stage rehearsal time for the yet untitled piece. Brown heard this prompt as "Newark!" which she likened to the bellowing of a train conductor, and made it the main title of the new dance. She then looked up this word in the *Encyclopedia Britannica*, and found that the original name for Newark, England, was "Niweweorce," a term that was used around 1055 or even earlier. Brown was taken by the words and sounds that could be found by extrapolating from this obsolete name — wow, wew, new, weorce (as in "worse"), and so on. *Nieweweorce* became the subtitle of the piece.[29]

SETS
Newark (Niweweorce), further developed the stage design Judd initiated with *Son of Gone Fishin'*. The drops are upstage in *Son of Gone Fishin'*; in *Newark* they use the entire stage.

Cadmium light red, burnt sienna, cadmium yellow, deep blue, and cadmium red. Drops rising and descending at different times, slightly alternating the amount of depth on the stage for the dancers. Hard edge.[30]
TRISHA BROWN

Donald Judd, **Untitled**, 1988.
Anodized aluminum
and Plexiglas,
19 5/8 x 216 x 19 5/8 in.
(49.8 x 548.6 x 49.8 cm)
Courtesy of PaceWildenstein.

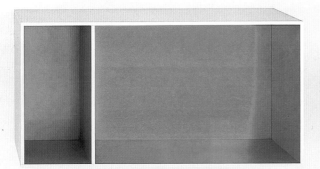
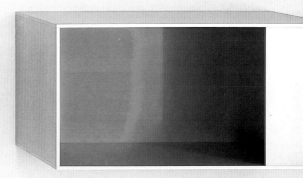

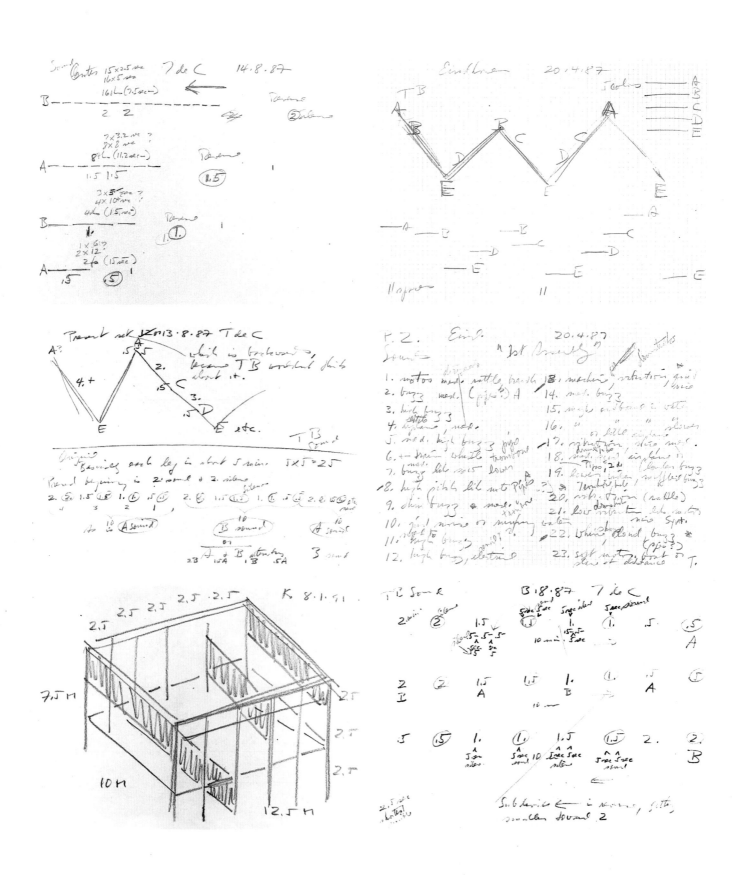

OPPOSITE PAGE
Each: Donald Judd,
Untitled, 1987.
Pencil on paper,
8 1/2 x 11 1/4 in.
(21.6 x 28.6 cm).
Collection of the
Judd Foundation.

THIS PAGE
Donald Judd, **Untitled**, 1987.
Suite of ten woodcuts,
22 5/8 x 31 1/2 in.
(56.2 x 80.0 cm) each.
Published in an edition
of 25 by Brooke Alexander
Editions. Courtesy
of Brooke Alexander,
New York.

LIGHTING
I was lucky to collabor-
ate with Trisha early in
my career. Her work, which
is always deeply explora-
tory, coincided with my
interests in exploring the
human body in space
through lighting. Trisha consistently challenged me
with her insight into form,
structure, and the rules
of systems in a way that
was not only engaging,
but truly enjoyable. I laughed a lot while I worked
with Trisha and still reflect
on her ideas and work
constantly.[31]
KEN TABACHNICK

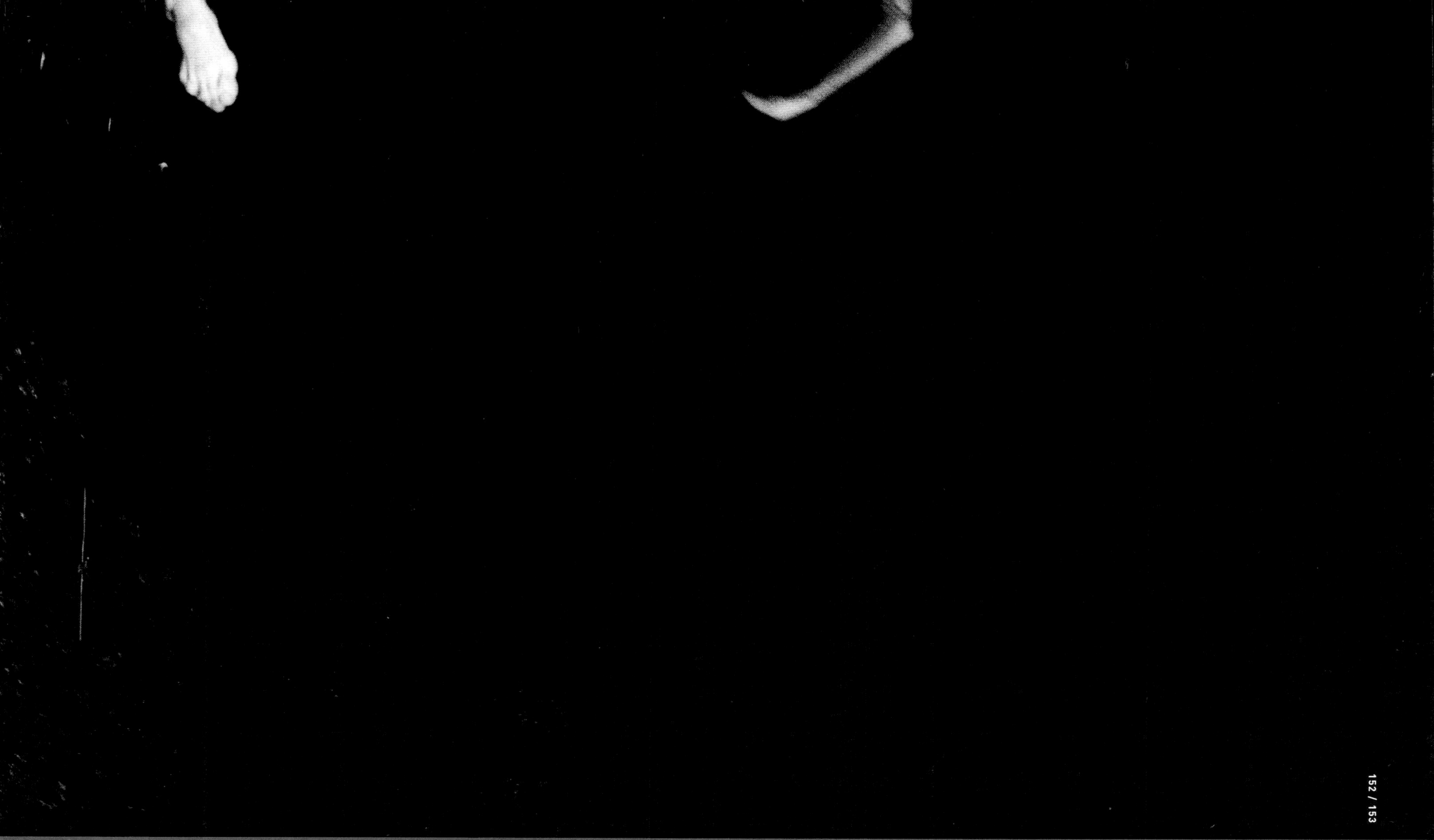

TITLE / DATE
ASTRAL CONVERTIBLE, 1989
CYCLE
VALIANT
LENGTH
32 MINUTES

MUSIC
RICHARD LANDRY
RECORDED MUSIC IS PART OF
A STEREO SENSOR SYSTEM
INSTALLED IN THE EIGHT FREE-
STANDING TOWERS OF THE SET.
VISUAL PRESENTATION
ROBERT RAUSCHENBERG
SETS
ROBERT RAUSCHENBERG
EIGHT TOWERS
PER BIORN, ENGINEERING AND
CONSTRUCTION; BILLY KLÜVER,
TECHNICAL CONSULTANT

COSTUMES
ROBERT RAUSCHENBERG
LIGHTING
KEN TABACHNICK WITH ROBERT
RAUSCHENBERG
AUTOMOBILE HEADLIGHTS
ON TOWERS
DANCERS
LANCE GRIES, NICOLE
JURALEWICZ, GREGORY LARA,
CAROLYN LUCAS, DIANE MADDEN,
LISA SCHMIDT, SHELLEY SABINA
SENTER, DAVID THOMSON,
WIL SWANSON

FIRST PERFORMANCES
PREVIEWED AT THE PALACE OF
CULTURE, MOSCOW, U.S.S.R.,
FEBRUARY 1, 1989
CITY CENTER, NEW YORK CITY,
MARCH 14, 1989
FESTIVAL DE MONTPELLIER, COUR
JACQUES COEUR, MONTPELLIER,
FRANCE, JUNE 22, 1989

I once sat in the last balcony of the old Sadler Wells
theater and its height
produced a nearly vertical
view from above. I realized
then that those poor souls
only saw the foreheads
of the dancers, no backdrop
and a lot of floor. For *Astral
Convertible*, I worked in
three levels, on the floor,
standing, and the level
exactly in between the two.
The floor dance always
gave the upper balcony
something to look at, as did
the standing dance for the
low seats in the orchestra.
The dancers powered
their way up and down
through the midlevel
phrases to the standing/
leaping material and
back down according to
choreographic design.
In fact, for the low seats,
the dancers could enter
by rising and exit by
dancing back down into
the floor. Valiance and
audience perception were
subject matter.[32]
TRISHA BROWN

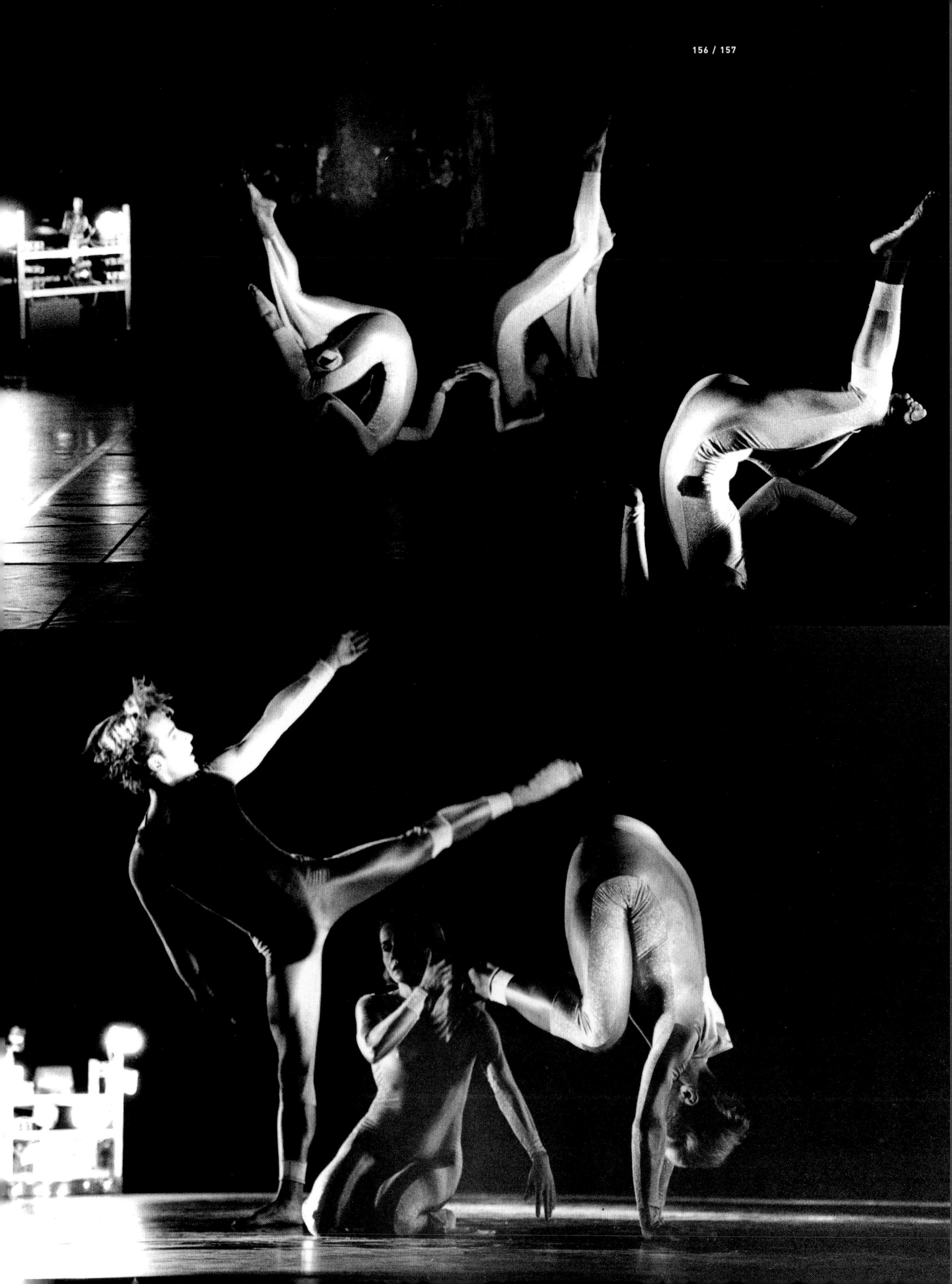

SETS

I wanted the dancers to be
in direct contact with the
sound and the lights. They
were in control of both.[33]
ROBERT RAUSCHENBERG

I learned of an unusual
dance circuit through Spain,
in which performances
were held out-of-doors in
town squares, bereft of
technical support. My
choreographies were not
invited. To gain access to
this circuit for reasons of
economics and romance,
I asked Bob [Rauschenberg]
to design an inflatable
set.... He came back with
a rejection of the inflatable
idea.... Instead, he pro-
posed eight metal tow-
ers...two each in heights
of two, four, six, and eight
feet.... They are self-con-
tained and house all our
theatrical gear, most of it
from the automobile indus-
try: car batteries, head-
lights, stereo systems,
sensors. The sensors are
positioned to trigger the
lights and sound to turn
on or off when a dancer
passes. Their small control
boards introduce a degree
of randomness into the
dancer-sensor relationship.
    Bob gave me the
title for the piece: "astral"
for skyborne, "conver-
tible" for the option
to change, and, of course,
for the pun.[34]
TRISHA BROWN

COSTUMES

The costumes Bob
designed are shiny, skin-
tight, silver-and-white
unitards marked by white
reflector stripes, which
augment in the piercing,
striated lighting of the
headlights. The women
each have a white
triangular piece of fabric
attached to the inseam
of their costumes,
suggesting a skirt.[35] TB

I wanted the dancers to
appear almost as filaments
of light bulbs.[36] RR

I was asked to collaborate
with Bob on a new piece
to be performed outdoors
at the National Gallery
of Art in Washington, D.C....
Another autonomous set
was needed.... I suggested
that we keep *Astral
Convertible*'s set and costumes, double the length
of the dance, include
moving towers, ask John
Cage to write new
music, and call it *Astral
Converted (55)*.[37]
TRISHA BROWN

It is rare to have the
chance to open a choreog-
raphy (*Astral Convertible*)
and create again, within
the context of the former,
something new (*Astral
Converted*). A significant
difference was achieved in
Astral Converted through
the technical stabilization
of the towers. Initially
we could not touch them.
Now we could push one
or more onto the stage or
into a dance or snag them
out of way of an oncoming
dancer. But most important,
in the context of an out-
door, unframed playing
area, we could reconfigure
the space at will.[38] TB

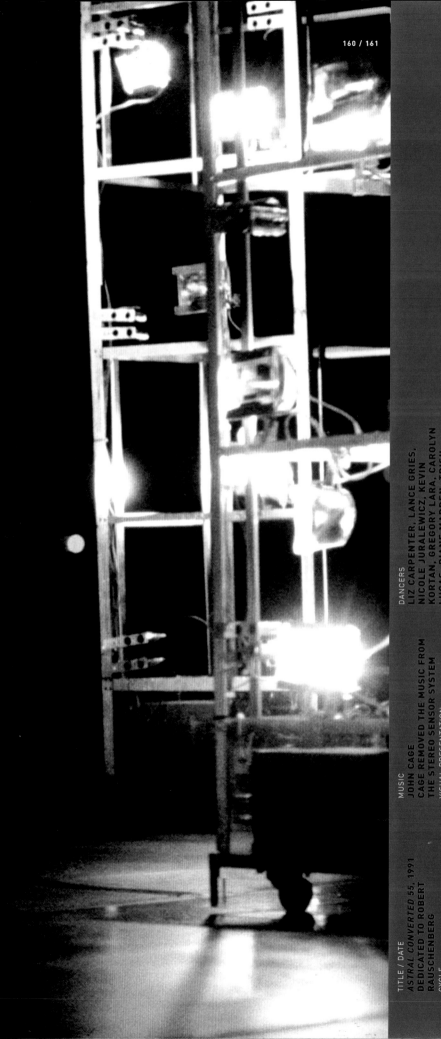

TITLE / DATE
ASTRAL CONVERTED 55, 1991
DEDICATED TO ROBERT
RAUSCHENBERG
CYCLE
VALIANT
LENGTH
55 MINUTES

MUSIC
JOHN CAGE
CAGE REMOVED THE MUSIC FROM
THE STEREO SENSOR SYSTEM
VISUAL PRESENTATION
ROBERT RAUSCHENBERG
SETS
ROBERT RAUSCHENBERG
COSTUMES
ROBERT RAUSCHENBERG
LIGHTING
SPENCER BROWN WITH ROBERT
RAUSCHENBERG

DANCERS
LIZ CARPENTER, LANCE GRIES,
NICOLE JURALEWICZ, KEVIN
KORTAN, GREGORY LARA, CAROLYN
LUCAS, DIANE MADDEN, TRISH
OESTERLING, LISA SCHMIDT,
WIL SWANSON, DAVID THOMSON
FIRST PERFORMANCES
NATIONAL GALLERY OF ART,
WASHINGTON, D.C., MAY 14, 1991
FERME DU BUISSON, NEAR PARIS,
FRANCE, NOVEMBER 24, 1992
CITY CENTER, NEW YORK CITY,
MAY 6, 1993

MUSIC
LOCAL MARCHING BAND
VISUAL PRESENTATION
ROBERT RAUSCHENBERG
SETS
ROBERT RAUSCHENBERG
COSTUMES
ROBERT RAUSCHENBERG
COSTUMES OF GOLD AND SILVER
WITH MARKINGS OF MAGENTA,
GREEN, ROSE, AND YELLOW

LIGHTING
SPENCER BROWN WITH ROBERT
RAUSCHENBERG
DANCERS
TRISHA BROWN, LANCE GRIES,
NICOLE JURALEWICZ, KEVIN
KORTAN, GREGORY LARA,
CAROLYN LUCAS, DIANE MADDEN.
TRISH OESTERLING, LISA
SCHMIDT, SHELLEY SABINA
SENTER, WIL SWANSON,
DAVID THOMSON
FIRST PERFORMANCES
BIENNALE DE LA DANSE DE LYON.

FRANCE, SEPTEMBER 22, 1990
WEXNER CENTER FOR THE ARTS,
OHIO STATE UNIVERSITY,
COLUMBUS, NOVEMBER 2, 1990
CITY CENTER, NEW YORK CITY,
MARCH 5, 1991

TITLE / DATE
FORAY FORÊT, 1990
CYCLE
BACK TO ZERO
LENGTH
28 MINUTES

Audience perception is a central concern in *Foray Forêt*. By the third piece in the Valiant cycle my dancers were lying in the wings on their backs at the end of a program heaving and hauling for air. They asked me to do something simpler and easier for the next choreography to balance the program, and I was ready. Back to Zero was a return to simple forms and a movement vocabulary in which I relinquished the artifice of cleverness. I developed a vocabulary of subconscious moves through the activation of gesture before the mind is engaged. I called them delicate aberrations. A marching band playing Sousa marched around the exterior of the theater and in some instances entered the lobby. (Each theater requires a different route for the band.) I thought about time: the audience member going back in time to a memory of a parade (Where are you?), while watching a choreography on the stage made of small details in combination with a larger more energetic vocabulary, while piecing together the location and path of the band outdoors or in the lobby (what do you see?).[39]
TRISHA BROWN

Trisha is doing a solo, and we're in the wings with just our tips showing. It was so hard to do that; what a struggle. Trisha's work looks so free but it sure doesn't feel free when you're trying to do it. She really desires very strict unison.[40]
CAROLYN LUCAS

MUSIC
At the first performance, the Fanfare de l'Ecole Centrale de Lyon, a local marching band, played outside the theater, approached, and disappeared again. On stage, during the section of the choreography when the dancers were dancing in the wings while all tried to maintain unison, they cued each other by whistling.

Bob Rauschenberg has functioned as my unofficial artistic director for many years. I told him that I had an idea that won't go away, that I wanted to test out on him. "I'm thinking of using a marching band playing Sousa as they march around the outside of the theater for the music in my next piece." He said, "I think that's the best bad idea you've ever had."[41] TB

COSTUMES
Bob told me, "Trisha, I've found you the cheapest, sleaziest looking fabric."[42] TB

FOR M.G.: THE MOVIE, 1991

TITLE / DATE
FOR M.G.: THE MOVIE, 1991
CYCLE
BACK TO ZERO
LENGTH
30 MINUTES

MUSIC
ALVIN CURRAN
MUSIC PERFORMANCE
ALVIN CURRAN, RECORDED PIANO
AND AMBIENT SOUNDS; WITH
SOME PERFORMANCES HAVING
LIVE PIANO ACCOMPANIMENT BY
CURRAN, OFFSTAGE RIGHT
VISUAL PRESENTATION
TRISHA BROWN
SETS
TRISHA BROWN
AVAILABLE BACKSTAGE CLUTTER,
FOG MACHINE, AND LIGHTS

COSTUMES
TRISHA BROWN
LIGHTING
SPENCER BROWN WITH
TRISHA BROWN
DANCERS
LIZ CARPENTER, NICOLE
JURALEWICZ, KEVIN KORTAN,
GREGORY LARA, DIANE MADDEN,
WIL SWANSON, DAVID THOMSON
FIRST PERFORMANCES
L'HIPPODROME DE DOUAI,
FRANCE, NOVEMBER 8, 1991
(UNDER THE TITLE *LEVER BEST*)

EGYPTIAN THEATRE, NORTHERN
ILLINOIS UNIVERSITY, DEKALB,
APRIL 16, 1992
CITY CENTER, NEW YORK CITY,
APRIL 28, 1993

Performed twice under the title *Lever Best* (L'Hippodrome de Douai, France, and Sadler's Wells, London). Title changed to *For M.G.: The Movie* after the death of Michel Guy to honor the French minister of culture who had invited Brown to France in 1973 to perform at the Musée Galliera, Paris.

Enigmatic events were my overarching metaphor. I wanted to slip dancers on and off the stage as they do in film, not to lumber in with their great big two-legged bodies. I wanted mystery. Sleight of body. I got those invisible entries by making a commotion downstage right while a figure eases into the space on the opposite side. There were four characters in the piece. The marathoner, Diane Madden, running in great looping spatial patterns ratcheting up in speed or down again to bank the corners just right, not using one iota of excessive muscle power. Everyman, Kevin Kortan, standing there with his back to the audience, while the choreography ebbs and flows around him. Wil Swanson, the voyeur, the one who accidentally finds himself too close to the subject of his desire and doesn't recognize it. He is wandering around in a duet (now trio), reaches for this and that passing gesture. Never quite connects. And then there is the bad girl, Trisha Brown, she is engaged in breaking the rules on "acceptable gesture." All of this put together with other mysterious strategies and wrapped in the most beautiful and evocative music.[43]
TRISHA BROWN

MUSIC

Now how's this for a collaboration tale.... We knew each other in Rome during Fabio Sargentini's [Galleria] L'Attico days (late 1960s) — Judson on the Tiber — but not very well. I figure my name must have come out of a hat, but there she was on the phone in 1991 asking me if I was interested in working with her on a new piece. Talmudically speaking, what else could I be interested in?

This happened to be an emergency where I would not have the time to view the dance beforehand, nor even see any videos (I was in Rome, she in NYC), and Trisha wanted some music, like, tomorrow. Armed with enormous amounts of patience and goodwill, she began to explain the inexplicable, from the little men to the tide tables. As we tested each other's ideas over an hour or so, I felt that a couple of handles appeared — some degrees of dissonance, angles of consonance, bumps of density, sprats of light, dark, and speed — but not much more. This was not about anything one could relate to a legal jury, she was trying to key me into her codes of pure Kabbalistic movement....

When I got off the phone all excited about this new project, I panicked, realizing that I'd understood absolutely nothing, not a word she'd said other than that the piece had to be 30 to 35 minutes long.... Later I figured it out. Trisha had used a magic strategy in this long-distance consultation — based on intuition and blind faith — that left me feeling as though she had offered me carte blanche to create a dreamwork with her, using anything that interested me at the moment — a collaborative process which she has cultivated time after time with remarkable success. Brilliant.

Whatever I had understood of Trisha's project, it was clear that she was goading me toward embracing personal and musical dangers. I approached her defiant abstraction with naive melody and met her ingenious structural tangles with quasinarrative, hoping that hers and mine — our sames and opposites, ironies and deceptions — would dovetail and ultimately become the other and the one.

So there I was back in the emergency room. I grabbed a dyslexic waltz — quintessential dance music — that was sitting half-finished on the piano and made it into what turned out to be a perfectly behaved classical rondo: successive repetitions of increasingly deformed synthesizer variations, interspersed with sonic tableaux of old fashioned lawn-mowers, the Nantucket Light Ship, mobs of crows, John Cage's inimitable voice, tin cans being kicked in a deconsecrated Venetian Church etc. etc. I whipped 35 minutes together in less than a week and, like a lottery ticket, sent the tape of *For M.G.: The Movie* off to New York.

Some 10 days later Trisha calls all laughs (a truly good sign with Trisha) and says:"Alvin you're not gonna believe this, I don't believe this, nobody is.... Your score fits like a glove, how did you do it?" "I don't know," I laughed back, "I just took some minimal, some maximal, some dirt from Satie's grave and some foghorns, shook it up in a martini mixer and put it in the mail." This was the start of a wonderful friendship. Artistically two more works followed (*One Story as in Falling* for the Bagouet company, and *Another Story as in Falling* for the Trisha Brown company), coming with much harder knocks, but come they did, and in the process we each learned a great deal about how the other works, and I learned the hardest lesson of all in dance, how to keep the music strong but invisible... whether completely rewriting my own string quartet or throwing together samples of bowling balls and Mozart clarinet trios. All of this in a very congenial environment of backbreaking perfectionism, where at the drop of a shoe Trisha would point her collaborators as she pointed herself, in one direction only: to unimagined, unthinkable inventions in their own art. I'm sure like any angel she has some faults, I've just never seen them.[44]
ALVIN CURRAN

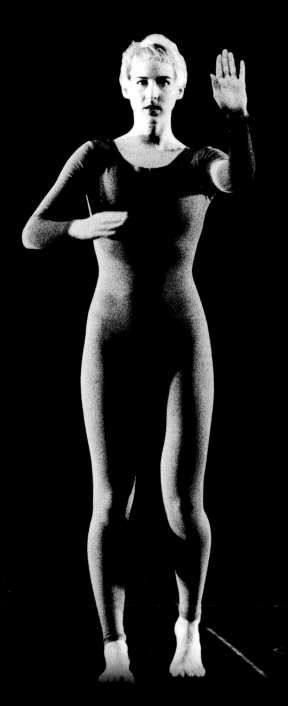

COSTUMES

Gray unitards were dyed a darker gray color everywhere but the sweat pattern of the individual dancer. By the end of the dance, with the addition of sweat, the costumes became monotone.

LIGHTING

In reflection on working with Trisha, many fond memories come to mind. As you may know I worked as a lighting designer and production manager for Trisha for nearly ten years.

One project that came to mind was collaborating with Trisha on *For M.G.: The Movie*. When we first started working on the piece, Trisha asked me if I could bend light. My first response was no, light rays are straight lines, but then I started thinking on reflecting light and using the rays of light to create an environment for the dancer to dance in. While we were in residency at U-Mass we worked on some base ideas. I created a wall of light in the back of the stage. And shot beams of light high in the air. We used a haze machine so the beams of light could be seen. With these first working ideas we took the piece to France, I forget what theater, but it was a theater in the round that was set up for proscenium-style performance. We had much room upstage. We left the back open to the structure of the theater and lit small parts just enough to be seen through the wall of light. I remember watching the piece there and thinking that we will never be able to make the piece work in other theaters. The exposed theatre structure was so wonderful I couldn't imagine being able to recreate this anywhere else. To my surprise I was able to make this idea work in most theaters that we took it to. Another element to the design was I worked with the idea that the lighting through the piece would always be moving. The movement is very slow. The idea was that the audience would know a change had happened but not know when. The lighting cues are in constant movement.

I had so many creative experiences with Trisha that it would take a book just to write them all.[45]
SPENCER BROWN

TITLE / DATE
ONE STORY AS IN FALLING, 1992

CYCLES
BACK TO ZERO IN MOVEMENT:
UNSTABLE MOLECULAR
STRUCTURE IN FORM

LENGTH
20 MINUTES

MUSIC
ALVIN CURRAN

MUSIC PERFORMANCE
ALVIN CURRAN, SAMPLER AND
KEYBOARD

VISUAL PRESENTATION
ROLAND AESCHLIMANN

SETS
ROLAND AESCHLIMANN

COSTUMES
ROLAND AESCHLIMANN
LARGE YELLOW SUITS AND BLACK
T-SHIRTS

LIGHTING
SPENCER BROWN WITH ROLAND
AESCHLIMANN

DANCED BY
LA COMPAGNIE BAGOUET:
HÉLÈNE CATHALA, MATTHIEU DOZE,
DOMINIQUE JÉGOU, SYLVAIN
PRUNENEC, FABRICE RAMALINGOM,
AND JUAN MANUEL VICENTE.
FOR THE FIRST PERFORMANCE IN
FRANCE, THE BAGOUET DANCERS
WERE JOINED BY TWO MEMBERS OF
THE TRISHA BROWN DANCE
COMPANY, GREGORY LARA AND
WIL SWANSON.

FIRST PERFORMANCES
CITY CENTER, NEW YORK CITY,
MAY 4, 1992
MONTPELLIER INTERNATIONAL
DANSE FESTIVAL 92, MONTPELLIER,
FRANCE, JUNE 24, 1992

Choreographed for the
dance company of
Dominique Bagouet during
a residency in Montpellier,
France. Marked the
first time Brown choreo-
graphed for a company
other than her own.

There is a kinship between
Dominique's work and
mine, and a respect. This
shall be a rare adventure —
six new dancers of another
aesthetic and technical
practice spanning five
months and two continents.
I foresee long days of hard
rehearsals, new experi-
ences, word salads in the
rehearsal room, and the
melding of our separate
stories, French and
American, into a coherent
new context for making
a dance.
   The Bagouet dancers
have this quality essential
for me: neutrality that
gives birth, through
abstraction, to characters.
I like their honesty, the way
they start a work they are
unfamiliar with. They start
to understand my dance,
which comes from a history
unfamiliar to them. I have
to find a delicate balance
between what I expect from
them and the way they
interpret my expectations.
Even more difficult today
as I am interested now
in areas unknown to me.
I seek a path; rather I look
for an airplane that would
bring my dance back to the
ground towards more
simplicity and maybe more
delicacy.[46]
TRISHA BROWN

It is perhaps the tension between proximity and isolation, between the sensitivity of the dancers to one another, that makes this tersely beautiful work generate kinds of characters, traces of sadness.[47]
DEBORAH JOWITT

VISUAL PRESENTATION

Born in Switzerland, Roland Aeschlimann belongs to a select group of influential Swiss designers who rose to prominence in the 1960s. Like many of his close peers, Aeschlimann developed strong ties with Japanese designers, and he spent two years working in Kyoto in the late sixties. Since 1976, his practice has focused on stage design, particularly for the opera. His work for the stage generally extends to all visual aspects of a production, including the costumes, lighting, and sets. Aeschlimann was influential in Brown's decision to work in the world of opera.

SETS

A monochromatic, partitioned area, delimited at each corner by an architectural element. A long rectangular shaft of light punctures the background. An immense plumb line moves very slowly, from the audience's right to left, across the stage space during the whole length of the performance, shifting invisibly.

The *Story* dances share a
very long phrase that is born
of an imaginary character,
Little Man, who is rather
bland, a steady worker, and
never gets riled. He has
a special walk, carefully
delineated gestures, and
takes his time. Together the
eight "little people" of the
company arrive on the set
one at a time or in clusters to
form a community of like
types, who move in and out
of the set in unison or not
as they improvise their
way through their very low-
keyed private adventures
with others. New costumes,
new set, new music
and new improvisation.[48]
TRISHA BROWN

TITLE / DATE
ANOTHER STORY AS IN FALLING, 1993
DEDICATED TO ADAM MARTELL
BROWN, TRISHA BROWN'S SON

CYCLES
BACK TO ZERO IN MOVEMENT;
STRUCTURED IMPROVISATION IN
FORM

LENGTH
24 MINUTES

MUSIC
ALVIN CURRAN
VSTO (LONG VERSION)
MUSIC PERFORMANCE
DAVID SOLDIER AND MARK
FELDMAN, VIOLINS; RON
LAWRENCE, VIOLA; MARGARET
PARKINS, CELLO; LIVE ONLY
AT FIRST NEW YORK PERFORM-
ANCE
VISUAL PRESENTATION
ROLAND AESCHLIMANN

SETS
ROLAND AESCHLIMANN
FLOOR-TO-CEILING WOODEN
FENCELIKE STRUCTURE WITH
MOVING SLATS. BEHIND IT, A
YELLOW SPHERE MOVES SLOWLY
FROM THE AUDIENCE'S RIGHT
TO LEFT ACROSS THE STAGE,
CONCURRENT WITH A PLAY
OF LIGHTS.

COSTUMES
ROLAND AESCHLIMANN
RED PANTS AND VEST WITH
LONG-SLEEVED GRAY T-SHIRTS

LIGHTING
SPENCER BROWN WITH ROLAND
AESCHLIMANN

DANCERS
LIZ CARPENTER, CAROLYN LUCAS,
NICOLE JURALEWICZ, KEVIN
KORTAN, GREGORY LARA, DIANE
MADDEN, KELLY MCDONALD,
WIL SWANSON

FIRST PERFORMANCES
ZELLERBACH AUDITORIUM,
UNIVERSITY OF CALIFORNIA,
BERKELEY, APRIL 3, 1993

CITY CENTER, NEW YORK CITY,
APRIL 27, 1993
DE SINGEL THEATRE ANTWERPEN,
BELGIUM, NOVEMBER 10, 1993

TITLE / DATE
YET ANOTHER STORY, 1994

CYCLE
BACK TO ZERO IN MOVEMENT AND
STRUCTURED IMPROVISATION IN
FORM.

LENGTH
18 1/2 MINUTES

MUSIC
ALVIN CURRAN
VSTO (LONG VERSION)

VISUAL PRESENTATION
ROLAND AESCHLIMANN

SETS
ROLAND AESCHLIMANN
THE STAGE IS OCCUPIED BY
PARALLEL, LOW-LYING
ELASTIC ROPES.

COSTUMES
ROLAND AESCHLIMANN
LARGE RED PANTS AND GRAY
LONG-SLEEVED T-SHIRTS

LIGHTING
SPENCER BROWN, WITH ROLAND
AESCHLIMANN

DANCERS
KATHLEEN FISHER, KEVIN
KORTAN, STANFORD MAKISHI,
DIANE MADDEN, GENA RHO,
WIL SWANSON, KEITH A.
THOMPSON, MING-LUNG YANG

FIRST PERFORMANCE
JOYCE THEATER, NEW YORK CITY,
MAY 3, 1994

LONG AND DREAM, 1994

Steve [Paxton] and I
worked together maybe
five sessions before
performance in Vienna.
Not enough time to coordi-
nate our improvising
impulses; I kept running
into him. In New York
City we again rehearsed in
advance. I encouraged
him to go ahead and throw
himself at my torso, I was
sure I could catch him,
and every time I dropped
him. He said that I looked
like a greyhound and he
was fearful he would hurt
me. On the contrary, in performance, he took very
good care of me on issues
of strength and stamina
and let me dance my little
heart out to dizzying
results.[49]
TRISHA BROWN

TITLE / DATE
LONG AND DREAM, 1994
LENGTH
25 MINUTES (APPROXIMATELY)

MUSIC
EXCERPTS FROM COMPAGNIA
DEL TRALLALERO, "LA SQUADRA
GENOISE," AT FIRST EUROPEAN
PERFORMANCE;
"BLUE" GENE TYRANNY,
"HARMONIC BRANCHINGS"
FROM *A LETTER HOME* (1976),
AT FIRST U.S. PERFORMANCE
LIGHTING
SPENCER BROWN
DANCERS
TRISHA BROWN AND STEVE
PAXTON

FIRST PERFORMANCES
VOLKSTHEATER, VIENNA, AUSTRIA,
AUGUST 12, 1994
NEXT WAVE FESTIVAL, BAM OPERA
HOUSE, BROOKLYN ACADEMY OF
MUSIC, BROOKLYN, NEW YORK,
OCTOBER 2, 1996

TITLE / DATE
IF YOU COULDN'T SEE ME, 1994
A SOLO BY BROWN DANCED
ENTIRELY WITH HER BACK TO
THE AUDIENCE
LENGTH
10 MINUTES

MUSIC
ROBERT RAUSCHENBERG
VISUAL PRESENTATION
ROBERT RAUSCHENBERG
COSTUME
ROBERT RAUSCHENBERG
LIGHTING
SPENCER BROWN WITH ROBERT
RAUSCHENBERG
DANCER
TRISHA BROWN

FIRST PERFORMANCES
JOYCE THEATER, NEW YORK CITY,
MAY 3, 1994
FESTIVAL DE DANSE,
CHÂTEAUVALLON, FRANCE,
JULY 1, 1994

Dear Trisha,

I wrote to Betsey Frederick [a mutual friend of Paxton and Brown's in Albuquerque] yesterday including something about your solo. And it lingered. I woke with your scapulae floating in that part of the brain which remembers such things.

Spencer, Bob and especially you have made a deeply satisfying artifact. The costume is exactly right. It is impossible to separate it from the light, because you are clothed in both. The revel and revelation of your spinus erectae, scapulae and delicate pearls of spinal processes in the lumbar, side-lit for maximum bas-relief, sent a gasp through the audience.

You cannot know, but may have heard from others, what the sculpture of your back can accomplish. It is Indonesian in line and volumes: richly shadowed, and starkly lit in its highlands, it became an abstraction shifting from an anatomical event with muscles like a whippet to a large looming face to a mask—something alien and frightening although weirdly comic as the rest of the body reconnects and we see again a back.

Bob's device [the idea of not facing front] gives us three things in the end. It refutes the frontal convention—as you did once before, with the standing figure in *For M.G.: The Movie*, so Magritte-like. It gives the solo a real task to accomplish—a simple idea, one we can examine for effects and learn from: for instance, the enlivening of the upstage space and how the black curtain is not just an expanse of dark background to contrast with your lit figure and push you toward us, visually. Your orientation declares it a dark vista, and it acquires a dimensionless depth.

And last, facing up relieves you of facing us. I believe that you are essentially a private person who almost perversely, moth-like, headed for the limelight. Your dances are never less than brilliantly constructed and (bless your excellent company) danced. Yet they do not yield to our gaze. They are hyperactive; over-rich in thrust, drop, dart, scamper, buck, throw, lift, swoop, twist. They don't settle happily onstage. They twist metaphorically too, subtlety and irony being common.

The performance style is sometimes like seeing animals in one's headlights, or an insect, however beautifully exotic, pinned. Who was that masked woman?

Facing upstage, you aren't blinking uncomfortably in the light of our avid eye. You know you cannot know or concern yourself with how you may look to us, and so try to deflect us. With that issue aside and privacy assured, you seem to relax and really put out. Lordy, how you dance. Pure, assured, full-bodied, wild and fully self-knowing.

We are not watchers but onlookers. You are not our focus exactly but a medium mediating between us and something, some unknowable or unthinkable vision in the upstage volume or, sometimes beyond *into* the velour fathom *into* which we project. This illusory upstage spatial pliability—from positive dancing figure on black to negative dancing figure in front of potenized unguessable empty space is deeply satisfying, mythic and wholly theatrical.

I grew fond of the music. It sets you up well, for one thing. We watch the front curtain lights, beginning to...drift, in spite of ourselves, then the curtain rises and the black is a color, not an absence. Our eyes see you and then the moonscape of your back, the chiaroscuro, which as you raise your arms, fascinates us, bringing us closer and rendering you enormous, a woman with a whole scene on her back. It is like puppets and how we adjust to their scale, along with the unsettling fact that the puppeteer's whole body is visible and active, too.

This is analogous to the figure-ground flipping revealed as the dance progresses—partial or full-figure, back is front, front is back, lookers as onlookers. When, in philosophy, so much is achieved and the means are minimal, the word used to describe the effect is "elegant." And so it is.

One quibble. The ending. We have gotten used to these materials, and having made your move, it is time to stop. The light again is dressing you. Your arms float high then drop and swoop to their asymmetrical positions beside you, fingertips alert to your surface and your figure's suddenly quiet mass. The light fades; just right. But the music—was it, too, faded out? It felt like acoustical short shrift. One further flip could be achieved if it played on for a moment in darkness—we could lose all our visual foci and be engulfed in the black you have sourced; so we might experience what we have seen beyond you on the stage, but only as a distance. We could be you in it, or experience what you might have felt as you played with it, faced it. The music would keep us entranced as our bearings fade, your visual surface recedes. We could shift from the specificity of the visual solids to more oceanic senses—the drone and the dark.

I run on. Let me just say that I think *Trillium* would be proud of you.
Looking forward:

Love, Steve[54]

MUSIC

I received a Yamaha electric piano for Christmas last year. I started playing and decided that only a good friend like Trisha could encourage me. I phoned her and sent a couple of tapes for a solo. She accepted.[50]
ROBERT RAUSCHENBERG

I wanted music not to sound like music.... Nobody in the audience stopped talking when it came on, and it began before the piece does. I wanted the music to be...additional sound.... The death of an artwork is when it's generally understood.[51] RR

VISUAL PRESENTATION

Trisha asked me, "What do you think would be the most difficult thing?" And I said, "For a dancer to dance with their back to the audience.... How can you surprise yourself if you know what it is?"[52] RR

COSTUME

A very scoop-backed dress with two long panels front and back, open on the sides, with a pair of shorts underneath.

LIGHTING

It was a very simple idea but such a wonderful piece. A single light cue with bright white down light and red side light. The movement of light comes through the dance and the white costume, which move with red hints from the side.[53]
SPENCER BROWN

TITLE / DATE
YOU CAN SEE US, 1995/1996
LENGTH
10 MINUTES

MUSIC
ROBERT RAUSCHENBERG
VISUAL PRESENTATION
ROBERT RAUSCHENBERG
COSTUMES
ROBERT RAUSCHENBERG
LIGHTING
ROBERT RAUSCHENBERG
DANCERS
TRISHA BROWN AND BILL T.
JONES (1995); TRISHA BROWN
AND MIKHAIL BARYSHNIKOV
(1996)

FIRST PERFORMANCES
MONTPELLIER DANSE 95,
MONTPELLIER, FRANCE, JUNE
28, 1995 (WITH BROWN AND
BILL T. JONES)
NEXT WAVE FESTIVAL, BAM
OPERA HOUSE, BROOKLYN
ACADEMY OF MUSIC, BROOKLYN,
NEW YORK, OCTOBER 1, 1996
(WITH BROWN AND MIKHAIL
BARYSHNIKOV)

Bill T. Jones asked me to make a solo for him for the best of reasons. He could see a logic in my work and wanted to know more about my thinking through the process of creation. I didn't have the time to make a new piece, but, honored by the request, suggested he learn my solo *If you couldn't see me* and we perform it as a duet with him facing the audience. Retitled *You can see us*. I liked the balance in all the opposites: front / back, man / woman, gay / straight, young / not so young, black / white, etc.

With Misha, I liked the training process, his analysis of sequence, daily conversations before rehearsal, often about Modern Dance history, and his approach to learning my style of movement, which was not in his training (ballet) or in mine either (back to audience, no turns for dynamic or momentum, and a splaying of gestures to the side of the body so the audience could see them).[55]
TRISHA BROWN

I didn't have the luxury of living four or five months with this piece; I had to simply learn it. So I looked for a phrase that was familiar and asked, How can I chain this? What comes next?... I'm not trying to act out every phrase by any means. But sometimes there's a mystery about [an abstract phrase] that gives it a strange kind of bouquet, and your body language is affected whether you want it to be or not, and that makes it more interesting.[56]
MIKHAIL BARYSHNIKOV

M.O., 1995

TITLE / DATE
M.O., 1995
CYCLE
MUSIC
LENGTH
55 MINUTES

MUSIC
JOHANN SEBASTIAN BACH
(1685–1750), FROM *MUSICAL
OFFERING* (BWV 1079):
RICERCARE À 3, CANON À 2
CANCRIZANS, CANON À 2 VIOLINI
IN UNISONO, PER MOTEM CON-
TRARIUM, PER AUGMENTATIONEM,
CONTRARIO MOTU, CANON À 2
PER TONOS, FUGA CANONICA,
CANON PERPETUUS, CANON À 2,
CANON À 4, TRIO SONATA,
RICERCARE À 6

MUSIC PERFORMANCE
KENNETH WEISS, HARPSICHORD;
MARC HANTAÏ, FLUTE; FRANÇOIS
FERNANDEZ, VIOLIN; PHILIPPE
PIERLOT, VIOLA DA GAMBA
VISUAL PRESENTATION
TRISHA BROWN
COSTUMES
IRIE
LIGHTING
JENNIFER TIPTON
DANCERS
KATHLEEN FISHER, KEVIN
KORTAN, DIANE MADDEN,

STANFORD MAKISHI, KELLY
MCDONALD, GENA RHO, WIL
SWANSON, KEITH A. THOMPSON,
MING-LUNG YANG
FIRST PERFORMANCES
THÉÂTRE ROYAL DE LA MONNAIE,
BRUSSELS, BELGIUM, MAY 21, 1995
SERIOUS FUN! FESTIVAL:
AMERICAN VISIONARIES, LINCOLN
CENTER FOR THE PERFORMING
ARTS, NEW YORK CITY,
JULY 19, 1995

In *M.O.* I seek to find the movement equivalent of the musical forms by first developing a movement vocabulary that maintains its identity inside the powerful sweep of Bach's music. With an attention to traveling phrases (in both space and time), the body was divided into two parts, upper and lower, then recombined in subsequent repetitions of the music, to locate both theme and counterpoint in one body. The options were endless. The test was to try to match Bach's purity.[57]

TRISHA BROWN

LIGHTING

Trisha Brown is an artist whose work is right down my alley. Her formal concerns are clearly focused, revealing the structure and organization of her work. Underlying this form is a human center giving each dance an emotional underpinning that is quite particular to the work. Each dance has a cool surface with warmth at its core. The balance of intellect and sensuality is perfect, as if a membrane separated them, allowing one to seep into the other to a greater or lesser degree depending on the circumstances of the dance. The challenge of capturing that balance in the light for a dance in a way that is unique to that dance has given me great delight in our years together.[58]

JENNIFER TIPTON

TITLE / DATE
TWELVE TON ROSE, 1996
CYCLE
MUSIC
LENGTH
25 MINUTES

MUSIC
ANTON WEBERN (1883–1945),
FIVE MOVEMENTS FOR STRING
QUARTET, OP. 5: NOS. I, III, AND
IV OF FOUR PIECES FOR VIOLIN
AND PIANO, OP. 7; STRING
QUARTET, OP. 28 (OP. 7 REMOVED
AFTER JULY 1999)
MUSIC PERFORMANCE
MEMBERS OF BROOKLYN
PHILHARMONIC ORCHESTRA:
ROBERT CHAUSOW, FIRST VIOLIN;
ROBIN BUSHMAN, SECOND
VIOLIN; SARAH ADAMS, VIOLA;

LANNY PAYKIN, CELLO; KENNETH
BOWEN, PIANO
VISUAL PRESENTATION
TRISHA BROWN
COSTUMES
BURT BARR
BLACK AND RED COSTUMES.
THOSE FOR THE WOMEN INCLUDE
A RED STRING RUNNING FROM
ONE ARM TO THE SKIRT ON THAT
SIDE, WHICH CAUSES THE SKIRT
TO LIFT WHEN THE DANCER
RAISES THAT ARM.

LIGHTING
SPENCER BROWN
DANCERS
KATHLEEN FISHER, DIANE
MADDEN, STANFORD MAKISHI,
MARIAH MALONEY, GENA RHO,
WIL SWANSON, KEITH A.
THOMPSON, ABIGAIL YAGER,
MING-LUNG YANG

FIRST PERFORMANCES
NEXT WAVE FESTIVAL, BAM OPERA
HOUSE, BROOKLYN ACADEMY OF
MUSIC, BROOKLYN, NEW YORK,
OCTOBER 2, 1996
ARSENAL DANSE, METZ, FRANCE,
NOVEMBER 26, 1996

When I listen to Webern's music, my brain spreads the way it does when I am choreographing. One of my favorite sections of this piece, during opus 5, [is when] a sextet enacts a form of rich flux, but along its course, it dissolves, as in film, and reappears at an earlier moment in the form that we recognize but we don't know how it got there.[59]
TRISHA BROWN

Accumulation with talking and excerpts from *For M.G.: The Movie*, *If you couldn't see me*, *Twelve Ton Rose*, *Astral Converted 55*, *Set and Reset*, and *Newark (Niweweorce)*.

A gala piece created for The Kitchen. It is a collage of excerpts from six chore-ographies and a full-scale version of *Accumulation with talking* performed by me. It was yet another addition to the good ship *Accumulation*.[60]
TRISHA BROWN

FIRST PERFORMANCE
THE KITCHEN @ 25, THE KITCHEN,
NEW YORK CITY, JANUARY 28, 1997

VISUAL PRESENTATION
TRISHA BROWN

COSTUMES
BURT BARR

LIGHTING
SPENCER BROWN

DANCERS
KATHLEEN FISHER, DIANE
MADDEN, STANFORD MAKISHI,
MARIAH MALONEY, GENA RHO.
WIL SWANSON, KEITH A.
THOMPSON, ABIGAIL YAGER,
MING-LUNG YANG

MUSIC
EXCERPTS FROM THE MUSIC FOR
THE DANCES, INCLUDING THE COM-
POSITIONS OF LAURIE ANDERSON
(SET AND RESET), JOHN CAGE
(ASTRAL CONVERTED [55], ALVIN
CURRAN (FOR M.G.: THE MOVIE),
ROBERT RAUSCHENBERG (IF YOU
COULDN'T SEE ME), ANTON WEBERN
(TWELVE TON ROSE), AND PETER
ZUMMO (NEWARK). PRODUCED BY
JIM DAWSON

TITLE / DATE
ACCUMULATION WITH TALKING PLUS
REPERTORY, 1997

MATERIAL
IMPROVISATION AND FIXED

LENGTH
45 MINUTES (APPROXIMATELY)

FOR MERCE, 1997

This dance was a structured improvisation based on very short thematic phrases for each bagatelle. The music is exquisite beyond comprehension. In the first performance, I got a bad start because the lights and music were not synched. I went and one of them didn't. There was stillness — (she's thinking) — and then quiet explosions of action — (she's surprised) — as I duked it out with FORM off the cuff. Fortunately, it was videotaped and relearned, and took its place in the repertory.[61]
TRISHA BROWN

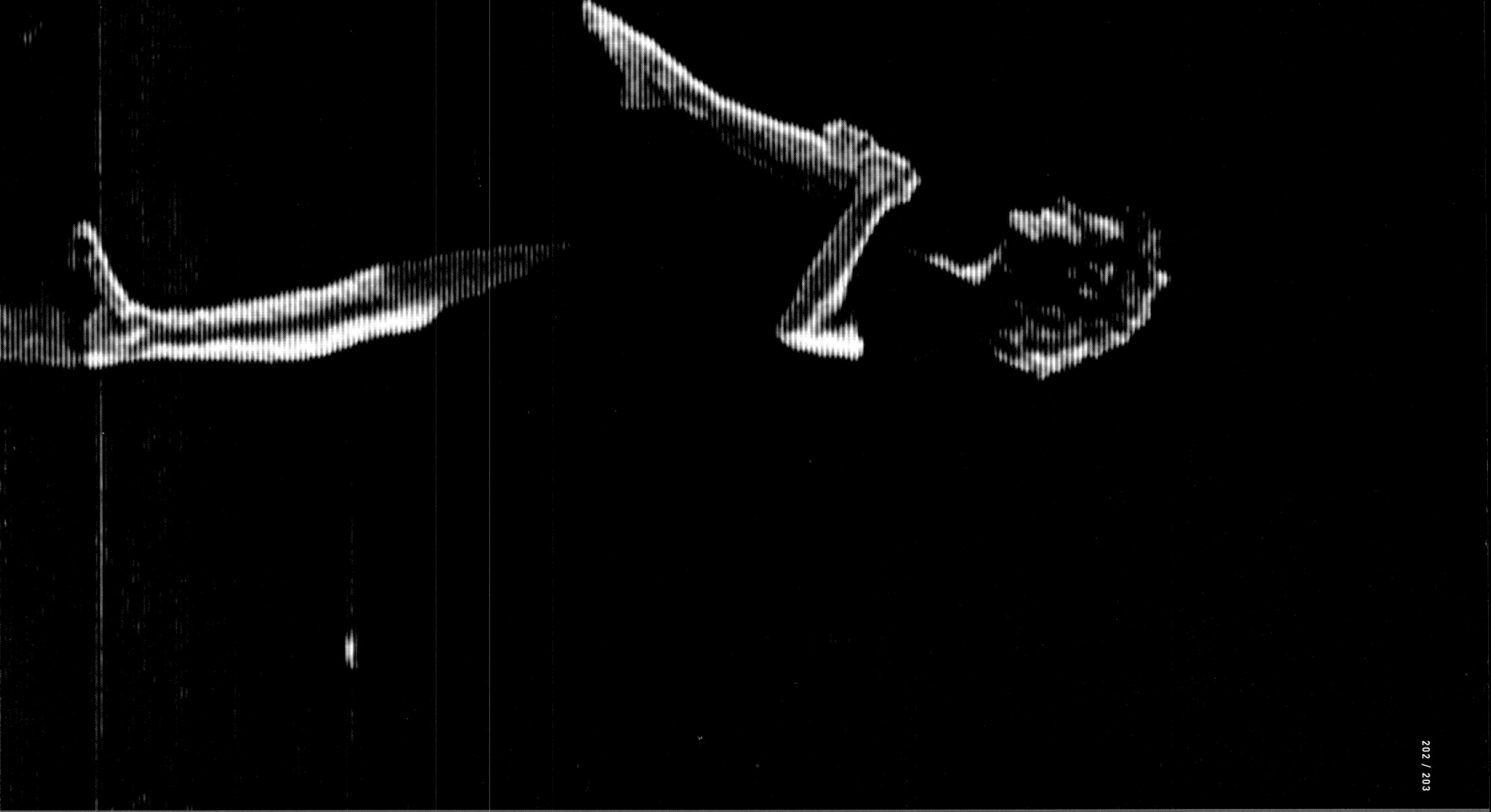

FIRST PERFORMANCES
TRIBUTE TO MERCE CUNNINGHAM,
BAM OPERA HOUSE, BROOKLYN
ACADEMY OF MUSIC, BROOKLYN,
NEW YORK, MAY 19, 1997
HEBBEL THEATER, BERLIN,
GERMANY, SEPTEMBER 16, 1998

MUSIC
ANTON WEBERN (1883–1945),
SIX BAGATELLES FOR STRING
QUARTET, OP. 9
VISUAL PRESENTATION
TRISHA BROWN
COSTUME
BLACK DRESS WITH RHINE-
STONES, SELECTED BY NANCY
GRAVES
LIGHTING
SPENCER BROWN
DANCER
TRISHA BROWN

TITLE / DATE
FOR MERCE, 1997
CYCLE
MUSIC
LENGTH
5 MINUTES

CANTO / PIANTO, 1997

The choreography carries
the story of Orfeo and
Euridice through a succession of dramaturgical
excerpts from the opera
L'Orfeo. There were dance
constructions, like an
eight-person snake, that
were made for the opera,
but not used in the end. In
addition, when the music
was far too long for the
dramatic moment, such as
Euridice following Orfeo
out of Hades and his
egregious error of looking
back at her, I used an
otherworldly electronic
sound track that better
suited the urgencies of the
story. We did not use
the set or costumes from
the opera.[62]
TRISHA BROWN

TITLE / DATE
CANTO/PIANTO, 1997
CYCLE
MUSIC
LENGTH
32 MINUTES WITHOUT FLYING
SECTION; 38 MINUTES WITH
FLYING SECTION

MUSIC
CLAUDIO MONTEVERDI
(1567–1643), *L'ORFEO*
MUSIC PERFORMANCE
RENÉ JACOBS, CONDUCTOR,
AND CONCERTO VOCALE AND
COLLEGIUM VOCALE GENT
SOUND EFFECTS
JAMES DAWSON
VISUAL PRESENTATION
TRISHA BROWN
COSTUMES
ROLAND AESCHLIMANN AND
BURT BARR

LIGHTING
JENNIFER TIPTON
DANCERS
KATHLEEN FISHER, MARIAH
MALONEY, BRANDI NORTON, SETH
PARKER, STACY MATTHEW
SPENCE, TODD LAWRENCE STONE,
KATRINA THOMPSON, KEITH A.
THOMPSON, ABIGAIL YAGER
FIRST PERFORMANCES
AMERICAN DANCE FESTIVAL,
DURHAM, NORTH CAROLINA,
JUNE 26, 1997

HEBBEL THEATRE BERLIN,
GERMANY, SEPTEMBER 16, 1998
JOYCE THEATER, NEW YORK CITY,
MAY 5, 2000

L'ORFEO, 1998

TITLE / DATE
L'ORFEO, 1998
CYCLE
MUSIC
LENGTH
120 MINUTES

MUSIC
CLAUDIO MONTEVERDI
(1567–1643), *L'ORFEO* (LIBRETTO
BY ALESSANDRO STRIGGIO)
MUSIC PERFORMANCE
RENÉ JACOBS, CONDUCTOR;
SIMON KEENLYSIDE AND CARLO
VINCENZO ALLEMANO, ORFEO;
JUANITA LASCARRO, EURIDICE/LA
MUSICA/ECO; GRACIELA ODDONE,
MESSAGGIERA; MAURO UTZERI,
APOLLO; MARTINA DIKE,
PROSERPINA; STEPHEN WALLACE,
LA SPERANZA; TOMAS TOMASSON,
PLUTONE; PAUL GÉRIMON,
CARONTE; ANNE CAMBIER AND
MARTINA DIKE, NINFE; YANN
BEURON, STEPHEN WALLACE,
JOHN BOWEN, PAUL GÉRIMON,
AND RENÉ LINNENBANK,
SHEPHERDS AND SPIRITS;
AND CONCERTO VOCALE AND
COLLEGIUM VOCALE GENT
VISUAL PRESENTATION
ROLAND AESCHLIMANN
SETS
ROLAND AESCHLIMANN

COSTUMES
ROLAND AESCHLIMANN
LIGHTING
ROLAND AESCHLIMANN AND GERD
MEIER
DANCERS
DIANE MADDEN (AS FLIGHT
OF LA MUSICA), WITH KATHLEEN
FISHER, STANFORD MAKISHI,
MARIAH MALONEY, BRANDI
NORTON, STACY MATTHEW
SPENCE, KATRINA THOMPSON,
KEITH A. THOMPSON, ABIGAIL
YAGER, MING-LUNG YANG

FIRST PERFORMANCES
THÉÂTRE ROYAL DE LA
MONNAIE, BRUSSELS, BELGIUM,
MAY 13, 1998
NEXT WAVE FESTIVAL, BAM
OPERA HOUSE, BROOKLYN
ACADEMY OF MUSIC, BROOKLYN,
NEW YORK, JUNE 10, 1999

I tried to make it dramatic. I couldn't stand the lack of energy on the opera stage, so I began to make forms that informed the audience of the story and the music. My boldness was replaced by innocence, knowing by not knowing. Can a singer do this?...I thought if I got the gestures right, I could empower them as performers.[63]

TRISHA BROWN

MUSIC

Right at the outset, Trisha made it plain that she was an abstract dancer/choreographer and not so much interested in a narrative. But I was a singer, and wholly unprepared, unskilled, and not a little unwilling to experiment in front of her in my reluctant body. What she said at that time didn't mean a lot to me. In any case, time passed, and during rehearsals Trisha had with her at all times a vocal score and a translator, and knew in detail the meaning of the Italian text. That got me thinking…maybe it got her thinking too? I don't know, but the result was that the movement (the dance) drifted from abstract to downright descriptive. She had this mercurial way of showing half-truths that might sometimes allude to the narrative or, alternatively, "comment" on some aspect of the character's personality, whilst he/she would be singing about something else entirely. Or a gesture could represent a character's state of mind…. There was always the feeling that it would never quite be pinned down to anything too specific…and, of course, those feints just made the whole thing more fascinating.

She also had this wonderful way of using the edges of the canvas as if it were peripheral vision…. You never leave unwatched the edges of a Trisha Brown stage. It may just be that she's talking to you, the audience, from the wings and other dark recesses of the stage.

The work *Orfeo* was largely built on her dancers before the beginning of our rehearsal period and then applied, where possible, to us singers. There was, of course, a fair degree of cutting and pasting at points where we found ourselves unable to recreate what they had worked out. This was unlike other collaborations that I had seen between dance and opera, where the singers (no doubt by necessity) end up, more or less, standing still, whilst the dancers…dance! Trisha did not want that. She wanted that the physical and musical languages would coexist…sink or swim together I suppose, and that meant that her dancers took on the role of teachers as much as of dancers, endlessly coaxing and goading us to get as close as we could to what Trisha had in mind. I think that what was more important to her, on this occasion at least, was the whole picture…. The drama…rather than to fully realize the physical and artistic potential of the dance troupe. That was a risk! And an enormous leap of faith, to entrust singers with a physical repertoire in which we are not schooled…but which, in her and her dancers' care, ultimately resulted in a most wonderful piece of art.[64]
SIMON KEENLYSIDE

SETS

If the décor is economical and pure, it enhances the essential elements of characters and space. I was the assistant of Joseph Swoboda, who was very sensitive about architecture and a master in the art of lighting to suggest the forms.[65]
ROLAND AESCHLIMANN

El Trilogy developed organically, with *Five Part Weather Invention* inspiring the next two parts. After *Rapture to Leon James* and *Groove and Countermove* were choreographed, the solos of interludes 1 and 2 melded the three parts together.

El Trilogy is actually in five parts. There are two interludes that function as a dynamic connection between the choreographies. They are meant to reveal stagehands at work in their normal practice of changing the stage over for the next piece. I augment the stage culture by placing a solo dance in their midst. This is where I usually am during the show, backstage. I get ideas looking at the sides of my dances. I think of these interludes as somewhat dark zones for the imagination to roam around.[66]
TRISHA BROWN

In El Trilogy she started a new thing with her dancing and its delivery to the dancers; she would do improvisations by herself more…. Most of those phrases she improvised from the beginning to the end, and she would just go one after another after another.[67]
CAROLYN LUCAS

TITLE / DATE
EL TRILOGY, 1999–2000
INCLUDES:
FIVE PART WEATHER INVENTION,
1999
INTERLUDE 1 (RAGE)
RAPTURE TO LEON JAMES, 2000
INTERLUDE 2 (LADDER)
GROOVE AND COUNTERMOVE, 2000
CYCLE
MUSIC
LENGTH
75 MINUTES

MUSIC
DAVE DOUGLAS
MUSIC PERFORMANCE
SEE INDIVIDUAL LISTINGS THAT
FOLLOW FOR MAIN SECTIONS;
INTERLUDE 1, SUSIE IBARRA,
PERCUSSION; INTERLUDE 2,
MARK FELDMAN, VIOLIN
VISUAL PRESENTATION
TERRY WINTERS
COSTUMES
TERRY WINTERS
FOR THE TWO INTERLUDES:
GRAY LEOTARD AND PANTS

LIGHTING
JENNIFER TIPTON
FIRST PERFORMANCES
AMERICAN DANCE FESTIVAL,
DURHAM, NORTH CAROLINA,
JUNE 29, 2000
LUZERNERTHEATER, LUCERNE,
SWITZERLAND, SEPTEMBER 28, 2000
LINCOLN CENTER FESTIVAL,
LAGUARDIA CONCERT HALL,
NEW YORK CITY, JULY 18, 2001

TITLE / DATE
FIVE PART WEATHER INVENTION, 1999
FIRST PART OF *EL TRILOGY*
CYCLE
LENGTH
20 MINUTES

MUSIC
DAVE DOUGLAS
MUSIC PERFORMANCE
CHARMS OF THE NIGHT SKY:
DAVE DOUGLAS, TRUMPET; GUY
KLUCEVSEK, ACCORDION; MARK
FELDMAN, VIOLIN; GREG COHEN,
BASS
VISUAL PRESENTATION
TERRY WINTERS
SETS
TERRY WINTERS
A BACKDROP WITH A BLACK-AND-
WHITE DRAWING, FILLING MUCH

OF THE STAGE AND, ALONG ITS
UPPER EDGE, A COLOR BAR AND
GRAY SCALE, WHICH ARE KEYED
TO THE COSTUMES.
COSTUMES
TERRY WINTERS
COSTUMES IN ONE OF FIVE COL-
ORS, YELLOW, WARM RED, CYAN,
AND GRAY, WITH SOME LAYERING
LIGHTING
JENNIFER TIPTON
DANCERS
KATHLEEN FISHER, MARIAH
MALONEY, BRANDI NORTON, SETH

PARKER, STACY MATTHEW
SPENCE, TODD LAWRENCE STONE,
KATRINA THOMPSON, KEITH A.
THOMPSON, ABIGAIL YAGER
FIRST PERFORMANCES
JACOB'S PILLOW DANCE FESTIVAL,
LEE, MASSACHUSETTS, JULY 7, 1999
DE SINGEL THEATRE ANTWERPEN,
BELGIUM, NOVEMBER 11, 1999
JOYCE THEATER, NEW YORK CITY,
MAY 2, 2000

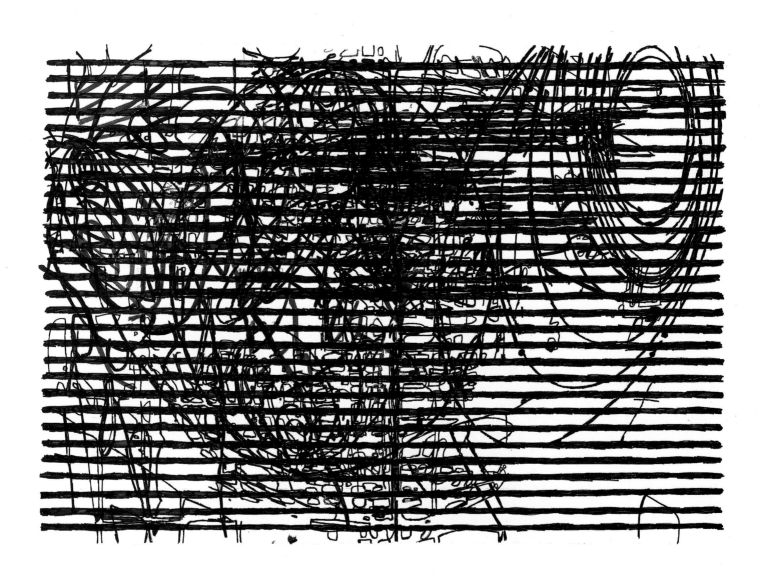

OPPOSITE PAGE
Terry Winters, **Linking
Graphics, 1**, 1999. Ink on
paper, 30 1/2 x 44 1/2 in.
(76.8 x 113.0 cm).
Collection of the artist.

THIS PAGE
Terry Winters, **Linking
Graphics, 2**, 1999. Ink,
graphite, and colored
pencil on paper,
30 1/2 x 44 1/2 in.
(76.8 x 113.0 cm).
The Museum of Modern
Art, New York.

Trisha had this idea about wanting to make a phrase that looked like weather and that had to do with foot patterns and rhythm.[68]
CAROLYN LUCAS

MUSIC
There's a story I'd like to share that maybe even Trisha doesn't remember:

It was the first or second rehearsal for *El Trilogy* and our hands and minds were full with the new material. The music was brand new, and I'm sure the dance vocabulary was fresh as well. It was exciting to be working on something so new with so many wide-open possibilities.

We were just trying things together in a very open and playful way when we stumbled on some issues that I can't even remember and in retrospect are probably unimportant. Trisha, caught up in the moment, was intently conferring with her dancers. Thinking that something in the music was throwing them, I walked over and asked if there was any way we might be able to help.

She turned around, smiled, and without hesitating said, "Honey, you just make the music KICK ASS!"

It seemed like a good motto under any circumstances, and I let it guide me through all of our work together.[69]
DAVE DOUGLAS

VISUAL PRESENTATION
Trisha Brown's abstract choreographies are moving constructions. From the vernacular to the spectacular, she has mapped a complexity of sensations through the use of open-ended narrations. Her story lines trace emotional states far from equilibrium yet somehow perfectly balanced. Keeping body and soul together, Trisha's high-wire act pushes the limits of performance. Always working without the benefit of a net — every time flying.[70]
TERRY WINTERS

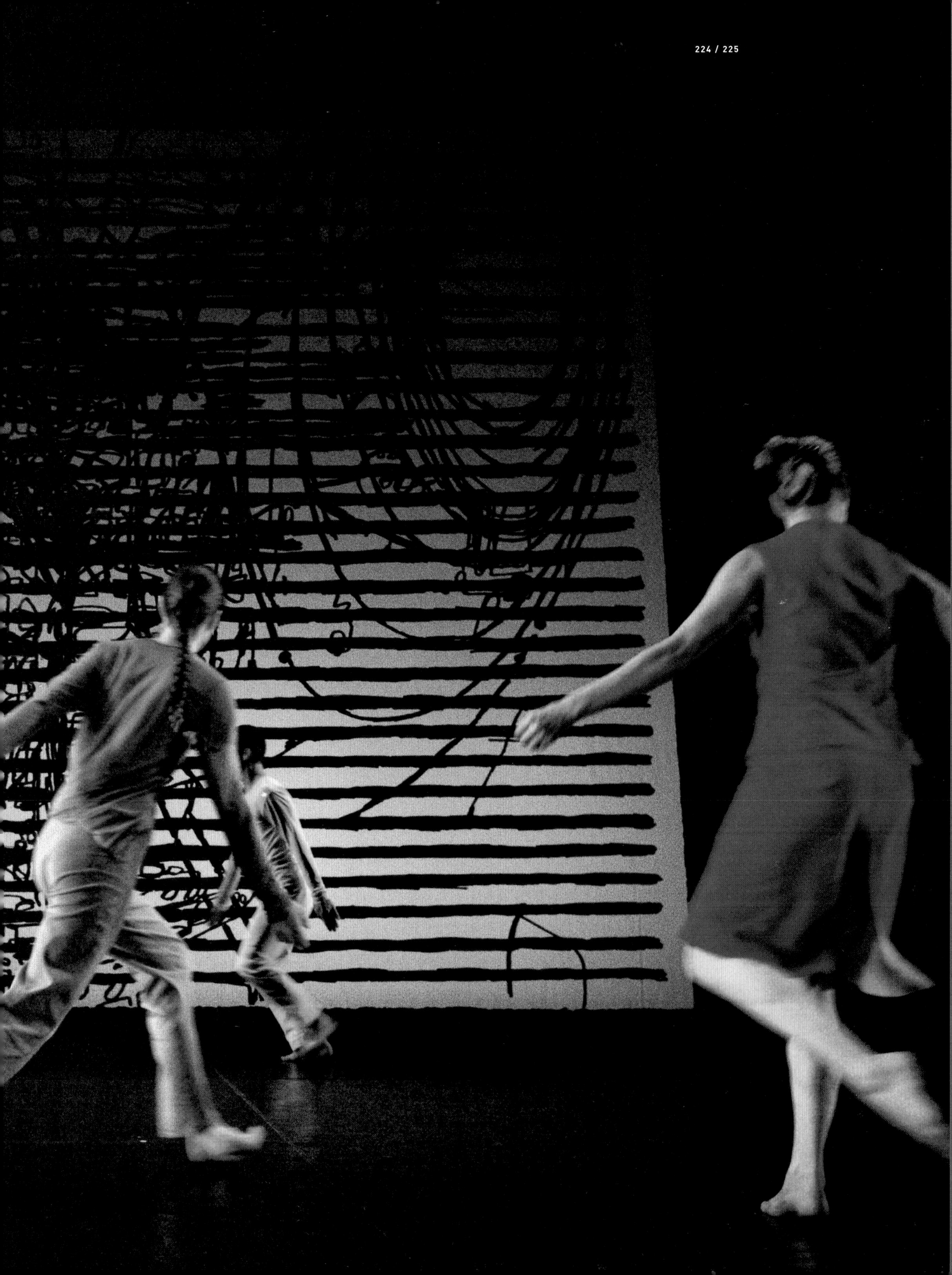

Interlude 1: House lights are partially raised; above stage, equally spaced industrial stage lights descend until they are fully visible. Backdrop for *Five Part Weather Invention* lifts, and a stagehand rolls in a cart with a stack of cymbals, which are attached to two wires and rise to the full height of the stage. Work lights are withdrawn.

TITLE / DATE
RAPTURE TO LEON JAMES, 2000
SECOND PART OF *EL TRILOGY*
CYCLE
MUSIC
LENGTH
24 MINUTES

MUSIC
DAVE DOUGLAS
MUSIC PERFORMANCE
DAVE DOUGLAS, TRUMPET;
GREGORY TARDY, TENOR SAXO-
PHONE AND CLARINET; GREG
COHEN, BASS; SUSIE IBARRA,
PERCUSSION
VISUAL PRESENTATION
TERRY WINTERS
SETS
TERRY WINTERS

COSTUMES
TERRY WINTERS
COSTUMES, IN A MIX OF BLACK,
WHITE, AND GRAY, THAT ARE REIN-
TERPRETATIONS OF SOCIAL-DANCE
CLOTHES FROM THE THIRTIES
LIGHTING
JENNIFER TIPTON
DANCERS
KATHLEEN FISHER, MARIAH
MALONEY, BRANDI NORTON, SETH
PARKER, STACY MATTHEW
SPENCE, TODD LAWRENCE STONE,

KATRINA THOMPSON, KEITH A.
THOMPSON, ABIGAIL YAGER
FIRST PERFORMANCES
EISENHOWER AUDITORIUM, THE
JOHN F. KENNEDY CENTER FOR THE
PERFORMING ARTS, WASHINGTON,
D.C., FEBRUARY 17, 2000
JOYCE THEATER, NEW YORK CITY,
MAY 9, 2000
LUZERNERTHEATER, LUCERNE,
SWITZERLAND, SEPTEMBER 28. 2000

Leon James (1913–70) was a famous Lindy Hopper, one of an elite group of African-American social dancers based at Harlem's Savoy Ballroom during its heyday in the late 1920s and 1930s. James was called for a time the "King" of the Savoy and was especially admired for his "break-away routines," or solo improvisations.

MUSIC
[For *Rapture*], I was improvising on a percussion score from an earlier recording of Dave's.... I was using the percussion like a grid of sound, and I was improvising inside that grid as a musical participant; and not only as one whole person, but as the subdivisions of my body. I was a little orchestra out there, one could say.... I got better and better at getting to all of my criteria...of dance-making on the moving body, but also I was interacting with a spirit of jazz and improvisation.[71]
TRISHA BROWN

VISUAL PRESENTATION
I think [pictorial space and movement] both involve a lot of the same issues. I'm interested in the pragmatic encounters that happen within the course of making a painting. There's a dynamic — especially with someone like Trisha or

Merce Cunningham, whom I'm working with now — in the way they articulate movements across the stage. Their approach has a lot to do with the kind of spatial configurations that I'm interested in. Also, I found the whole notion of working with Trisha and Dave Douglas interesting because of the added temporal dimension.[72]
TERRY WINTERS

SETS
Eight cymbals increasing in size from bottom to top are suspended from two cables placed downstage. Projection of light washing the backdrop relates to the costumes for *Groove and Countermove*. Sometimes the cymbals are used to create circular shadows on the backdrop.

EL TRILOGY: INTERLUDE 2 (LADDER), 2000

Interlude 2: House lights
are partially raised, and
work lights appear.
Cymbals from *Rapture to
Leon James* are brought
down, restacked onto a
cart, and rolled offstage,
while the backdrop for
Groove and Countermove
appears.

GROOVE AND COUNTERMOVE, 2000

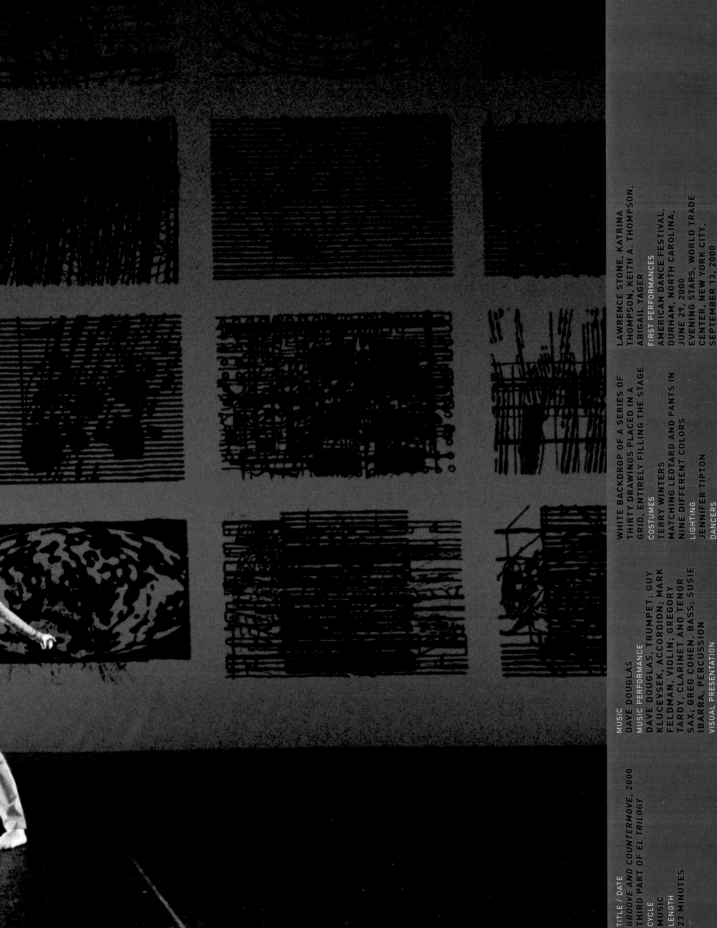

TITLE / DATE
GROOVE AND COUNTERMOVE, 2000
CYCLE
THIRD PART OF *EL TRILOGY*
MUSIC
LENGTH
23 MINUTES

MUSIC
DAVE DOUGLAS
MUSIC PERFORMANCE
DAVE DOUGLAS, TRUMPET; GUY
KLUCEVSEK, ACCORDION; MARK
FELDMAN, VIOLIN; GREGORY
TARDY, CLARINET AND TENOR
SAX; GREG COHEN, BASS; SUSIE
IBARRA, PERCUSSION
VISUAL PRESENTATION
TERRY WINTERS
SETS
TERRY WINTERS
DIGITALLY PRODUCED BLACK-AND-

WHITE BACKDROP OF A SERIES OF
THIRTY DRAWINGS PLACED IN A
GRID, ENTIRELY FILLING THE STAGE.
COSTUMES
TERRY WINTERS
MATCHING LEOTARD AND PANTS IN
NINE DIFFERENT COLORS
LIGHTING
JENNIFER TIPTON
DANCERS
KATHLEEN FISHER, SANDRA
GRINBERG, MARIAH MALONEY,
BRANDI NORTON, SETH PARKER,
STACY MATTHEW SPENCE, TODD

LAWRENCE STONE, KATRINA
THOMPSON, KEITH A. THOMPSON.
ABIGAIL YAGER
FIRST PERFORMANCES
AMERICAN DANCE FESTIVAL,
DURHAM, NORTH CAROLINA,
JUNE 29, 2000
EVENING STARS, WORLD TRADE
CENTER, NEW YORK CITY,
SEPTEMBER 13, 2000
LUZERNERTHEATER, LUCERNE,
SWITZERLAND, SEPTEMBER 28, 2000

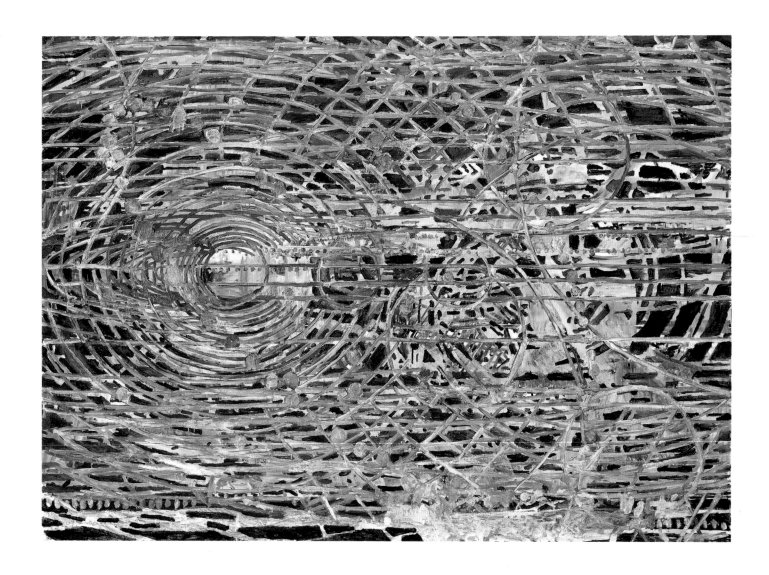

OPPOSITE PAGE
Terry Winters,
Source Wave Reference,
1999. Oil on linen,
82 5/8 x 116 1/4 in.
(209.9 x 295.3 cm).
The Eli and Edythe L.
Broad Collection.

THIS PAGE
Terry Winters, **Untitled**,
1999. Oil on linen,
82 5/8 x 116 1/4 in.
(209.9 x 295.3 cm).
Collection of
Mr. and Mrs. Lawrence
Liebowitz, Dallas.

3

7

10

11

16

18

20

21

26

27

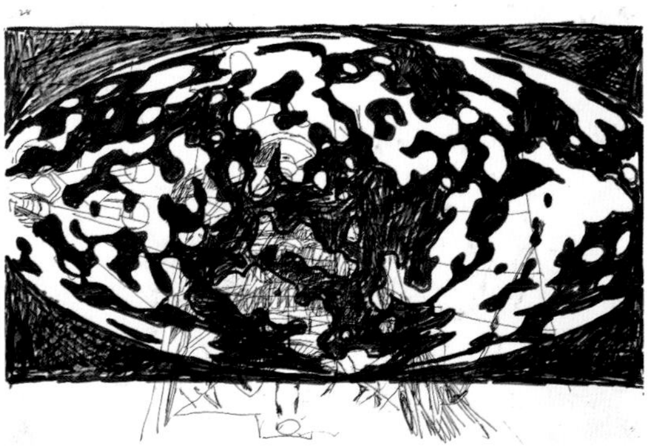

28

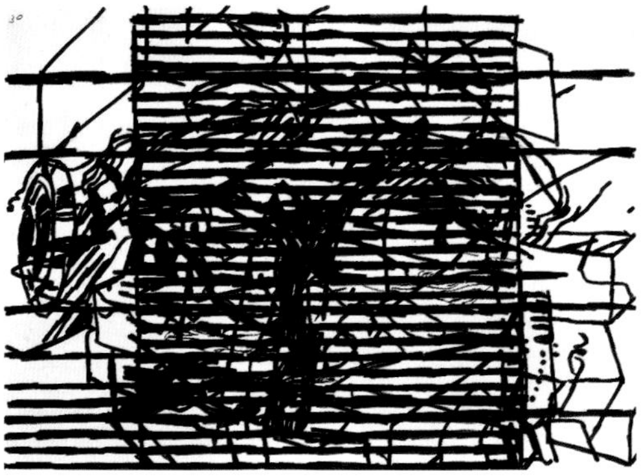

30

Each: Terry Winters,
Location Plan, 1999. Ink on
vellum, 11 1/2 x 16 3/8 in.
(29.2 x 41.6 cm). Collection
of the artist, courtesy of
Matthew Marks Gallery,
New York.

Groove and Countermove is summary of all that comes before in [*El Trilogy*] plus new material. There is a savvy improvisation on a score that repeats the theme then slides into improvisation a number of times for both dancers and musicians. The aerial work is over the top in more ways than one, and so is the music. A line of nine dancers, each in a different color, reject unison by a hair's breadth in a simultaneous explosion of nine heads, eighteen arms and eighteen legs, as they progress in a line (upstage to downstage) traveling from stage left to right. All of this plus more leading into the great continuing crescendo of a Dave Douglas finale. All hands and lips on strings and bows and horns and sticks as the dancers hit the deck with more body parts than mentioned before cruising head first on their bellies into the wings. La Fin.[73]

TRISHA BROWN

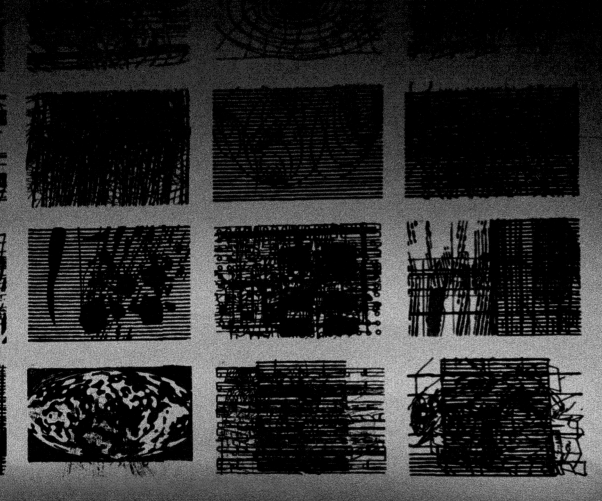

MUSIC

Trisha asks questions. Trisha listens, she makes my work hers. Everyone's eyes could remain closed to the world, but Trisha opens it to her enthusiasm.

It might seem strange, but it doesn't often happen that a collaboration among artists transforms itself into a real exchange, into a meeting of much resonance. I feel gratitude and affection for Trisha Brown, besides all the admiration that she deserves.[74]

SALVATORE SCIARRINO

I met Trisha Brown for the first time during the production of Salvatore Sciarrino's opera for La Monnaie in Brussels. In the preparatory workshop it became immediately clear to the opera singers that she had high expectations of our abilities to perform also as "dancers." Trisha Brown had created a complex abstract choreography for Sciarrino's composition. At the same time, full of curiosity, Trisha watched her new performers and tried to grasp their individual personalities intuitively. Although her choreographic works apparently don't tell stories, her formalized movement structures frame a universe of meanings and associations that seem to emerge incidentally. Over the time

of our collaboration an atmosphere of mutual confidence developed. It enabled us to find creative freedom within the strict choreographic architecture and to make room for our personal expression.

For me as performer this work became a wonderful experience. I reached my physical limits and at the same time, paradoxical as it might seem, I found within this highly constructed body language a maximum of individuality. The text of Salvatore Sciarrino's opera is equally condensed. It is a highly abstract (and very colorful) musical language that opens a wide space for multiform layers of meaning. For this reason, Trisha Brown staged successfully a congenial corresponding scenic composition.[75]

ANNETTE STRICKER

TITLE / DATE
LUCI MIE TRADITRICI, 2001
CYCLE
MUSIC
LENGTH
75 MINUTES

MUSIC
SALVATORE SCIARRINO
BASED ON *IL TRADIMENTO PER
L'ONORE* BY GIACINTO ANDREA
CICOGNINI, 1664, WITH AN ELEGY
BY CLAUDE LE JEUNE
MUSIC PERFORMANCE
LA MONNAIE SYMPHONY
ORCHESTRA, KAZUSHI ONO,
MUSICAL DIRECTOR
VISUAL PRESENTATION
ROLAND AESCHLIMANN
SETS
ROLAND AESCHLIMANN

COSTUMES
ROLAND AESCHLIMANN
LIGHTING
ROLAND AESCHLIMANN AND
ROBERT BRASSEUR
PERFORMERS
ANNETTE STRICKER (LA
MALASPINA), PAUL ARMIN
EDELMANN (IL MALASPINO),
JOHN BOWEN (UN SERVO DELLA
CASA), LAWRENCE ZAZZO
(L'OSPITE)

FIRST PERFORMANCES
THÉÂTRE ROYAL DE LA MONNAIE,
BRUSSELS, BELGIUM,
MARCH 16, 2001
LINCOLN CENTER FESTIVAL,
LAGUARDIA DRAMA THEATER, NEW
YORK CITY, JULY 10, 2001

"THE VOICE IS A MUSCLE": TRISHA BROWN AND OPERA

GUILLAUME BERNARDI

IN ITALY DECEMBER IS TRADITIONALLY THE MOST EXCITING MONTH FOR OPERA AFICIONADOS. After the long summer break, the opera houses reopen, always with glamorous new productions. One of the most anticipated premieres of the 1986–87 season was the production of *Carmen* at one of Italy's most venerable theaters, the Teatro San Carlo of Naples. The production brought together some prestigious newcomers and some exciting concepts. The director was popular, iconoclastic Italian filmmaker Lina Wertmüller. Rumors had it that in her first opera production she would transpose Bizet's opera from the early nineteenth century to the 1920s. Thus, in act 5, Carmen would meet her tragic fate in an automobile, a mild shock for the San Carlo's "abonnés." More intriguingly, she had asked the postmodern, abstract choreographer Trisha Brown to participate as a choreographer and performer in the production. For her first opera venture, Brown would be on stage for most of the piece. In the program, her role was listed as "La Bruja," the sorceress: she would represent the dark forces at work in the opera.[1] Last but certainly not least in the land of bel canto, the now-deceased Lucia Valentini-Terrani, then at the height of her young glory, would make her debut in one of the most dramatic roles of the opera repertoire, Carmen, quite a challenge for a mezzosoprano known for her coloratura singing.[2] Although the production was a great success, the collaborations didn't quite pan out. The Italian critics struggled to understand Brown's approach and insisted that Brown's dances, the rhythm of which never coincided with the music, felt disconnected from the opera.[3] More distressing, Valentini-Terrani dramatically left the production days before the opening, creating one of those opera scandals that Italy loves so much. The alleged cause of her withdrawal was the singer's refusal to share the stage with Brown during her entrance aria, the famous "Habanera." There is no doubt that for Brown, *Carmen* was a tough but transformative experience. Later, when asked to explain her interest in opera, she always referred to *Carmen*, but in Naples she had had to work under very difficult conditions, pressed for time, and in a milieu ultimately closed to the ideas of postmodern dance. The crisis with Valentini-Terrani illustrated the difficult rapport between opera and the other arts, between tradition and modernity. It was a clear sign that for such collaborations to be productive, careful thinking was necessary.

Ten years later, Brown started a much happier, and still ongoing,[4] partnership with the Théâtre Royal de la Monnaie in Brussels, which has resulted in two landmark productions, Monteverdi's *L'Orfeo* in 1998 and Salvatore Sciarrino's *Luci mie traditrici* in 2001.[5] Bernard Foccroulle, the artistic director of La Monnaie, played a key role in those successes. First, he gave Brown full control as director and choreographer of the productions.[6] He was also an ever-present, fully supportive partner. The main lesson of Naples was that Brown should be able to work on her own terms. Brown negotiated with La Monnaie a rehearsal process of unheard length in the opera milieu.[7] She also brought to Brussels her team of assistants and her dancers, who, on a one-on-one basis, taught the singers the parts developed by Brown

Previous spread: *Glacial Decoy*, 1979. Sets and costumes by Robert Rauschenberg. Pictured: Trisha Brown, Nina Lundborg, Lisa Kraus. Photograph by Babette Mangolte.

Opposite page: *Carmen* by George Bizet. Directed by Lina Wertmüller, Teatro di San Carlo, Naples, 1986. Pictured: Trisha Brown. Photograph by Luciano Romano.

1. *Carmen* was one of the least seen and documented works of Brown's mature production. There were only ten performances, attended mainly by local audiences. A thirteen-minute video by Burt Barr, *Trisha and Carmen* (1988) captures a short dance in rehearsal and in performance. Maybe more importantly, it depicts the context of this production: the opulence of the San Carlo and its rituals, the sense of displacement of Trisha Brown and her dancers, heavily made-up and clad in Hispanic costumes. Apart from reviews, the only substantial article on *Carmen* is Klaus Kertess, "Dancing with Carmen," *Art in America* 75, no. 5 (April 1987): 180–85. I relied heavily on this article and on personal communications from Trisha Brown and some of the dancers who participated in the production: Irene Hultman, Carolyn Lucas, and Diane Madden.
2. Lucia Valentini-Terrani (1949–99) was famous for her vocal virtuosity and acting talent, in particular in Rossini. Her untimely death saddened the Italian opera community.
3. See, for instance, the comments of Sandro Rossi in *L'Unità*: "The much-awaited choreography by Trisha Brown to us felt nearly always foreign to the economy of the show, and even at times a disturbance (Quasi sempre estranee all'economia dello spettacolo ci sono sembrate, poi, le attese coreografie di Trisha Brown, quando addirittura non hanno costituito un elemento di disturbo)"; quoted in Silvana Ottolenghi, ed., *Opera '87* (Turin: E.D.T., 1988), p. 146.

in the peace of her New York studio. The experience of *Carmen* also had demonstrated the importance of finding operas with real affinities with Brown's work. The hyperdramatic *Carmen*, steeped in melodrama and in fantasy Spain, was probably too jarringly discordant with Brown's aesthetic, whereas both *L'Orfeo* and *Luci mie traditrici* had an authentic kinship with Brown's world. In *L'Orfeo* (1607), the earliest opera still regularly performed, the emphasis is less on the dramatic action than on the emotions aroused by the tragic events that befall Orpheus and Eurydice. Similarly, in *Luci mie traditrici* (1998), Sciarrino condensed the complex action of the original seventeenth-century play in eight enigmatic scenes in which again the inner world of the characters is more important than the few actual events. Bernard Foccroulle provided a foundation that ensured his initiative to associate a postmodern, abstract, New York choreographer famous for her resistance to "drama" and to narrative with a genre as entrenched in tradition as opera was not just a publicity coup but rather the occasion for an important artistic event. It was then up to Brown, now in the director's chair, to resolve those paradoxes and bring the productions to success.

In Brussels, Brown's greatest achievement was probably to have tenaciously maintained her artistic identity and to have resisted first the dominant system of production of opera and then its dominant dramaturgy. Brown's directorial practice reflected deeply her personal history, as a performer and as a choreographer. Her very understanding of her role as director came from her previous experiences, not from standard opera practice. Consequently her productions would indeed be closer to her world than to standard opera fare.

At the Judson Church, Brown's artistic path started with simple, radical questions (What is dance? What happens if all parts of the body are treated equally?) and with improvisation

Opposite page: Rehearsal of *Luci mie traditrici*, 2001. Sets and costumes by Roland Aeschlimann. Pictured: Eric Tipler, Guillaume Bernardi, Annette Stricker, Carolyn Lucas, Trisha Brown, Sybile Wilson. Photograph by Johan Jacobs.

This page: *Skunk Cabbage, Salt Grass, and Waders*, 1967. Pictured: Trisha Brown. Photograph by Peter Moore.

4. *L'Orfeo* was remounted at La Monnaie in May 2002. At the time of writing, discussions were under way between Brown and La Monnaie for a new project in 2004.
5. Both productions received many performances in various cities and are well-documented (see the "Dance and Art in Dialogue" section and the bibliography and videography in this volume).
6. Whereas for *Carmen*, Trisha Brown participated as choreographer and performer, for *L'Orfeo* she was credited as choreographer and director, and for *Luci mie traditrici* simply as director, a significant evolution.
7. Brown started working on *L'Orfeo* in 1995. Apart from the standard six weeks of rehearsal, the process included lengthy preparatory rehearsals with the Trisha Brown Dance Company and a two-week workshop with the principal singers.
8. On Cage's influence on Brown, see: "Dancing and Drawing, Trisha Brown–Hendel Teicher interview," in *Trisha Brown: Danse, précis de liberté* (Marseille and Paris: Musées de Marseille and Réunion des musées nationaux, 1998), p. 14.

as her primary tool. Brown's approach to opera followed the same route. She challenged preconceived ideas on the form and through improvisation introduced countless new solutions to classic opera staging problems. Another essential asset was her rich and original understanding of collaboration. In many ways, Brown's opera work was a continuation of her collaborative practice. Just as *M.O.* was a dialogue of equals between Brown and Bach, *L'Orfeo* and *Luci mie traditrici* were indeed dialogues between Brown and Monteverdi and then Brown and Sciarrino. She was less intent on furthering the expression of their ideas (the goal of traditional opera directors) than exploring the possibilities of the dialogue. Brown, probably influenced by John Cage in this respect,[8] was able to envision the relationships between the various components of an opera with an immense sense of freedom, each element responding to the others but keeping its own identity. In Brown's dramaturgical vision, opera functions by associations, as a metaphoric system rather than a mimetic one. The implications of Brown's innovative approach to directing were most strongly felt in the way she dealt with three key elements: the set and costume design, the narrative, and the singers.

In Brown's productions, both the mythological world of *L'Orfeo* and the castle of *Luci mie traditrici* became monochrome, strongly shaped transcendent worlds, haunted by beings dressed in muffled colors. The nymphs and shepherds of *L'Orfeo* were indistinguishably dressed in white pajamas, whereas in *Luci mie traditrici*, the beige and cream 1920s costumes erased all class distinctions between the aristocrats and their servants. Abstraction, a defining concept for Brown, had an essential dramaturgical impact. By removing basic markers that are essential to realistic staging—the establishing of time or locale but also gender and social class—abstraction conferred on the design an autonomy from the outside world and from the original text of the operas. As the performers didn't utilize the set in a realistic manner, it soared to a life of its own, offering to Brown a challenging but essential source of inspiration. Brown's collaboration with designer Roland Aeschlimann must be thought of as resembling her work with Donald Judd on *Newark (Niweweorce)* rather than as the standard relationship between director and designer. Rather than requesting from her designer a set that would fulfill *a priori* her staging needs, she worked with Aeschlimann's creation: she developed movement and meanings from it, thus inverting the usual relationship between set and staging. The result was extraordinary. In *L'Orfeo*, for instance, Aeschlimann envisioned a sweeping move of a wall across the entire stage to represent the passage from the earth to the underworld. Brown then imagined that the moving wall pushed away the rolling, entangled bodies of the infernal spirits. Brown went one step further in *Luci mie traditrici*. Its set was a steep, silvery hill crossed diagonally by seven toothed, moving blades. Brown devised a complex aleatoric system of movements for the blades that metamorphosed the set into a kind of huge, slow-breathing, coiled, primitive monster. On it, she adjusted the movements of the singers in order to create a sense of the different locations required by the libretto: a rose garden, a bedchamber, and so on. That process created a deeply organic relationship between the singers and the set; they used all its potential. At the same time, the frictions between the singers and the set as autonomous entities produced clusters of novel metaphors.

Brown's aesthetic choice to allow a multiplicity of meanings to emerge was also perceptible in her treatment of narrative. Academics have postulated that the original production of *L'Orfeo* had a different conclusion from the version published in 1607. The earlier version followed more closely the original myth: instead of Orpheus being transported to heaven by the god of music, Apollo, he was murdered and torn apart by the Maenads. In her production, Brown chose to present both endings in succession. Apollo did appear and speak with Orpheus, but then there was an abrupt change: during the concluding *Moresca*, the Maenads made a wild entrance and dismembered the demigod. Brown's democratic approach to narrative was even more deeply perceptible in her treatment of musical structures. Opera, as a genre, functions on the parallel drives of drama and music, but usually drama through plot and characters get most of the director's attention. The underlying musical structures often remain buried under the dramatic actions. Brown instead strove to express the musical structures on stage. It was easy for Brown, after the lessons learned from Bach when choreographing *M.O.*, to bring out the musical forms used by Monteverdi. In acts 1 and 2, the Italian composer devised a wealth of forms (such as ritornelli, duos, trios) that Brown exploited in the choreography of the vocal ensembles. She created a complex choreography, she called it "a machine," that moved singers and dancers around the stage in a continuous flow. Rather than emphasizing dramatic motivations, the choreography created another formal system of meaning, in parallel to text and to music. Brown's use of the set and her multilayered approach to narrative certainly loosened up dramatic tension. At the same time though, her approach freed the spectators from the intense, obsessive emotions of opera: it allowed them to see and to relate to the singers in new ways.

A disconcerting thing happened on the first dress rehearsal of *L'Orfeo* at La Monnaie. The chorus came on stage wearing their costumes for the first time, but also in Louis XVI powdered wigs and thick white makeup: none of the singers was recognizable any more. By the end of the rehearsal, Brown had decided to cut the wigs and to drastically reduce the makeup.

It was essential for her that the individuality of each chorus member showed on stage. Brown's attention to the singers' bodies and personalities was truly exceptional. During the whole rehearsal process, all the singers received daily in-depth movement classes with the dancers of Brown's company, who also taught them their parts with extreme care. After having studied meticulously not only the music but also the words (a new territory for Brown) of the beautiful librettos of *L'Orfeo* and *Luci mie traditrici*, the choreographer had developed eloquent, moving "dances" for them. The singers relinquished their tired vocabulary of rhetorical gestures, so much associated with opera, to embody a new, complex, richly metaphoric gesturality. As Brown's approach grew more assured, the source of inspiration for the movement vocabulary became freer, more in touch with her intuitive associations. In some cases, when she could establish a deeper rapport with singers like Simon Keenlyside (Orfeo), Graciela Oddone (Messaggiera in *L'Orfeo*) or Annette Stricker (La Malaspina in *Luci mie traditrici*), the performers themselves generated some of the movement material. The conflict between dance and singing that had plagued *Carmen* was now resolved. The audiences responded with utter fascination to these singing and dancing performers, who could capture their full attention. Traditional operatic intensity had been relinquished to give place to new emotions, to new aesthetic territories. In Brown's productions, all the elements grew together and at the same time blossomed with a life of their own. The magic balance between harmony and diversity proved that Trisha Brown, the opera director, was indeed "La Bruja."

Following spread: Trisha Brown, Pages from choreographic notebook, 1997. Pencil on paper, 11 3/4 x 7 3/4 in. (29.8 x 19.7 cm). Collection of Trisha Brown.

I would like to thank Thérèse Barbanel, who provided me with rare reviews of *Carmen*, Jean Conon-Unda for listening, Antonio Torres-Ruiz for his support, and, of course, Trisha Brown for her trust and immense generosity.

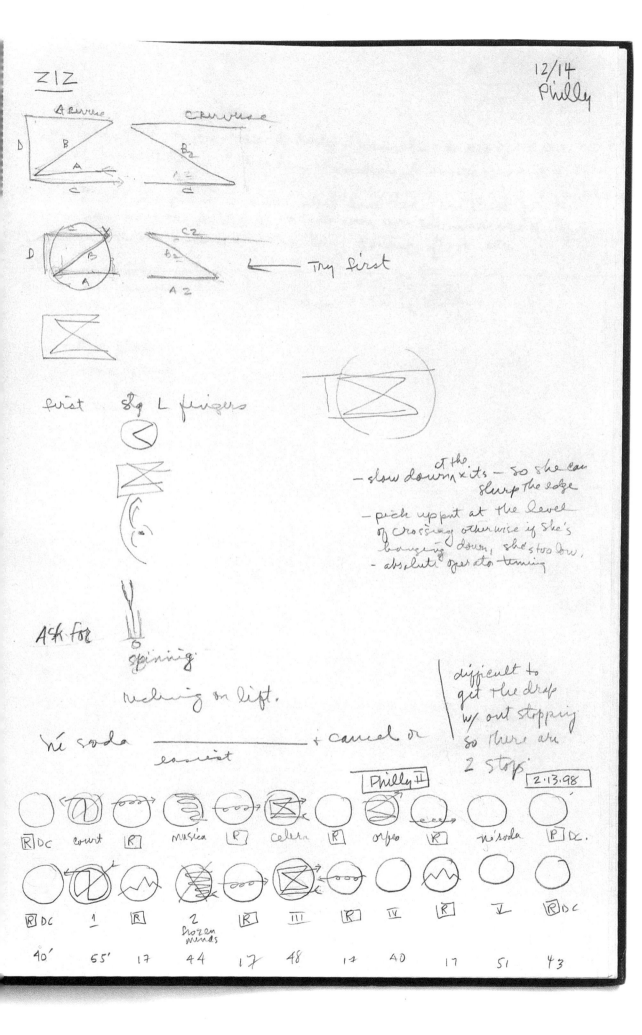

ZIZ

A REVERSE   C REVERSE

← Try first

first   lg L fingers

- slow down at the exits — so she can slurp the edge
- pick up pnt at the level of crossing otherwise if she's banging down, she's too low.
- absolute operator timing

Ask for

spining

reeling on lift.

né soda ———————— + cancel or
       easiest

difficult to get the drop w/ out stopping so there are 2 stops

Philly II   2.13.98

R DC	court	R	musica	R	celera	R	orfeo	R	né soda	P DC

R DC	1	R	2 frozen minds	R	III	R	IV	R	V	R DC

40'   55'   17   44   17   48   17   40   17   51   43

WHEN SHE WAS EMBROILED IN THE EBULLIENTLY RADICAL WORK OF NEW YORK'S JUDSON Dance Theater, physical expertise—along with bravura performing—was something a dancer kept under wraps. Yet here was a woman who, orchestrating the mundane acts of sitting, lying, and standing in *Trillium* (1962), her first Judson piece, found herself attempting to lie down in midair. "I did not," she said later, "notify myself of my intentions in advance of performance."

If one takes "virtuosity" to mean not empty display but mastery of a form and expansion of its frontiers, then Brown certainly was already demonstrating it in the 1970s. Walking on walls via harnesses, ropes, pulleys, and tracks tested her dancers' stamina even as it derailed spectators' expectations about gravity in relation to visual information. Once she returned to the ground to choreograph, the basic vocabulary that she built on the bending, straightening, and rotating of joints was subjected to complex structural permutations that demanded extraordinarily nimble minds on the part of the performers. Watching Brown perform her 1979 *Accumulation with talking plus Watermotor*, in which she slips back and forth between two earlier solos and between two anecdotes she tells about her past, you feel viscerally the pulse-quickening delights of risk, the daunting job of memory.

Like her colleagues of the 1960s (Steve Paxton, Yvonne Rainer, David Gordon, Simone Forti, and others) Brown initially rejected enhancing lights, decor, costumes, drama, and fiction, along with traditional use of music. Gradually, she found ways to come to terms with some of them. The collaborations with artists and composers that she began in 1979 with Robert Rauschenberg's designs for *Glacial Decoy* have been rigorously untraditional. Rather than being simply decorative, the decor for her pieces ignites formal analogies with her own processes. The translucent, variously colored backdrops by Donald Judd that rose and descended during the 1987 *Newark (Niweweorce)* altered the space, confining and pressurizing some sections of dancing. The only music for *Foray Forêt* (1990) was provided by a marching band circling the block outside the theater—first heard faintly, becoming louder, then dying away to leave us in a deeper silence; what we heard enhanced the visual imagery of appearance and disappearance: movement flickering between still figures, light glancing off Rauschenberg's gold and silver costumes.

Crucial to Brown's work is her famously silky style. Although initially reticent about her influences, she once said something offhand about growing up in a forest. Aberdeen, Washington, is on a bay of the Pacific. Nothing about her dancing or her choreography thrusts itself at you head on. It's like something glimpsed between trees, influenced by tides. "I'm always trying to deflect your focus," she said in an interview with her old friend and colleague Yvonne Rainer. Her dancing—considered completely inimitable until she took it upon herself in the early eighties to transfer it to remarkable dancers like Eva Karczag, Vicky Shick, Stephen Petronio, Diane Madden, Lisa Kraus, and others—incites water analogies. You feel movement running through her body—spurting here, flowing there, diverted by new currents, but always delectably free and supple.

Opposite page: *Son of Gone Fishin'*, 1981. Sets by Donald Judd and costumes by Judith Shea. Pictured: Diane Madden, Eva Karczag. Photograph by Joshua Adams.

From the 1980s, her dances have also reflected that complex fluidity in the ways the dancers intersect; almost colliding, slipping past or glancing off one another, setting up impulsive new lines of transit. Movements give the illusion of leaping across the stage, alighting on one dancer, then another. Brown refers to *Opal Loop/Cloud Installation #72503* (1980), *Son of Gone Fishin'* (1981), and *Set and Reset* (1983) as "Unstable Molecular Structures." Watching those combustible dances, your eye grazes on almost constant flux.

The audience for Brown's work of the 1970s could grasp her structures. In 1973, dance fans and lunchtime loiterers were watching her and three dancers perform *Group Primary Accumulation* in the sunken plaza of the McGraw-Hill Building. "Come *on*! Let's go," a construction worker urged his buddy; having grasped the 1, 1-2-, 1-2-3 pattern, the other shook him off: "Wait a minute. My favorite movement's coming up."

Gradually the structures became secret agents. Performers in *Set and Reset*, for example, kept dancing out of the main performing area, where they remained visible through Robert Rauschenberg's translucent side panels. To create this come-and-go play with the official edges of the stage, Brown created three phrases; two traveled the perimeter of the stage, along one side and across the front; another moved up the other side away from the audience and across the back. The dancers improvised upon these phrases—heeding guidelines like "be invisible" or "line up"—until Brown liked what she saw and set it. The perimeter phrases also "delivered" choreographed solos, duets, and trios to the center of the stage.

Her dancers have become increasingly virtuosic in the traditional sense (many with the kind of conservatory training her first company lacked), but mental agility is still a requirement. They can reverse the phrases she choreographs and perform them to either side. They can splice part of phrase A into phrase B, say, and then jump-cut to the end of phrase C and start

Opposite page: *Lateral Pass*, 1985.
Sets and costumes by Nancy
Graves. Pictured: Diane Madden,
Stephen Petronio, Vicky Shick,
Randy Warshaw, Iréne Hultman.
Photograph by Babette Mangolte.

This page: *Newark (Niweweorce)*,
1987. Sets and costumes by
Donald Judd. Pictured: Diane
Madden, Jeffrey Axelrod, Lance
Gries, Carolyn Lucas. Photo-
graph by Tristan Valès/Agence
Enguerand, Paris.

through it backward. Brown developed a method of building a dance in part as if she were a
chef—calling for and assembling known ingredients to produce unforeseen consequences.

With the dances she called the Valiant cycle—*Lateral Pass* (1985), *Newark (Niweweorce)*
(1987), and *Astral Convertible* (1989)—prowess vaulted into a new dimension. *Newark*, which
premiered in the Nouveau Théâtre d'Angers under the auspices of France's Centre National
de Danse Contemporaine, marked the first time in which Brown made a distinction between
male and female styles. She had two superb men dancers, Lance Gries and Jeffrey Axelrod.
She'd also had a streak of bad luck; her response to this last, she said in 1990, was "to work
with very powerful, emphatic movement—the way I got into it was by shoving furniture
all around the studio like a stevedore (the dancers thought I was off my rocker)—and that
segued into an interest in men's bodies, like really saying, 'Okay, what do I think looks elegant
on them? What can they do that I cannot because of my body structure?'" The opening unison
duet for the two consisted of heroically strong, blocky moves, elegantly designed. For the
first time in what seemed like years, Brown engineered pauses, allowed the viewer's eye to
alight, or travel around the same body for seconds at a time. However, *Newark* didn't capitu-
late to conventional dance machismo; the men were lyrical in their power, and the women's
fluidity didn't preclude strength. At one point, Madden spun while balancing Gries on
her shoulder.

Having segued out of these heroic displays of mind-body virtuosity via *Foray Forêt*, with
its mix of stillness and vibrant motion, Brown quieted herself down further with *For M.G.:
The Movie* (1991), dedicated to the recently deceased Michel Guy, the French minister of culture
who had so admired her work. For the entire dance, Kevin Kortan stood motionless, his back
to the audience, and Nicole Juralewicz stood beside him for much of it. This spare work began

with the magnificent Madden simply running and running and running in paths that traced an invisible web on the floor. Quietness abounded. For *One Story as in Falling* (choreographed in 1992 for the French group run by the late Dominique Bagouet) and its 1993 version, *Another Story as in Falling*, Brown even abandoned much of her springy vocabulary, creating a long sequence of clear moves and gestures she dubbed "Little Man." The unemphatic rhythms generated an image of multiple, everyday Joes plodding quietly through their separate lives (the baggy red men's suits created by Roland Aeschlimann added to the effect). In its functional look, the piece seemed a kind of throwback to the 1970s. It was as if Brown were paring down from lushness to simplicity in order to reconsider her path.

It has often been her practice to dig into her past and present previous material in a new way. Perhaps the tantalizing vision of the dancer with his back to the audience in *For M.G: The Movie* influenced her enigmatic 1994 solo, *If you couldn't see me*, in which she danced without ever facing the audience—knowable only by her spine. In the early 1970s, she and her dancers had walked on walls, down pillars and trees; some ten years later, *Set and Reset* began with a group of performers carrying Madden laid out, head to the audience, across the rear of the stage, "walking" on air. In one section of *Lateral Pass*, Randy Warshaw was suspended from above on an elastic harness, amid Nancy Graves's hanging sculptures, sometimes dipping down to touch the ground beside his associates. Defying gravity reached an apogee of theatricality in the opening scene of the Monteverdi opera *L'Orfeo*, which Brown directed in 1998. During an aria praising Orpheus's musical gifts, dancer Katrina Thompson sailed across a circle of blue sky glimpsed through an "eye" in the black frontcloth. On almost invisible equipment, she flew joyously out of sight, tumbled back, and somersaulted away again—the very embodiment of music. And of Trisha's spirit.

The gorgeous vision also embodied Brown's pleasure in testing the perimeters of space and orchestrating games between the seen, the half-seen, and the unseen, as she had in *Glacial Decoy*, *Set and Reset*, and *Foray Forêt*. In this last, when she performed her final thoughtful solo, dancers appeared intermittently, half in and half out of the wings, like elusive memories.

Brown's experience choreographing Lina Wertmüller's 1986 production of *Carmen* made her reconsider the possible delights of working with pre-existing music. Ten years later, in *M.O.*, she tackled Bach's *Musical Offering*, and the following year set *Twelve Ton Rose* to the works of Anton Webern. In collaborating with famous dead composers, she did not simply allow her body to sing along with their melodies, but studied their forms and textures. She taught herself baroque polyphonic composition and matched her zest for counterpoint to Bach's. She captured both the sparsity and compression in Webern's pieces by rapidly coalescing and dissolving highly organized patterns.

Although Brown makes non-narrative dances, directing *L'Orfeo* meant she had to consider emotional content. Mixing singers and dancers together, she reflected the tale of doubly lost love through groupings, pattern, and gesture: finding her own equivalents for the flow of happiness and plunges into grief, as well as for the ornamental filigrees and long plangent lines of Monteverdi's music. In *Canto/Pianto*, the dance that she made for her company using music and movement material drawn from the opera production, she expressed the emotions in even more condensed ways, especially in a remarkable and almost stationary solo for Kathleen Fisher. The two halves of Fisher's body seemed at odds with each other—one flowing, one cracking: the expressed lament and the inexpressible inner tumult.

Brown's most recent works—three collaborations with visual artist Terry Winters and innovative jazz composer Dave Douglas—have presented a different challenge. We are used to choreographers who set dances to jazz accommodating the music's insistent beat, syncopations, and get-down tone. But Brown approached *Five-Part Weather Invention* (1999) and *Rapture to Leon James* and *Groove and Countermove* (both from 2000), armed with her own loose-limbed, witty vocabulary and her keen eye for form. In the first of the three pieces, for example, she plays lively games with the jazz practice of improvising around a known tune. The dancers all know a set phrase for the feet, but must work to top it with the arm patterns Keith Thompson is making up on the spot.

Some artists tackle "serious" subjects and dark narratives. Brown, an extremely serious artist—a master, a virtuoso—has never lost that heightened playfulness that marked her task structures of the 1960s and early 1970s. Wildness may crop up in her dances; so may risk and explosiveness. Never anger, never violence inflicted by one person on another. Amid the postmodern preoccupation with text, eclecticism, and sociopolitical commentary, her work shines with a particularly clear light.

Opposite page: *Astral Convertible*, 1989. Sets and costumes by Robert Rauschenberg. Pictured: Nicole Juralewicz, Wil Swanson, Carolyn Lucas. Photograph by Geneviève Stephenson.

Following spread: *Rapture to Leon James* (2000) from *El Trilogy*, 1999–2000. Sets and costumes by Terry Winters. Pictured: Keith A. Thompson, Todd Lawrence Stone, Abigail Yager, Stacy Matthew Spence, Seth Parker, Kathleen Fisher, Brandi Norton, Mariah Maloney, Katrina Thompson. Photograph by Joanne Savio.

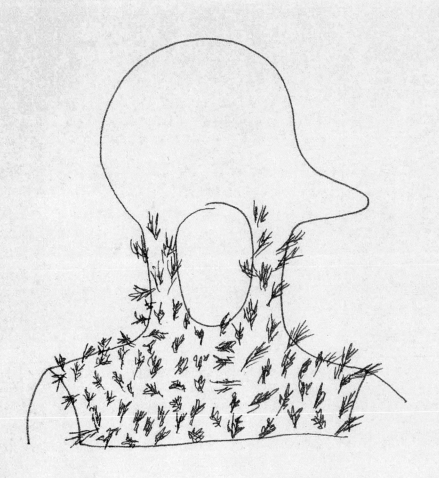

THE DANCE WITH THE DUCK'S HEAD

Half bird, Half woman.

Paper maché skirt in sit down position.

Made a cotton skirt, full. Made a human model by stuffing old ~~stocks~~ pants w/ paper. ~~Set~~ Put the skirt on the model and sat the whole thing up in a chair. Sprayed it w/ epoxy several times. Carefully — ~~preason~~ precisionly layed on paper strips honoring every fold and crease. It worked.

Left a 1/4" wide strip on one side to function as a hinge → and basted together seam on the other side. To be opened for putting on and sewed into for performance. It worked. Same process.

BIRD/WOMAN/FLOWER/DAREDEVIL: TRISHA BROWN
HENDEL TEICHER

IN DECEMBER 1968, TRISHA BROWN PERFORMED *THE DANCE WITH THE DUCK'S HEAD* at The Museum of Modern Art in New York. She entered the space wearing a yellow papier-mâché skirt shaped so that the knees remained bent as if seated, a rigid bra (to "cure anyone from ever wearing a bra again," as Brown has suggested), a large collar made of chicken feathers, and a helmet in the shape of a duck's head, also adorned with chicken feathers. It had taken Brown weeks to build her costume, layer by layer, and during this process she also spent time drawing and writing several "idea/images" about the choreography. In the opening moments of the performance she moved across the stage in a crouch and sat down in a chair. Soon after, a staged "violent fight" broke out in the audience between two performers situated there. As calm was restored, Brown's duck-lady stepped into a pair of logging boots bolted to a metal frame.[1] The frame was then lifted by four men who walked around the space turning, twisting, and rolling the frame with Brown in it—even turning it upside down—to achieve "the look of free flight."[2] The fifteen minutes during which Brown was stuck in her boots being swirled upside down and around the space reveal the multiple layers that still reverberate in her work. *The Dance with the Duck's Head* was at once refined and raw, humorous and poetic, and on a more intimate level addressed the relations between men and women. In this work, she began to devise for herself an original path inside the "soft" and malleable space of dance. She knew how to fly out of the yoke of that stiff costume.

Decades later, Dominique Frétard began an article on Trisha Brown by stating that "one could nickname her the Woman of Iron for her character. And the Bird/Woman for the way she takes off from the ground."[3] The image and idea of a half-bird/half-woman can be traced back to Brown's childhood in Aberdeen, Washington. Brown explains in unpublished notes written in the early 1970s:

> It's funny with all the hunting I did as a kid that I should identify with birds. Witness a few of the dances I've made. Well, shooting doves is excellent target practice because they are small and fast…. There was one thing that happened too often. A downed dove may appear to be dead but only be wounded, and after you put it in the game pocket on the back of your vest a few minutes later this fluttering would start up. Like inside my shirt. There was one moment though when I ran over to retrieve a dove I'd shot to find a dead robin. I realized that I killed a birdie.[4]

Brown's formative years shaped a spirit and a body without fears. Her world then had no boundaries; dangerous and forbidden games were played in total innocence. The simple, childlike, and birdlike motions of catching/throwing, moving fast/slow, fluttering/being still, and flying/falling became the premises of her dance language. The various topologies of nature found in her childhood—moss, grass, leaves, trees, earth, water, air, fog, rain, and sun—weave the texture of memory into her dances.

Previous spread: Trisha Brown, Drawings and notes for *The Dance with the Duck's Head*, 1968. Ink on paper, 11 x 8 1/2 in. (27.9 x 21.6 cm) each. Collection of Trisha Brown.

Opposite page: *The Dance with the Duck's Head*, 1968. Performance at The Museum of Modern Art, New York, December 6, 1968. Pictured: Steve Carpenter, Peter Poole, Trisha Brown, Elie Roman, Melvin Reichler. Photograph by J. Raman.

1. Brown made six pages of notes and drawings in preparation for *The Dance with the Duck's Head*. In her notes, Brown describes a "violent fight."
2. From the drawings and notes for *The Dance with the Duck's Head*.
3. Dominique Frétard, "Le corps géometrique et le corps animal," *Le Monde*, 1 March 1990.
4. Choreographer's notes, not dated.

Trisha Brown
Oct 80

Left hand drawn by right hand #1

Token for Bob #1

Trisha Brown
Oct 80

Opposite page from top: Trisha Brown, *Left hand drawn by right hand #1*, October 1980. Pencil on paper, 11 3/8 x 16 in. (29.9 x 40.6 cm). Collection of Trisha Brown.

Trisha Brown, *Token for Bob*, October 1980. Pencil on paper, 11 1/2 x 16 in. (28.9 x 40.6 cm). Collection of Robert Rauschenberg.

This page: Marie Chabelska as the Little American Girl in *Parade*, 1917. Ballet by Jean Cocteau, score by Erik Satie, choreography by Léonide Massine, sets and costumes by Pablo Picasso. Photograph Musée Picasso.

Performance photo of Suzushi Hanayagi.

Accumulation with talking plus Watermotor, 1979. Pictured: Trisha Brown. Photograph by Nathaniel Tileston.

5. Bruce Chatwin, *The Songlines* (New York: Viking, 1987), p. 272.
6. Deborah Menaker Rothschild, *Picasso's Parade* (London: Sotheby's Publications, 1991), p. 268.
7. She wore a navy blue sailor jacket, a short white pleated skirt, and was sporting a large white bow in her hair.
8. Gustave Fréjaville, *Au Music-hall* (Paris: Editions du Monde nouveau, 1923), p. 138.

The loss and celebration of her childhood is an active memory and a source of inspiration for Brown. In his book *The Songlines* Bruce Chatwin reminds us of Proust's perspicacious belief that the "walks" of childhood form the raw material of our intelligence.[5] The physical freedom that Brown experienced growing up amid unspoiled and powerful nature was a gift that nurtured her constant curiosity about different worlds. Over time, those forays layered her work. Consistently, like stringing pearls, Brown began constructing units of earthbound and celestial events. One of these units culminates thirty years later in the Prologue to *L'Orfeo* by Monteverdi when La Musica flies in an ethereal blue sphere, offering us simultaneously memories of Tiepolo's baroque ceilings and yearnings for dreams of flying—or swimming—in a free, open space.

The legendary choreography of Léonide Massine in the 1917 work *Parade* brought together an avant-garde team of collaborators: the score was written by Erik Satie, the ballet arranged by Jean Cocteau, and the costumes and décor designed by Picasso. A description of *Parade* by Guillaume Apollinaire from his program note to the 1917 production said, "*Parade* will upset the ideas of quite a number of spectators. They will be surprised, to be sure, but in the pleasantest way, and fascinated, they will learn how graceful modern movement can be— something they have never suspected.... The American girl [a character in the ballet], by turning the crank of an imaginary automobile, will express the magic of their everyday life."[6] Picasso's costume design for the American girl[7] would likely have been recognized by the audience as similar to that of the Eight Allissons, an American acrobatic team that was touring Europe at the time. The frenetic movements of the *Parade* girl were certainly reminiscent of the Allissons' "flips, somersaults and pirouettes without stop."[8]

The image of the American girl's pantomime in which she rotated her wrists outward with thumbs extended brings to mind a similar gesture Brown included in her choreography for *Accumulation* (1971) and its subsequent elaborations. According to Brown, the work raised the

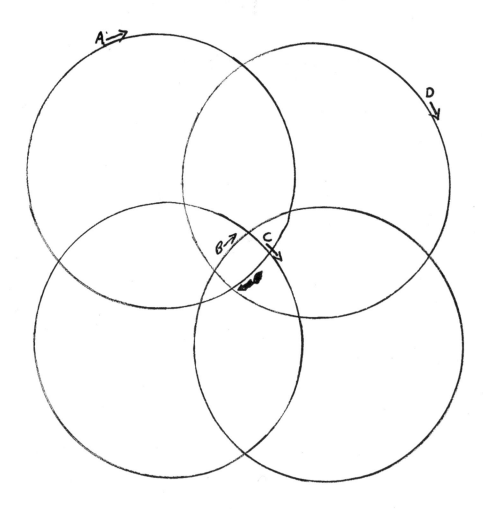

Dancers A and B are partners and travel on parallel
circular tracks. Partners C and D travel on parallel
circular tracks different from A and B. The four
dancers carry their heads centered and do not look to
the right or left. When no one is in their vision
they initiate movement. When 1, 2, or 3 other dancers
are in their vision, focused and peripheral, they
copy the movements simultaneously.

Opposite page: Trisha Brown,
Circles, 1973. Ink on paper,
11 x 8 1/2 in. (27.9 x 21.6 cm).
Collection of Trisha Brown.

This page: Photograph of Brown's
brother, Gordon Brown, by Lee
Friedlander, c. 1951.

9. Interview of Trisha Brown by the
author, "Dancing and Drawing,"
in *Trisha Brown: Danse, précis de
liberté* (Marseilles and Paris:
Musées de Marseilles and Réunion
des musées nationaux, 1998), p. 19.
10. Cynthia J. Novack, *Sharing
the Dance: Contact Improvisation
and American Culture* (Madison:
The University of Wisconsin Press,
1990), p. 230.
11. Representing a tree composed
of feet, hands, and a heart, the
Grand Union logo was designed
by Carol Michaud.

questions, "Is rotating a fist acceptable? Is dropping my right arm down acceptable?," some of
which she explored in drawings.[9] The humorous aspect of the performance and the straight-
forwardness of a series of quotidian, nondecorative gestures add to the mysterious, abstract
sign language that unfolds. It is between rawness and refinement that many of Brown's secrets
lie. She is, on the one hand, that "American girl," the nature girl from the Pacific Northwest,
engaged in down-to-earth activities and "hands-on" day-to-day tasks. On the other hand, she
empowers those activities by adding mysterious new meanings.

Trisha Brown's parents encouraged their children to play sports. Brown fondly recalls being
a devoted supporter of her brother, Gordon, who played on the school basketball team.
The photographer Lee Friedlander, also a native of Aberdeen, took numerous pictures, both
live-action and posed, of Gordon's number 33. In her remarkable book, *Sharing the Dance:
Contact Improvisation and American Culture,* Cynthia J. Novack argues that "the audience
for sports crosses class, racial, and ethnic lines, just as its participants do. It is no wonder
that American dancers and audiences are aesthetically influenced by athletics: Sport is our
most prominent visual referent for physical skill."[10] Brown's passion for American sports
is certainly a visible thread throughout her choreography, which incorporates multiple speeds,
daring passes, precarious flights, and powerful physical encounters, as well as an affinity
for close group formations.

    Brown and her Grand Union peers, a group of choreographers active in New York in the
early seventies, shared a fascination with Native American cultures. In 1974, the group
produced a leaflet combining pictures of their performances, their union logo,[11] and photographs of the ceremonial performances of the Kwakiutl, Nootka, and other tribes. Brown's
vocalizing in *Medicine Dance* (1967), which she has described as "anguished," was doubt-
lessly influenced by her interest in cathartic, shamanistic rituals that she imaginatively
embraced in her own coming of age. In other pieces choreographed by Brown, the inspiration
behind the symbolic rituals of tribal dances find their way into movements described by

12. See Paxton, "Brown in the New Body" in this book.
13. Interview of Diane Madden by Hendel Teicher, December 2001.
14. See transcript from Brown's performance of *Accumulation with talking plus Watermotor* reprinted in this volume.

lines, circles, and geometric patterns. Resembling a sand painting, a drawn score by Brown of *Circles*, a part of *Accumulating Pieces* (1973), displays a central intersection of four circles that are dancers' paths. This simple, geometric drawing embodies a ritual full of symbolic meanings of time and space.

Brown's cultural references were not only American. Since the early seventies, she has had a long-standing friendship with the Japanese choreographer and dancer Suzushi Hanayagi. Their correspondence speaks about personal subjects as well as containing an intense and fruitful exchange about their work. While in New York, Hanayagi was part of John Cage's artistic orbit, creating her own choreography and keeping alive the theatrical dance style of Kabuki from the Edo period. The minute gestures and, to her, exotic movements of this Japanese tradition intrigued Brown, who with her abstract vocabulary freely adopted similarly precise and contained metaphoric language. Her immersions into other cultures can also be seen in her choreography for such works as *Spanish Dance*, part of *Accumulating Pieces* (1973); Monteverdi's opera *L'Orfeo* (1998); and *Rapture to Leon James* (2000). Each of these projects is a way to look into, learn, and transform the riches of flamenco, baroque opera, and the ballroom dances of African-American communities of the late 1930s.

Brown shows us how the body is the place and space of identity. Throughout her career, she has consistently incorporated new concepts about the body into her work, including elements of Ideokinesis (where a thought or image is used as a facilitator of a movement) and the teachings of the movement therapist Susan Klein, who emphasizes initiating actions from the bones instead of the muscles. As Steve Paxton notes in his essay in this volume, by the advent of the Judson Dance Theater in 1962, "a multitude of ways and thoughts about the body were in the air…. The Body had currency. The Cartesian split, pitting the mind versus the body, was not an issue for us."[12] Diane Madden, who has been dancing with Brown's company since 1981, maintains that Brownian gestures have more content, since they are "done from the bones and have a very different effect from a gesture done muscularly. [They come] from a deeper place and have a lot more meaning, or it communicates more. It has to do with weight. It has to do with your skeleton. It has to do with energy and connection through your body."[13]

The body stores memory; the body is the passage to memory made visible. Brown demonstrated this phenomenon when she spontaneously began to dance during a lecture she gave at the American Center in Paris in October 1973. Her movements were based on the Accumulation series and the piece became known as *Accumulation with talking*. She then added to it again, making *Accumulation with talking plus Watermotor*, which was first performed at Oberlin College in February 1979. In this work Brown poignantly provides an example of how the body, movement, and memory work together when she states: "In that first lecture in Paris I said that my father died in between the making of this move and that move. I was amazed that my body had stored a memory in a movement pattern"[14] For Brown, dance embodies memories that can be brought back through either repetitive movements that function as reminders, or through improvisation, which allows past experiences to surface spontaneously and abstractly. Repetition and improvisation became strategies for Brown to explore the emotional characteristics of the temporal dimension. It is in the space between the dance as energy and the body as the tool of the unpredictable that one finds Brown

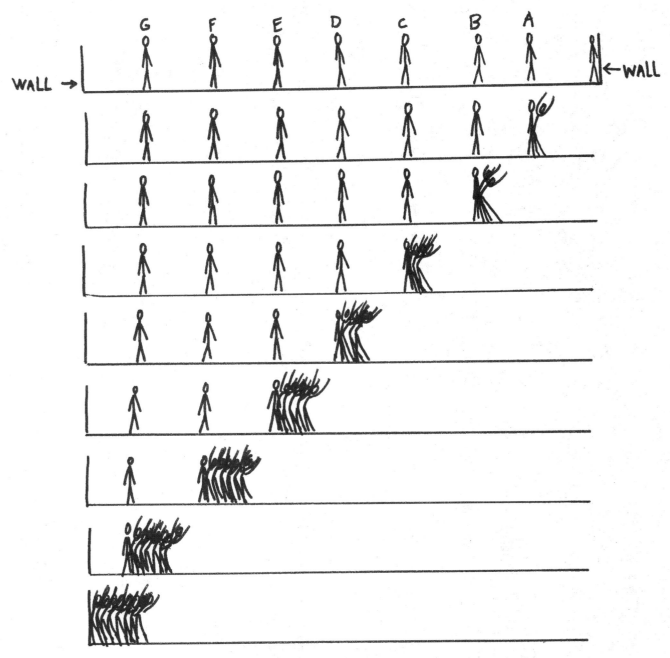

Dancer A slowly raises arms like a magnificent Spanish dancer
and travels forward in time to Bob Dylan's "In the Early Morning
Rain." When dancer A touches up against the back of dancer B,
dancer B slowly raises her arms like a magnificent Spanish dancer
and the two travel forward, touching up against the back of
dancer C, etcetera until they all reach the wall.

working most comfortably. The animation of emotions and their development from individual units into structured networks keeps Brown's choreography moving into unforeseen spaces and times.

Looking back at Brown's career, one sees that in 1968—the year she created *Planes*, *Falling Duet [I]*, *Ballet*, and *The Dance with the Duck's Head*—her journey into choreography could easily have changed course and veered toward sculpture or performance art. Brown was experimenting with kindred ideas: the body as a field of investigation, notions of gravity and disorientation, the interaction of abstraction and narrative, and the blurring of boundaries between art forms. In Brown's *Planes*, Jud Yalkut's aerial film of New York was projected onto a wall that contained concealed hand- and foot-holds for the dancers. The dancers moved across the wall and sometimes revolved slowly upside down as the film played, appearing to fly through the city. Brown and the other two dancers, Michelle Stowell and Simone Forti, perfected the creation of the appearance of ease, as if they were free from gravity within this filmic space. Adding to this effect of disorientation were the jumpsuit costumes, which were black on one side and white on the other. When the white side was shown to the audience, the dancer disappeared into the light play of the projection; when the black side surfaced, the dancer reappeared as a moving shadow. Brown's experimentation with movement and film in the late sixties was echoed by contemporaneous investigations in film and video by visual artists, particularly the work of Bruce Nauman, who stated, "I wanted to find out what I would look at in

Previous spread: Trisha Brown, Drawing for "Spanish Dance," part of *Accumulating Pieces*, 1973. Ink on paper, 11 x 8 1/2 in. (27.9 x 21.6 cm). Collection of Trisha Brown.

Opposite page: Denishawn Dancers in the costumes made for them in Bombay for Ruth St. Denis's *In Bunnia Bazaar*, 1926. Pictured: Pauline Lawrence, Anne Douglas, Edith James, Jane Sherman, Georgie Graham (Martha Graham's younger sister), Ernestine Day. Collection of Jane Sherman.

This page: *Line Up*, 1976. Pictured: Lisa Krauss, Mona Sulzman, Trisha Brown, Wendy Perron, Elizabeth Garren. Photograph by Babette Mangolte.

15. Bruce Nauman quoted in Coosje van Bruggen, *Bruce Nauman* (New York: Rizzoli, 1988), p. 225.

a strange situation, and I decided that with a film and camera I could do that."[15] Nauman's interest in disorientation extended to his work in video. In *Revolving Upside Down* (1969), he used the video camera as an extension of his body: as he turned while hanging upside down, the camera turned with him. In so doing, he allowed his actions to be choreographed from the camera's point of view.

On a parallel track to Brown's investigation of gravity, Richard Serra's massive lead sculptures *Prop* (1968) and *One Ton Prop (House of Cards)* (1969) showed gravity as a structural, sustaining force. By depending solely on gravitational force, Serra did away with the traditional methods of shaping and affixing metal sculptures, such as welding and riveting. His works thus became dramatic demonstrations of the pragmatics of process as a working principle rather than an applied aesthetic. Brown's *Falling Duet [I]* (1968), which she danced with Barbara Dilley, was an improvisational use of gravity as the primary movement generator of the duet. One dancer would cause herself to fall, allowing gravity to take over, and the other would catch her or fall under her, depending on the length of time available for a reaction. The dance went on until the point of exhaustion; just as gravity initiated the movements, it also brought the piece to a close after having "acted on" the dancers, literally wearing down their ability to continue moving. Also in 1968, Brown choreographed a complex work titled *Ballet*. (Brown has forgotten many of the specifics of this piece, some of which have been reconstructed through photographs. In this dance, two parallel ropes were strung

horizontally, approximately eight feet above the floor. Dressed in a pink tutu, Brown reached the ropes by a ladder and then traversed them on all fours, with her hands holding on and her legs in a necessarily awkward version of the "second position" used in ballet training. In addition to the spectacle of this playful acrobatic feat, Brown used slide projections throughout the performance. Some of the slides show her in the same position that she used to cross the ropes and others are details of colorful knitted sweaters that cast a kaleidoscopic light across the stage and onto Brown. Still others show the tutu, with its stiff layers of frills, as an object, which through a series of images she manipulates by progressively opening the circular waist. Appropriately, Brown called the blossoming costume "flowers." In *Ballet*, sexual analogies hover in the air, while humorously dispelling the rigid traditions of ballet. The conventional lexicon of classical dance is subjected to the primitive movements and desires of the animal kingdom. Brown likes to stand at the edge of possibilities. As both a dancer and a visual artist, she keeps herself "off-balance," remaining open and focused on the choreographic process. Her unconventional use of film, slides, lighting, costumes, and props is integral to the development of her dances. Brown's instincts are often sculptural in nature: a Volkswagen as a lighting device for *Motor* (1965); slippers and the straps from a baby carrier holding a projector on her back for *Homemade* (1966); a horizontal grid of ropes threaded with old clothes for *Floor of the Forest* (1970); harnesses and ropes for *Man Walking Down the Side of a Building* (1970); and a mattress, chairs, and stones for *Pamplona Stones* (1974).

By the mid-1970s, Brown's choreographic vocabulary had reached a point where a decision needed to be made regarding her future development. "It was a crossroads; I had to decide whether to go on in this quasi-sculptural direction or go back into dance, as I've been trained. I went into the direction of what I knew."[16] As Marianne Goldberg observes in her text included in this volume, the choreography for *Locus* (1975) finds Brown focusing again on movement and also brings together cross-media experimentation between linguistics, invented geometric shapes, autobiography, and the "environment" of the dancer (this time inside imaginary cubes).[17] At this time for Brown, drawing occupies a critical position: the performance of *Locus* was preceded by eight drawings that are among the rare instances when she created a score of a dance. An open cube with 27 numbers on it is correlated to the alphabet: 1 representing A, 2, B, and so on; the number 27 represents a space between words. The dance gestures spell out sentences, which remain invisible to the spectator and as Brown says, they are "personal gestures, things that have specific meaning to me but probably appear abstract to others."[18] Drawing is the access that leads back and forth to dance. In such a highly public and collaborative world as dance, the solitary and private act of drawing holds an appeal. Parallel to her major dance productions, Brown has quietly developed a body of drawings over the past thirty years, which provides her with another way of staying "off-balance." Process is used as the generator of form and image. As Brown has remarked, she finds "ideas in the drawings, and all those ideas infiltrate the dance process…. The movement now functions as a drawing."[19]

Another creative involvement is Brown's use of language. The titles of her choreographies often incorporate word plays that resonate with the actual movements of the dance. Several of her pieces interweave movements with spoken text, such as her seminal work *Accumulation with talking plus Watermotor*, which is, in Brown's words, the performing of "two dances and the telling of two stories at once. I shift back and forth between these four elements according to impulse in performance. I never stop dancing."[20] Another example of the power

Previous spread: *Ballet*, 1968. Pictured: Trisha Brown. Photograph by Peter Moore.

Opposite page (in pairs): Top, *Ballet*, 1968. Pictured: Trisha Brown. Photographs by Peter Moore; middle, Trisha Brown rehearsing *Ballet*; bottom, *Flower*, from a series of slides projected during the performance of *Ballet*.

16. Interview of Brown by the author, February and March 1998.
17. See her "Trisha Brown, U.S. Dance, and Visual Arts: Composing Structure" in this volume.
18. Trisha Brown, *Locus* (1975), reprinted herein.
19. Interview of Brown by the author, February and March, 1998.
20. Trisha Brown, Notes on *Accumulation with talking plus Watermotor*, 1980, reprinted in this volume.

Brown finds in language is represented by her unique choreography, *Skymap* (1969). In a completely dark theater, a twenty-minute text by Brown, recorded in her own voice and played for the audience, invites the listeners to mentally construct an aerial map of the United States. Her text offered multiple layers of information, ranging from the personal to the geographical (see reprint in this volume).

In 1979, Brown took on the challenge of performing on the proscenium stage. Inviting visual artists to join her, these collaborations bore a heightened sense of adventure, as for some artists it was their first experience working in the theater. The dialogues between Brown and Roland Aeschlimann, Nancy Graves, Donald Judd, Fujiko Nakaya, Robert Rauschenberg, and Terry Winters have been a joining of diverse visions and were integral to the development of her choreography. In Brown's collaborative process, she encourages and celebrates complexity, allowing for unpredictable events to surface. Each of these projects is a way towards making chaos visible. In his concept of "choreographic impurity," Guy Scarpetta points out that Brown's recycling of some classical elements—for example, returning to the stage— "has not resulted in a 'sobering down,' but rather the reverse: an abandoning of asceticism, an increased insolence, an additional exuberance."[21] And one must add sexuality. As best described by Madden in her running solo *For M.G.: The Movie* (1991), "It's just about weight shifts, that there's an incredible sensuality and eroticism in how you shift your weight. In my own body I feel that…like you see a woman walking down the street and they're very fully and comfortably in their body and sort of manifesting all those earthy qualities and their pelvis is alive and they have their weight, they're comfortable with it. It's that kind of sexy."[22] Being out of balance generates many of Brown's movements, which are often described as mercurial. Meanings are captured in the "in-between" movements, movements of open possibilities. Brown's long-time dedication and love for improvisation speaks to her own acceptance of the unknown. "Beauty is a rare thing," remarked the jazz musician Ornette Coleman. This is especially true in the fleeting worlds of music and dance where improvisation is precious.

Brown has speculated: "If it could be said that each artist works from a single idea or image and later gauges the success of a work in comparison to that image. Not that it would look like the original, but that it would be of equal power. If this is true, then for me it is the forest, a memory of dampness, broken light, unbelievable density, stillness and secrets."[23] One of Brown's secrets involves a flower, and a childhood connection. As always, memory helps to shape and give form to her work. *Trillium* was Brown's first public solo performance, which took place in March 1962 at the Maidman Playhouse in New York. Only three minutes long, it was accompanied by abstract vocal music composed and sung by Simone Forti. Her friend and colleague Yvonne Rainer noted that in the piece, Brown "gave herself the tasks of sitting, standing, and lying down while in the air or upside down, again demonstrating her innate kinetic humor and fearlessness."[24] A trillium is a three-petaled wildflower, usually white but also on occasion lavender, that is native to the forests of the Pacific Northwest. As Brown explains, "It grows in the spring…[and] is this beautiful creature down in the forest when you're walking through all this dark…. I tried to transplant it to my mother's garden and it would never take. It would never go into conformity in a garden. It grew wild."[25]

Trisha Brown, the American girl and daredevil, keeps alive that wildness and spirit of the Northwest. She has cultivated trillium in the streets of New York—for all to see.

Opposite page: *Trillium*, 1962.
Pictured: Trisha Brown.
Photograph by Al Giese.

21. Guy Scarpetta, *L'Impureté* (Paris: Grasset, 1986), p. 196.
22. Madden interview, December 2001.
23. Choreographer's notes, not dated.
24. See Yvonne Rainer, "A Fond Memoir with Sundry Reflections on a Friend and Her Art," in this publication.
25. Interview of Trisha Brown by Hendel Teicher, December 2000.

TRISHA BROWN: PROFILES

Opposite page: *If you couldn't see me*, 1994. Visual presentation and costumes by Robert Rauschenberg. Pictured: Trisha Brown. Photographs by Joanne Savio.

BURT BARR

Asking me to write about Trisha is like asking the beach to write about the tide. We're that close.

However, the analogy of the sea is apt.

She is always in motion. She does not stop. She comes and she goes. Ours is a house with open drawers and doors ajar — doors to rooms yes, but cabinets and closets also, many at a time, faucets left running, water boiling away, pots melting down, caps unscrewed, things just going, brimming over. At times she may not be here. It's like searching for a cat that may be perched or just gone. The place has been riddled with moves. It hardly began on a dance floor.

Long before one called it everyday movement or pedestrian movement or whatever, Trisha destroyed the artists' cliché "of going into the studio, to get some work done." She ripped that chronic bleat apart by dancing at the edges, on the walls, hanging like a bat, and when that was exhausted (the work, not her) she went up to the roof and did a piece there, then down the side of the building for another. Into the trees and over the water and up in the air. All these moves and places became actual works and are known and named elsewhere.

She is a protean artist. She has, as it's known, excelled in dance. But she has excelled in opera, in music, and very much so now, in drawing. And excelled in the best video ever shot on dance, *M.G. Shot from Backstage*, shooting it herself from backstage. Excelled as not only one of the best choreographers (or rather, as many in the know can attest, the best), she is also one of the very few supreme artists around. It's something that one (I) can easily say.

CAROLYN LUCAS

I joined Trisha Brown's company in 1984. Over the past eighteen years, I have been continually inspired by her process, both as a dancer and as her assistant. During the ten years I danced with Trisha, I rarely repeated the same movement twice; a reference to another work was the exception to the rule. The rule being: explore new territory to create, beginning at the foundation — the movement. With a passion for geometry, respect for the body's organic function, and an acute attention to detail, Trisha Brown has pioneered her own movement vocabulary. Her movement is so unique, traditional dance language does not apply. Instead, we take descriptions from imagery like "rodeo," "the bell life," "flag," "fireman," and "the web." As both a dancer and assistant, I have watched her draw from this vocabulary, honing phrases to perfection move by move or through improvisation. Phrases lead to sections, sections to dances. Her ambition to reinvent herself with each new work has produced an immense body of material. For this, I have great respect.

STEPHEN PETRONIO

I met TB in New York City 1979 while working as stage manager for a benefit performance for Movement Research. I had never seen her work at that point. When she arrived, I greeted her at the door of the theater. She smiled as I took her white metal makeup case and walked her to her dressing room. I can't remember the conversation, nothing much was said — but on that brief walk she completely won me.

That night she danced *Watermotor* and a short excerpt of the work in progress that would later become *Glacial Decoy*. I was floored by what I saw and not only for its exhilarating beauty — her language was startlingly new: a twisted blend of wild-ass, intuitive sensuality and cool rigor — but somehow I recognized it on a genetic level. I was instantly hooked and somehow knew I was home.

The first male in the company to stick, I remained for seven years (1979 – 86). A sweating, snorting bull in the china shop alongside of one of the most intelligent and silky bodies on the planet, I was duly challenged. Fortunately, Trisha had a kind of alchemical effect on me from the beginning. (I'm not alone in this respect.) She continually asked me to think and dance beyond my grasp. More often than not, and to my great surprise, I would find myself doing it.

The company in those days was filled with heady ambitious individuals and T reigned masterfully. I come from working class Italian roots, but she worked harder than anyone I had ever seen. When she was after something in the studio, she was relentless, patient, and worked with a curious calm. She created an environment of trust, humor, and ownership. Each dancer felt the realness of contributing to creation. The language she built was methodically written yet maddeningly illusive. She then coupled it with improvisational problems that demanded that each dancer employ that language on a primary creative level. This was a dancer's dream challenge. We worked hard and laughed loudly through creative periods (*Opal Loop*, *Son of Gone Fishin'*, and, most notoriously, *Set and Reset*). I vividly recall lingering in a kind of feverishly creative state throughout the rehearsals for *Set and Reset* and well after, into the night, only to wake up and jump back in the next day. It was sheer bliss for a twenty-five-year-old to go to work and find himself dancing next to a woman in the fullness of her creative power and to be making something with her that we all sensed was momentously potent. Dancing with her always seemed like an endless series of doors. If you were up to the challenge of walking through them, the benefits were huge.

Trisha smashed the mold both artistically and personally to forge a new movement model that is her own. It is a spherical, snaking, and elusive language, more subtle than any before it. During my years in her company my eye was trained to see the intelligent invention that the body is capable of. Now, fifteen years later, a choreographer with my own company, I walk into her theater and am amazed again and again by the inventions she continues to unearth.

DIANE MADDEN

I wish I could give some grand perspective of the overall importance of Trisha in the field of dance. But I'm unable. I'm an insider and the knowledge I have is intimate and encyclopedic of the extraordinarily valuable impact Trisha has on dancers.

I want to unabashedly say that, for a dancer, Trisha is the best. But how can I be so egocentric? Because not one dancer makes a commitment to work with another choreographer after working with Trisha. There just isn't anything better. Sure, dancers go on dancing for themselves after years of maturing with Trisha. And yes, some do projects with other choreographers, but not with the same investment, because there just isn't the same return.

So what is it we get from Trisha? A movement vocabulary that continues to evolve through formal explorations you can sink your teeth into with physical integrity always at its core. It's one of those rare situations when the better you realize the movement the more you deeply understand about yourself. There's a truth to this movement, so rich yet nothing superfluous. It's made me a lifelong believer in the expressive power of abstraction. Whether it tickles and/or tortures you, you know that if you keep working on it you won't just do it better, you'll become a better dancer.

Why is this movement so good? Because Trisha is a profoundly vivid dancer. Because she understands how energy moves and how structure is manifest in the body. Because she respects her dancers' potential and creates with that.

There's this simple thing that Trisha does when she choreographs that lends insight to why she's so good for a dancer. When she's done everything she can to help dancers realize an idea and they're still not taking the ball and running with it, she will very quietly and calmly threaten to give up and take away the opportunity to create. Awakening the dancers' hunger to grow, without them even noticing, she's saying, "Don't do this for me, do it for yourselves." And the dancer jumps at it. It works 99 percent of the time.

I see my little boy running, falling, banking, and skittering backwards and I say, "My God! It's the *For M.G.* running solo! That's me!" But I wouldn't have known it's me without Trisha. Who would Stephen be without *Set and Reset*? Who would Carolyn be without *Foray Forêt*? Who would I be without *Line Up* or *Son of Gone Fishin'* or monster phrase or message or pitch and catch or AC floor phrase or Carmen or Rage or spiriti or *Another Story* or *Orfeo* flying or Rage or the ladder dance or or or ad infinitum. It's unimaginable. With each dance Trisha brought me around the world to myself. Only a hugely generous genius could do that.

MERCE CUNNINGHAM

Trisha Brown's work has an air of immediacy about it to my eye. The slips of balance, the weight oddly off but not looking distorted. The sudden catch of equilibrium to send it out in another direction. The group activity often gives the inventive look of children as they fall into groups. There is buoyancy about it that hurtles it along.

Her own dancing has a strength in it, a woman moving with complete confidence from one shape to another, a quiet humor always present and the expressive presence of the movement made apparent.

The dances remain in one's eye and mind.

HOW TO MAKE A MODERN DANCE WHEN THE SKY'S THE LIMIT

TRISHA BROWN

Opposite page: Trisha Brown in rehearsal, Avignon, France, 1982. Photograph by Guy Delahaye.

LEARNING HOW TO DANCE STARTS YOUNG, even in the small town of Aberdeen, Washington (pop. 20,000). There was, of course, the first teacher, Marion Hageage, who taught tap, ballet, acrobatics, and yes, I could do a front roll and end up with my ass on my head. It was my specialty. Some days Marion would play the piano all to herself, cigarette in mouth, coffee cup and ashtray above the keyboard, then rise to take the floor in a slinky, blues-drenched style, eyes closed. This prepubescent girl, perhaps ten, not knowing what she was supposed to do, tagged along behind, more a puppy than a dancer, trying to catch those moves. I spent hours in her studio, agog. Not exactly the academy, but then, neither were the movies. Mitzi Gaynor, Cyd Charisse, Marge and Gower Champion, Carmen Miranda, Esther Williams. There I was in the movie theater, a death grip on the armrests. Why? Holding myself down in fear of popping straight up into the chandeliers?

Aberdeen has two dazzling edges, the Pacific Ocean due west and the Olympic National Forest due north, and almost nothing in the center of town anymore. The forest was my first art lesson. I learned to look there. Sitting in a small clearing, my eye fell first on the big things, the base of a forty-foot cedar tree, perhaps, then it periscoped down to the creek and over to an ancient tree trunk rotting on its severed roots, and then, oh lord, the whole world would open up to layer upon layer of teeming ecosystems on legs, or many legs, or wings, or belly-feet to crawl upon or buzz the myriad mosses attached to trees and rocks or other florae made lush and large by rain. All of this lit by shafts of light in a state of constant change.

On the less contemplative side, I climbed trees, pole-vaulted, played football and basketball under the tutelage of my older brother, dug razor clams, hiked, hunted geese, duck, pheasant, fished the local rivers, the Queets, the Quinault, the Hoh, for salmon, steelhead, and cutthroat trout. I did all this for all of my childhood and then went away to Mills College to major in modern dance, whatever that was.

I received a traditional modern dance education based on Graham technique and Louis Horst composition guided by four extraordinary women, Marion Van Tuyl, Eleanor Lauer, Doris Dennison (music), and Rebecca Fuller. Beyond the study of choreography to music and story, they taught me that I was not tired, I had enough time, and I could do it.

Add into this brew two summer sessions with Louis Horst, the formalist, at the American Dance Festival located at Connecticut College, and one with the improvisation wizard Anna Halprin located in Marin County, California, on an outdoor dance deck. Here I encountered, for the first time, the mercurial surges of an intuitive process where physical proposals and responses were dished and dashed on a whiz-by playing field. She also introduced ordinary task as formal structure, which found me sweeping the deck with a push broom for hours until I crossed over into levitation. Simone Forti and Yvonne Rainer, the brilliant ones from the Northeast, urged me to come to New York City to study composition with Robert Dunn. It was January 1961. Goodbye, my beloved Northwest, the sweep was total.

The story goes that John Cage asked Robert Dunn, a musician and accompanist at the Cunningham studio, to teach a dance composition class based on Cage's legendary series at the New School for Social Research, "Composition of Experimental Music." It was in Dunn's class that I was introduced to the notion that a chance procedure, such as the roll of the dice, can be the organizing principle in a choreography. The dice usurp the composer's role to choose, and in so doing, reposition the units of motion that make up a phrase. They become objects that can now be put together in any order, random or determined. Abstraction seeps in. The personal choice in a well-tooled phrase that a dancer is trained to create is upended. But, beyond the issue of how to transition from one disjunct unit into the next, this assignment cracked open the door of new possibilities for me. I understood, for the first time, that the modern choreographer has the right to make up the WAY that he/she makes a dance. Later that summer, I attended John Cage's lecture "Indeterminacy," which blew that door mentioned earlier right off its hinges. I got it. I got the rest of it, how form interacts with content.

A composition that is indeterminate, that is, not precisely fixed, further pries the author's hands off the performance. Some years later, the choreography *Accumulation with talking plus Watermotor*, half improvised, half choreographed, would fly off the wrist of that hand like a falcon gaining altitude in a tumultuous mix of form battling to keep on top of the measured addition of multiple elements to a point of overload and the subsequent erosion of this dancer/choreographer's intentions.

The assignments fulfilled in Bob Dunn's class were eventually organized into programs that were launched at Judson Church on July 6, 1962. It was a phenomenal period of experimentation—mostly by educated white people, hubris along the history chain—and olde modern dance, exhausted by the battering it took on all fronts, keeled over like an elephant, too big for me to dissect in this context, rested, then rose again, changed forever.

I was smitten by improvisation, you know, and pursued the elusive practice by working with Simone Forti outside of Bob Dunn's class. We developed structures (a.k.a. rulegames) to impose coherence and a measure of control to the great unknown of anything goes. How to capture esprit and do it again another day. Improvisation was not a respected endeavor in 1961. Louis Horst thought it was comparable to turning out the lights and announcing happy hour. I loved the give and take between idea and physical enactment with instinct sorting out the problems along the way. The body solves problems before the mind knows you had one. I love thinking on my feet, wind in my face, the edge, uncanny timing, and the ineffable.

To this day, I exploit instinctive behavior when building vocabulary (dance phrases) for a new choreography. I put two dancers on a possible collision course, camera running to capture the masterly maneuvers their bodies conduct in an effort to get past an impending accident while staying on their phrase. A blend of memorized and instinctive movement occurs. The camera is there to record the event for future rehearsals. The dancer/body will never go that close to danger again. They know too much. They have to see it on videotape to recreate the harrowing interlace and proximity.

The transition from improvisation (you'll never see that again) to choreography (a dance form that can be precisely repeated) required great effort and leaves me thinking that I am self-taught. If one is working with form and not formula, then the ideas take a visual presence in the mind and one must find a method to decant that vision. I start by describing the idea to the dancers, they query the request (I don't blame them), I say the same thing with other words, they try, I articulate what is missing, they try again, process is in motion. We keep heaving ourselves at each other like this until one or the other breaks through. We have a beginning. The metaphor is physically in existence. Now we have a template as reference to complete the phrase (theme).

I work simultaneously on form and vocabulary. One influences the other. After working for a decade or so, I noticed that my dances tended to cluster together in cycles. I take a compositional subject that intrigues me, work on it over two or three pieces until I have my answers, and then I move on. The early sixties were about discovery in the realm of improvisation versus form. I came back to that subject in the Unstable Molecular Structure cycle of work, *Opal Loop/Cloud Installation #72503* (1980), *Son of Gone Fishin'* (1981), and *Set and Reset* (1983). All of these dances were created by the dancers through a complex process of improvisation, repetition, and memorization of the aleatoric enactment of phrases according to instructions provided by me. During the choreographic process, I stepped out of the dance to view the work as it evolved, to make editorial decisions.

For *Set and Reset*, I made a very long phrase that circumnavigated the outside edge of the stage, serving as a conveyor belt to deliver duets, trios, and solos into the center of the stage. All of the dancers were taught the phrase and given the following set of five instructions: 1. Keep it simple. (The clarity issue.) 2. Play with visibility and invisibility. (The privacy issue.) 3. If you don't know what to do, get in line. (Helping out with downtime.) 4. Stay on the outside edge of the stage. (The spatial issue.) 5. Act on instinct. (The wild card.) We started upstage left, more or less pouring onto the stage with a feathering of gestures from the top of the phrase, and I turned, sat down on the floor, and rolled up through my spine to a shoulder stand. The dancer behind me gently pushed my pelvis with her foot, I rotated 180 degrees on my shoulders, rolled back down, and stood up to join the phrase. The shoulder stand was not in the phrase. The choreographer gives a nonverbal instruction to the dancers and the gauntlet is down.

The proscenium stage is something like a wasteland when you approach it without light, costumes, and set. I turned to Robert Rauschenberg, a painter and sculptor with extensive experience in the theater, to supply the missing elements, to create the stage picture that the audience encounters when the curtain goes up. This picture shifts in tandem with the reeling out of choreographic forms over time. In our collaborations, I was a lightning rod for Bob's theatrical projections. He described them to me as they occurred to him, often calling in the middle of the night. I would, in turn, picture the descriptions proffered, and in some cases choreograph with the spatial notion of the set he described to me in mind. Inevitably, each new design would be replaced by another, in an elegant procession of visual ideas, until he saw a rehearsal of the piece. At this point, galvanized by what he had assimilated through more systems than just sight, the final design would become manifest.

In *Set and Reset*, Laurie Anderson, music, and Beverly Emmons, lighting design, joined Rauschenberg in the rehearsal process from the beginning. There were many ideas and proposals along the way, but not until the nature of this new choreography could be identified, felt, did the alchemic brew begin to cook. Early on in the choreographic process, Bob saw some scrappy pieces of black velour hanging along the sides of the studio, trying to look like the legs (the lengths of fabric that form what are commonly called the stage's wings). They were placed there to dispel in the dancers the usual sacrosanct behavior required by theater stagehands, who admonish performers not to touch them, as if they were glass and might break. One of my choreographic themes was visibility/invisibility, and the more familiar we became with the legs, the more opulent were the opportunities. In fact, in the end, with Bob's help, they became props. The stage's velour legs have been reconstituted as see-through black scrim edged with a vertical stripe of ice-white satin, which demarcates the difference between onstage behavior and off. Our sanctuary is gone, invisibility dashed, downtime on display. To this situation Bob added gorgeous filmy white transparent costumes, silkscreened with pale-gray-to-black urban industrial images. No blue jeans. No underwear either. He did not want lingerie lines to interfere with the body as a body.

Laurie mixed the sound tracks in her studio while she watched a videotape of the nearly completed choreography. A clang is constant throughout, so is the lyric "Long Time No See," along with instrumentation and sound effects that fit the dance like a gauntlet to a hand, or not. There are wry correspondences between music and dance, the sound of plates breaking at the moment dancers collide, an embellished reference to the impact, but also to the phrase itself, which was fragmented by the uncanny overlay of gesture and improvisational high jinks now memorized.

Set and Reset was the sweetheart of my work in the 1980s and a hard act to follow. Now what? Shall I put the formula into production? Or shall I try something new? "New" was the answer, but "what" was the question. In general, I had been creating vocabulary based on the simple vertical and horizontal of the spine, arms, and legs, perpendicular or parallel to the floor. All gestures traveled to and from that infrastructure in a sequential, ongoing flow with democratic attention to equal air time to all parts traveling in all directions, high, low, front, back, side, side. The initiation of a gesture could come from any place on the body, unlikely or obvious, fingertips leading or the whole arm. All of this was spiced with the drama of balance: "Will she fall, or won't she?"

Transition pieces, between one cycle and the next, are interesting because they necessarily bring along the old patterns as I attempt to forge an entire new system of choreography. I decided to investigate the opposites of *Set and Reset*, to foreground the infrastructure, interrupt the sequential flow of gestures, drop improvisation, and "construct" a number of phrases, each of a different character, to be "mixed," phrase against phrase, into choreographic "units," quartets and duets, etc. This approach led to *Lateral Pass* (1985), with the collaborators Nancy Graves, set and costumes, Peter Zummo, music, and Beverly Emmons, lighting design. The choreographic units were mixed into the final dance with a consideration of all elements active in the collaboration. This was the beginning of a new choreographic cycle, which would fully arrive with my next collaboration.

The second piece in this new cycle was *Newark (Niweweorce)* (1987), with set, costumes, and music by Donald Judd, a sculptor I had collaborated with to make *Son of Gone Fishin'*. In both instances that we worked together, Judd brought his Minimalist aesthetic to my stage. A residency at the Centre National de Danse Contemporaine in Angers, France, gave Don and me, plus Peter Zummo, music production, and Ken Tabachnick, lighting design, the crucial gift of time on stage to choreograph with the set and lights every day, six days a week, for six weeks. I began my search for vocabulary by pushing furniture around in the studio. This behavior translated into a resolve to push myself and my dancers into powerful movement and carefully designed body-geometries, initially similar to furniture. The Valiant cycle, which had its beginning in *Lateral Pass*, was now fully established. Not only will she fall, the dancers will slam into the floor.

Don's stage design comprised five proscenium-size drops in the three primary colors plus brown and another shade of red. They split the stage into sections forming four corridors, which could alternately block and reveal the dance. Don devised three separate mathematical systems to determine what drops, in what order, would come in where and for how long.

The music, which consisted of nonreferential sounds found by Peter Zummo, was on yet another system all of its own. I had unwittingly allowed Judd to usurp the choreographer's territory of time and space. He could cut off a dancer flung high in an arc, or confine us in a narrow strip on the downstage light line, five feet deep and forty wide. My choreographic solution was to visually design the dance into the motional elements of the set, albeit adapting a few aspects to my favor. Why did I put up with it? Too late to change for one, but remember that abstract modern dance, unfettered by story and music, is, necessarily, in search of a logic or rationale to reduce the proliferation of options that hang around winking at us. The *Newark* set did impose tough dialogues and severe internal limitations, but it also delivered a spatial and temporal score that forced invention and resulted in one of the most striking pieces in our repertory.

This choreographic method continued until music and narrative entered the process, bringing with them a new consideration of character, gender, and the play between meaning and non-meaning in abstraction. In fact, they had already arrived, concurrent with my work on *Newark*, through the experience of choreographing my role as the Maga in Georges Bizet's opera, *Carmen*, directed by Lina Wertmüller.

I have continued the practice of question, analysis, and resolution through cycles of dance throughout my career. But, in 1995, I realized that I had more years behind me than lay ahead —unless I should have the misfortune to live to be 119. So I asked myself the question, What have you not done, that you will regret in the waning hours of your end game? The answer was opera. I had not yet directed an opera. To facilitate this terrifying desire, I chose J.S. Bach's *Musical Offering* and proceeded to teach myself baroque polyphonic composition with the assistance of Hans Theodore David's book on the history, interpretation, and analysis of that music. I wanted to make myself and my dancers accountable to the music, note by note. I worked to understand the structures in Bach's composition, some surprisingly familiar to my own earlier inventions, and then to find relevant structures in the dance idiom to ensure a parallel dialogue with Mr. Bach. This Modus Operandi would serve as the model for my research on all of the pieces in the burgeoning Music cycle: J.S. Bach, *M.O.* (1995); Anton Webern, *Twelve Ton Rose* (1996) and *For Merce* (1997); Claudio Monteverdi, *L'Orfeo* (1998) and *Canto/Pianto* (1997); Dave Douglas, *El Trilogy* (1999–2000); and Salvatore Sciarinno, *Luci mie traditrici* (2001) and *Geometry of Quiet* (2002).

There once was an extraordinary weekend in the south of France in July of 1998. My opera, *L'Orfeo*, was playing at the Festival International d'Art Lyrique in Aix-en-Provence. A day or so later, and nearby, an exhibition of my drawings opened at the Centre de la Vieille Charité in Marseille, as my dance company prepared to open in full theatrical regalia at the Théâtre du Gymnase across town. Life has not been the same since. Actually, it has not been the same since an earlier rehearsal day of *L'Orfeo* when I walked out into the center of my studio to improvise Orfeo's speech to Caronte in the monumental aria "Possente Spirito." I had sorted out my identity. I was both Orfeo asking for permission to enter Hades and the words he sang. I was primed with music, text, poetry systems, literature. I was the faithful shepherd (Guarini, Il Pastor fido), the Spirit was with me and, most of all, I could also arpeggiate my body in the clear place of a compositional mind that does operate on its own when Trisha is busy with a handful of other aesthetic concerns. I knew, at that moment, the long haul of my apprenticeship in choreography was over.

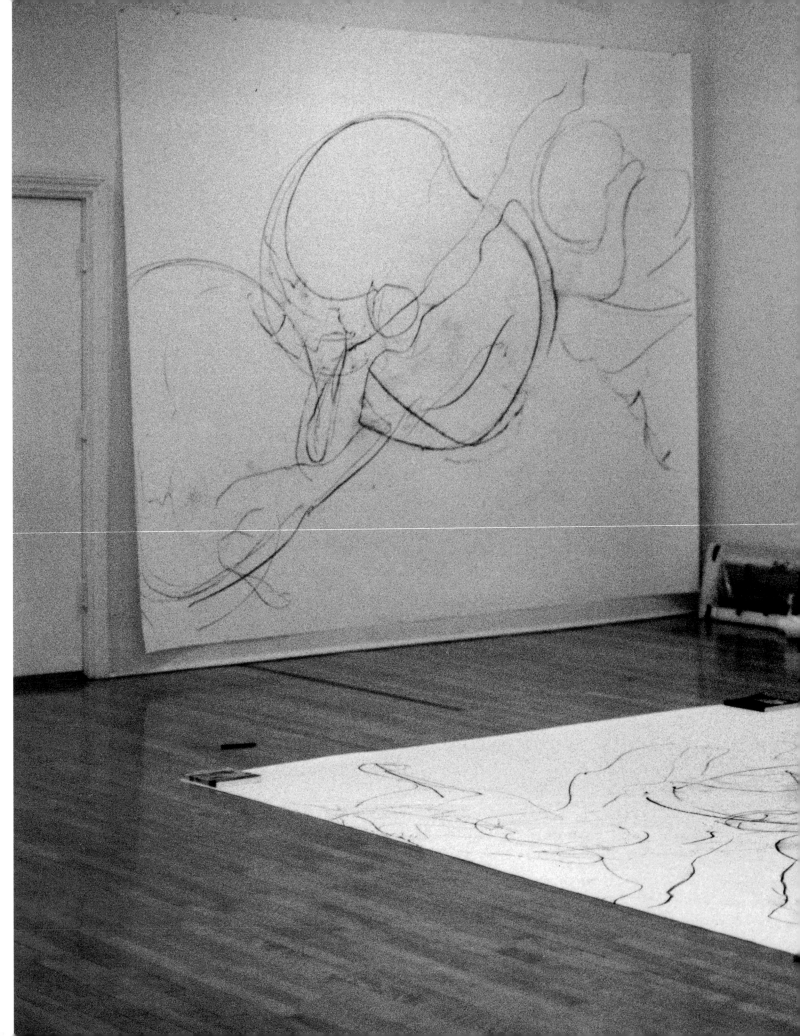

Trisha Brown was born on November 25, 1936, in Aberdeen, Washington, the third and youngest child (after siblings Gordon and Louisa) of Dorothy Abel and Martell Brown. Her father ran an ice delivery service and a cold storage facility known as the Ice Palace. Her mother taught high school English. Aberdeen is located near the Olympic National Forest and numerous waterways, an environment that Brown grew up exploring and references to which would later make their way into her dances. Her movement studies began in 1947 with Marion Hageage, with whom she studied acrobatics, jazz, ballet, and tap. In 1954 she enrolled in Mills College in Oakland, California, where she majored in dance. At Mills, her training included Martha Graham technique and Louis Horst composition, and she also took African dance classes taught by Ruth Beckford in Berkeley. Brown spent three summers at the American Dance Festival, then based at Connecticut College, where she studied with Louis Horst, José Limón, and Merce Cunningham. After graduation from Mills in 1958 she taught at Reed College, in Portland, Oregon, for two years, during which time she began to experiment with improvisation. In the summer of 1960, Brown participated in a six-week workshop with Ann Halprin, in Kentfield, in Marin County, California. Halprin furthered Brown's interest in improvisation by urging her to explore ordinary activities as sources of movement, and to incorporate verbalization into the creative process. This workshop was influential in Brown's development of "structured improvisation," an improvisational technique based on an initial movement framework or loose pattern. Two other participants in the workshop, Yvonne Rainer and Simone Forti, urged Brown to move to New York City, which she did in early 1961. In that same year she joined an experimental dance composition class taught at the Merce Cunningham studio by Robert Dunn. Encouraging an environment of non-judgmental discussion and analysis, Dunn developed choreographic assignments that applied the Cagian concepts of chance and indeterminacy. This class led to a series of performances at the Judson Memorial Church on Washington Square Park, the first of which took place on July six of that year. These performances were a radical reinterpretation of contemporary dance. Married to the dancer Joseph Schlichter from 1962 to 1970, Brown gave birth to their son, Adam, on February 24, 1965. She has been married to the artist Burt Barr since 1974.

In the 1960s and 70s, Brown was an active participant in the rich cultural life of downtown New York, which included visual artists, writers, and filmmakers, many of whom participated in Happenings. Reflecting her interest in other artistic disciplines, she began to make drawings in the late 1960s, a practice she continues today. In 1968, Brown created the choreography *Ballet*, in which she began to use equipment such as ropes in order to defy gravity. In other works from the late sixties and early seventies, she used mountaineering harnesses, among other devices. These groundbreaking works came to be known as the Equipment Pieces and are the first of a series of choreographic "cycles" that Brown describes in her work. In 1970, she was invited to join the experimental choreographic group Grand Union, which also included Rainer, Barbara Dilley, Douglas Dunn, David Gordon, Nancy Lewis Green, and Steve Paxton. In that same year, Brown founded her own company with three female dancers: Carmen Beuchat, Caroline Goodden, and Penelope.[1] With this group she began to develop her own choreographic vocabulary while also verging into the realm of performance art and even sculpture. By the mid-1970s, Brown had decided to focus on dance with the understanding that other disciplines, such as the visual arts, remained an active part of her creative thinking.

The following chronology provides an in-depth listing of her choreographies and improvisations prior to her decision, in 1979, to create works for the proscenium stage. This account of Brown's early life and work is based on my discussions with the choreographer, consultation of her own archive, and outside research. As in the main section of the book, which is devoted to Brown's dances from 1979 and after, I have incorporated statements by the choreographer or her contemporaries where appropriate. Many of Brown's early works were performed only once (this is particularly the case with the improvisations) and they took place in highly untraditional venues such as parks, plazas, rooftops, galleries, and churches. Adding to the difficulty of piecing together this early history is, of course, the ephemeral natural of dance, particularly before the now-common use of video. Although efforts have been made to gather all available information, this chronology nonetheless contains unavoidable omissions including, in some instances, the lengths of the pieces, the dancers involved, the costumes worn, and so on. This chronology ends in 1979 and is followed by miscellaneous information pertaining to the dances by other choreographers that Brown has performed in, the names of the dancers she has worked with, and dances she has choreographed that are now in the repertory of other companies.

Hendel Teicher

Previous spread: Trisha Brown's studio/home, New York City. December 2001. Photograph by Burt Barr.

Notes for this section begin on page 319.

TRISHA BROWN AND GROUP

2PM

JUNE 24, JULY 1

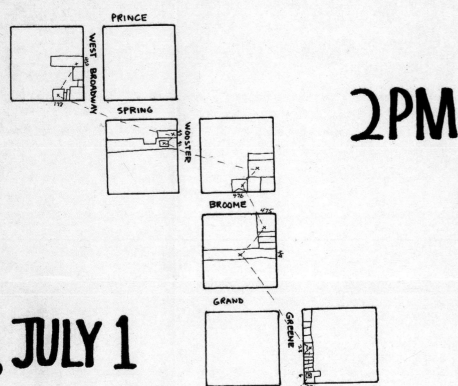

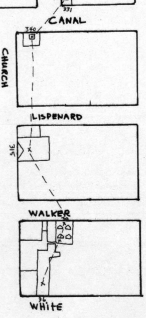

for reservations call Art Services 989·4953
Come prepared for the weather
This project is supported by a grant
from the National Endowment for the
Arts in Washington D.C. with the help
of the Experimental Intermedia Fndn.

CHRONOLOGY OF DANCES 1961–1979

STRUCTURED IMPROVISATIONS WITH SIMONE FORTI AND DICK LEVINE, 1961

The rehearsals leading up to this concert were engaged in the invention of a structure or game plan that was understood by all participants. One structure that came from Simone was to identify something in the room that could function as a score that we would interpret simultaneously. We wanted answers to the question of what to do in time, space, and intensity. In performance, one dancer pointed in a random direction with eyes closed. I must say my heart sank when I traced the point to a barrel-shaped wood-burning stove. But, in those days, I was shot out of a cannon in improvisations, especially in front of an audience, so, likely, fire, smoke, and chimneys were just right. Simone told me that [during rehearsals] we used to do the "floor-plans of fairytales in about five seconds" as a structure and might have included them [in the performance] as well. I [also] used this structure for *Inside* [in] 1966.[2] Trisha Brown

LENGTH Approximately 45 min.
SOUND Some verbal improvisation
COSTUMES Dance work clothes
DANCERS Trisha Brown, Simone Forti, Dick Levine
FIRST PERFORMANCE Chambers Street Loft Series, Yoko Ono's loft, 112 Chambers Street, New York City, May 26–27, 1961

TRILLIUM, 1962
STRUCTURED IMPROVISATION

Trillium [is] a structured improvisation of very high energy movements involving a curious timing and with dumb silences like stopping dead in your tracks. I was working in a studio on a movement exploration that moved to or through the three positions of sitting, standing, and lying. I broke those actions down into their basic mechanical structure, finding the places of rest, power, momentum, and peculiarity. I went over and over the material, eventually accelerating and mixing it up to the degree that lying down was done in the air.[3] Trisha Brown

There's a great bit of talking to the audience (without making any sound), an intimate story accompanied by all sorts of nervous and descriptive gestures. There are some bracing hard movements of the arms that knock out the dancer's breath. I recall some difficult-looking whipping turns and falls, and handstands that melt into a crumple on a shoulder and the back. Whatever it looked like, it had never been done before.[4] Jill Johnston

LENGTH 3 min.
MUSIC Simone Forti
MUSIC PERFORMANCE Simone Forti; a composite of all the different sounds that could come out of Forti's throat and mouth, including pitches, screeching, and scraping.
COSTUME Leotard and tights
DANCER Trisha Brown

[*Trillium*] had a handstand in it and a lot of very beautiful, indulgent movement. Trisha told me that a trillium was a flower that she had found in the wood…. She said she used to pick them in the woods, but by the time she got home they would be wilted and faded. And that's what she thought about movement—it was wild; it was something that lived in the air. It was odd to see a handstand in dance at that time. It was odd to see people off their feet doing anything but a very controlled fall.[5] Steve Paxton

When I saw *Trillium* I decided that Trisha didn't know about gravity and therefore gravity had no hold on her.[6] Elaine Summers

FIRST PERFORMANCE Maidman Playhouse, New York City, March 24, 1962

LIGHTFALL, 1963
STRUCTURED IMPROVISATION

Using the simple action of waiting (football style, hands on knees) as a recurrent "base," the dancers initiated a spontaneous series of interferences—ass-bumping and back-hopping—which were artless, playful excursions in quiet expectancy and unusual surprises.[7] Jill Johnston

I had seen the piece in rehearsal when we were up in the country. Trisha asked me for a title and it just came—*Lightfall*. The quality of the piece had so much to do with body weight and yet it was so light when they perched on each other's backs.[8] Yvonne Rainer

There is a performance quality that appears in improvisation that did not in memorized dance as it was known up to that date. If you are improvising with a structure your senses are heightened; you are using your wits, thinking, everything is working at once to find the best solution to a given problem under pressure of a viewing audience. In contrast, at that time, modern dancers glazed over their eyes, knuckling down behind that glaze to concentrate and deliver their best performance—an understandable habit but unfortunately resulting in a robot-look. At Judson, the performers looked at each other and the audience,

Opposite page: Invitation poster for *Roof and Fire Piece*, 1973. 22 x 17 in. (55.9 x 43.2 cm). Collection of Trisha Brown.

they breathed audibly, ran out of breath, sweated, talked things over. They began behaving more like human beings, revealing what was thought of as deficiencies as well as their skills.[9] Trisha Brown

LENGTH Unknown
SOUND Ambient
COSTUMES Leotards and tights
DANCERS Trisha Brown and Steve Paxton

Trisha's duets with Steve Paxton were extraordinary. In *Lightfall* the two were just bouncing all over and under each other. The choreography seemed to be based on how much risk they could take.[10] Robert Rauschenberg

FIRST PERFORMANCE Judson Memorial Church, New York City, January 30, 1963

NUCLEI FOR SIMONE FORTI, 1963
STRUCTURED IMPROVISATION

The improvisation was based on a set of "dance instruction poems" by Jackson Mac Low. Each card had 1 to 10 words typed in black small print at the top and 1 to 5 actions typed in red CAPITAL LETTERS at the bottom. There were about 60 cards in all. The cards were enigmatic and just the right balance in leeway and specifics to set off improvisational fireworks.[11] Trisha Brown

LENGTH Jackson Mac Low: "The running time is entirely up to the performer and the circumstances of the performance."[12] Running time of Yam Festival version unknown.
SOUND Some verbal improvisation
SETS Jackson Mac Low: "Anything that the performer chooses. In [Brown's] performance, one or two chairs."[13]
COSTUME Dance work clothes
DANCER Trisha Brown
FIRST PERFORMANCE Yam Festival, Hardware Poets Playhouse, New York City, May 12–13, 1963

During the month of May 1963, a number of Fluxus participants and other artists put on the Yam Festival ("May" spelled backwards), which was sponsored by the Smolin Gallery. Performances took place throughout New York City and at George Segal's farm in North Brunswick, New Jersey.

IMPROVISATION ON A CHICKEN COOP ROOF, 1963
LENGTH Approximately 15 min.
SOUND Some verbal improvisation
COSTUMES Street clothes
DANCERS Trisha Brown and Yvonne Rainer
FIRST PERFORMANCE Yam Festival, George Segal's farm, North Brunswick, New Jersey, May 19, 1963

LA CHANTEUSE, 1963
A solo in which Brown took the fourth position— a ballet pose with legs and arms in opposition— and then proceeded to fall over, "dead weight, like a tree cut down" while saying "oh no."[14]

LENGTH Approximately 3 min.
SOUND Some vocalization
COSTUME Leotard and tights
DANCER Trisha Brown
FIRST PERFORMANCE Benefit for the Foundation for Contemporary Performance Arts, Pocket Theater, New York City, June 10, 1963

TARGET, 1964
Duet, set phrases of movement and events like *La Chanteuse* were performed. The order and duration were altered by verbal cues given in the form of questions by the performers such as "What time is it?"[15] Trisha Brown

LENGTH Approximately 5 min.
SOUND Some talking
COSTUMES Dance work clothes
DANCERS Trisha Brown and Joseph Schlichter
FIRST PERFORMANCE Humboldt State College, Arcata, California, April 13, 1964

RULEGAME 5, 1964
STRUCTURED IMPROVISATION

In this dance five performers proceed along seven paths demarcated by seven rows of masking tape laid down in an area of 21 by 21 feet. Starting erect, each performer must lower his/her height so that when they reach the seventh path they are at their lowest possible height (possibly on their stomachs). This adjustment should be made at equal intervals on a scale of one to seven. The performer may pass another performer parallel to themselves only if he/she is crouched lower than those players on the "up" side and higher than those on the "down" side.[16] Trisha Brown

LENGTH 10–15 min.
SOUND Verbal instructions between performers to achieve the correct height for passage
COSTUMES Street clothes
DANCERS Trisha Brown, Walter de Maria, Alex Hay, Steve Paxton, Robert Rauschenberg, Joseph Schlichter, probably Olga Kluver and Simone Forti
FIRST PERFORMANCE First New York Theater Rally, television studio formerly used by CBS, Broadway and 81st Street, New York City, May 5, 1965

MOTOR, 1965

Duet with skateboard as timing device and partner, performed in a parking lot, lit by a Volkswagen, driver unrehearsed.[17] Trisha Brown

LENGTH Approximately 6 min.
SOUND Skateboard wheels and Volkswagen motor
VISUAL PRESENTATION Trisha Brown
EQUIPMENT/PROPS Volkswagen Beetle and skateboard
COSTUMES Street clothes
LIGHTING Beams from Volkswagen headlights
DANCERS Trisha Brown (and driver)
FIRST PERFORMANCE Once Again Festival, Maynard Street Parking Structure, University of Michigan, Ann Arbor, September 18, 1965

HOMEMADE, 1966

I used my memory as a score. I gave myself the instruction to enact and distill a series of meaningful memories, preferably those that impact on identity. Each memory-unit is "lived," not performed, and the series put together without transitions that are likely to slur the beginning and the end of each discreet unit. The dance incorporates a film of itself by Robert Whitman. A projector is mounted on the back of the performer and the film of the dance is projected onto the wall, floor, ceiling, and audience in synchronization with the "live" dance.[18] Trisha Brown

An earlier version of *Homemade*, which did not incorporate film, was performed at the First New York Theater Rally, May 5, 1965. It has been described by Brown as a "solo of microscopic movement taken from everyday activities, done so small they were unrecognizable."[19]

LENGTH 3 min.
SOUND Sound of projector
VISUAL PRESENTATION Trisha Brown and Robert Whitman
SETS Trisha Brown and Robert Whitman
COSTUME/PROPS Black leotard and projector worn on back using the straps off a baby carrier
DANCER Trisha Brown
FIRST PERFORMANCE Judson Memorial Church, New York City, March 29, 1966

[Trisha's] first wonderful kindness … [was] performing in a few pieces of mine in the early sixties, not caring if these were not going to be the parts of a lifetime. Being as committed to them as if it was her own work, as inventive.

Especially the kind of unafraid physicality, which we now almost take for granted. In fact in one case scaring people.

Gleeful solemnity, serious good times.[20]
Robert Whitman

INSIDE, 1966

To make … *Inside*, I stood facing a wall in my studio at a distance of about twelve feet and, beginning at the extreme left, I read the wall as a score while moving across the room to the far right. Any question that arose about the speed, shape, duration or quality of a move was determined by the visual information on the wall. An odd distribution of actions and gestures emanated from the architectural collection of alcove, door, peeling paint and pipes. After finishing the first wall, I repositioned myself in the same way for the second wall and repeated the procedure, [then] for the third and fourth. Therefore, in performance, I moved along the edge of the room, facing out, on the kneecaps of the audience, who were placed in a rectangular seating formation duplicating the interior of my studio. I was marking the edge of the space, leaving the center of the room empty, the movement concretely specific to me, abstract to the audience. And I looked at them. I added the problem of looking at the audience, not "with meaning," but with eyes open and seeing.[21]
Trisha Brown

LENGTH 5–8 min.
SOUND Ambient
COSTUME Dance work clothes
DANCER Trisha Brown
FIRST PERFORMANCE Judson Memorial Church, New York City, March 29, 1966

SKUNK CABBAGE, SALT GRASS, AND WADERS, 1967
STRUCTURED IMPROVISATION

In 1963 Brown had titled Robert Rauschenberg's choreography *Pelican*; in 1967 Rauschenberg contributed the name to Brown's structured improvisation that dealt with her childhood memories of duck hunting with her father.

LENGTH Approximately 15 min.
SOUND Taped monologue written and recorded by Brown as well as talking and ambient sounds
PROPS Bucket filled with water, chair
COSTUME "Dripping wet" white cotton dress[22]
DANCER Trisha Brown
FIRST PERFORMANCES Spring Gallery, New York City, May 14, 1967; Galleria L'Attico, Rome, June 22, 1969

Opposite page from top: Trisha Brown and her mother, Dorothy Abel Brown, in the Ice Palace owned by the Brown family, Aberdeen, Washington, c. 1942. Photograph by Jones Photo Co.

Trisha Brown, August 20, 1941.

Trisha Brown and her sister Louisa (Brown) Adams, c. 1946.

MEDICINE DANCE, 1967
IMPROVISED FLOOR WORK
LENGTH Approximately 5 min.
SOUND "Vocalized anguish and growling"[23]
COSTUME Dance work clothes
DANCER Trisha Brown
FIRST PERFORMANCE Sun Dance, Upper Black Eddy, Pennsylvania, August 26, 1967

PLANES, 1968

A film of aerial footage [by Jud Yalkut] is projected on an 18-foot-long, 13-foot-high wall which has concealed holes spaced at equal intervals across its entire surface. Three performers traverse the surface of the wall in slow motion, giving the illusion of falling through space.[24] Trisha Brown

Strength was a serious problem for [the] women. There were techniques for hooking your foot and slithering down, but you could get caught in a position, difficult to sustain, that could be quite dangerous. Going upward it was all power. If we were upside down and in pain because the instep of the foot was supporting most of the body weight on a half-inch of plywood, we could not acknowledge it—we did not show that tension.[25] Trisha Brown

Planes is an exploration of the corollaries between psychic space and the psychical escape of consciousness beyond the earth's biosphere. Conceive of the theater as vertical tunnel in which the audience is suspended in planes of rows. The city as centralized magnetic center, whose momentum is perpendicular, becomes the escape valve for a continuous ascent, spanning the poetics of macro- and micro-cosm, culminating in the brief and rapid deceleration of re-entry.[26] Jud Yalkut

LENGTH 20 min.
MUSIC Simone Forti; voice and vacuum cleaner: Forti vocalized the different pitches she could hear in the drone of the vacuum (taped).
VISUAL PRESENTATION Trisha Brown

I wasn't around theaters—I was in rooms and on the street. I began to have fantasies about how those surfaces could be used. *Planes* began by devising the technology that allowed me to support myself on a surface that was a near-perfect vertical. The technology delivered the movement that delivered the image that created the piece.[27]
Trisha Brown

There was complete devotion to the imagery. I was working against gravity, appearing to be free-falling—there was a twist there. We practiced this slo-mo keeling. When you rolled, the imagery on the film made you appear to be plummeting downwards. The more time you spent in a vertical position, the more you destroyed the setup of the roll. I was very aware that I was making a bold step, that I was doing something very large and out of the ordinary. So much of woman's work was in her lap. This was monumental structure—the scale, the steepness, and the difficulty of it.[28] Trisha Brown

SETS Trisha Brown; false wall, very slightly slanted, with hand- and foot-holds, onto which was projected a 16mm film by Jud Yalkut.
COSTUMES Trisha Brown; workman's suits altered to be black on one side, white on the other. When white side was shown to the audience, the dancers seemed to disappear into the film.
DANCERS Trisha Brown, Simone Forti, Michelle Stowell
FIRST PERFORMANCES Intermedia '68, State University of New York at New Paltz, February 24, 1968; Galleria L'Attico, Rome, Italy, June 22, 1969

SNAPSHOT, 1968
STRUCTURED IMPROVISATION
LENGTH Unknown
SOUND Ambient
COSTUMES Cloth bags (for one section) and dance work clothes
DANCERS Trisha Brown, Simone Forti, Michelle Stowell
FIRST PERFORMANCE Intermedia '68, State University of New York at New Paltz, February 24, 1968

FALLING DUET [I], 1968
STRUCTURED IMPROVISATION

One dancer falls over like a tree cut down (deadweight); the other dancer gets (scrambles) underneath and makes a soft landing with the total body surface, not hands. Stand, change roles, and repeat until too tired to continue.[29] Trisha Brown

The two women walk out and stand on a big tumbling mat. One falls; the other must catch her; they take turns. Their trust in each other is phenomenal and neither faller tries to make it easy.... It's beautiful: one woman very still, trying to feel which way her body wants to fall; the other eyeing her warily, maybe edging around her; then the slow, tree-like leaning that gathers speed (or the sudden plunge); the rapid move of the catcher; the slow tumble to the mat in a tangle; the pause to renew strength and breath; the rise to begin again.[30] Deborah Jowitt

LENGTH Approximately 5 min.

SOUND Ambient
COSTUMES Dance work clothes
DANCERS Trisha Brown and Barbara Dilley
FIRST PERFORMANCE Riverside Church Theatre,
New York City, June 19, 1968

BALLET, 1968

"A collection of images and movement ideas, including *Falling Duet*."[31]

CYCLE Equipment pieces
LENGTH 15–20 min.
SOUND Ambient
SET/EQUIPMENT Slides of colored fabrics projected
on white costume, parallel "high wire" ropes,
and a ladder
COSTUMES For Brown, pink tutu, leotard, and tights
DANCERS Trisha Brown and one other dancer
(unrecorded)
FIRST PERFORMANCE Riverside Church Theatre,
New York City, June 19, 1968

THE DANCE WITH THE DUCK'S HEAD, 1968

Dancer enters wearing a papier-mâché skirt fixed
in a sit-down position and a helmet in the shape
of a duck's head. She walks in a crouch across
the space and sits down in a chair. A violent fight
breaks out in the audience. When calm is restored,
the duck-lady steps into a pair of logging boots
that are bolted to a metal frame. Four men hoist
the apparatus with dancer and careen it around
the space turning it over in a cumbersome sort
of flight.[32] Trisha Brown

LENGTH 20 min.
SOUND The sounds of a "violent fight" at the
beginning of the dance
COSTUME Trisha Brown; papier-mâché duck's head
with feathers, papier-mâché brassiere ("will proba-
bly cure anyone from ever wearing a bra again"[33]),
and papier-mâché skirt in a seated position
DANCER Trisha Brown; with four "carriers" (Steve
Carpenter, Peter Poole, Melvin Reichler, Elie Roman)
and two "fighters" (David Bradshaw and Joseph
Schlichter)
FIRST PERFORMANCE The Museum of Modern Art,
New York City, December 6, 1968

YELLOWBELLY, 1969

I asked the audience to yell "yellowbelly," which
means "coward" in Aberdeen, Washington; performed the piece twice. The first time they were
very sweet about it so I stopped and I asked them
to yell in a nasty way and they did. They started
jeering and yelling. I was improvising and absolutely frozen and I have not any idea what I did,
although I had a few amorphous possibilities prepared. When I stopped, they really jeered at me,
so I started up again and finally we both stopped.
It was terrifying because it was confronting the
performer's fear that you will get up before an
audience and forget what you are doing. The point
was to set up precisely that situation and it
certainly tested both me and the audience. The
second time I performed it in Rome and had them
yell in Italian. It was a more sophisticated audience
and they just would not yell. When they sat back
and refused to yell, I refused to move. Then when
someone would yell, I would start, and
stop moving when they stopped yelling. It was the
most amazing relationship until they got very
angry and all began to yell....I started spinning
and continued until I was totally dizzy, then I
stopped and tried to do a beautiful articulate
dance, but without any success. That relationship to the audience was certainly rough and
symbiotic.[34] Trisha Brown

LENGTH Variable
SOUND Dialogue between Brown and the audience
COSTUME Leotard and tights
DANCER Trisha Brown
FIRST PERFORMANCES Newark State College, Newark,
New Jersey, April 10, 1969; Galleria L'Attico, Rome,
Italy, June 22, 1969

SKYMAP, 1969

A piece in which Brown did not dance; rather, in
a darkened space, she, "informed the audience how
to mentally construct an overhead map. The text
was recorded. My voice went to the ceiling."[35]

I had performed on the walls, the floor, and at
eye level, I knew that the ceiling was next, but I just
couldn't bring myself to enter into that kind of
physical training with that kind of danger below.
I sent words up there instead.[36] Trisha Brown

The text for Skymap *can be found on page 81.*

LENGTH 15–20 min.
SOUND Recorded text written and read by Brown
FIRST PERFORMANCES Newark State College, Newark,
New Jersey, April 10, 1969; Whitney Museum of
American Art, New York City, March 30–31, 1971

Opposite page from top: Trisha
Brown and her son Adam Brown,
Napanock, New York, 1968.

On the Hoh River, Washington
State, 1969. Pictured: guide;
Brown's father, Martell Brown;
Trisha Brown; Adam, her son.

THE WASHINGTON GALLERY OF MODERN ART

PRESENTS

CONCERT OF DANCE NUMBER FIVE

AMERICA ON WHEELS

WASHINGTON, D.C.

MAY 9, 1963

CHOREOGRAPHERS*
AND DANCERS

Carolyn Brown Trisha Brown* William Davis*
Judith Dunn* David Gordon* Barbara Lloyd
Robert Morris Steve Paxton* Yvonne Rainer*
Albert Reid* Jennifer Tipton Robert Rauschenberg*
Valda Setterfield Per Olaf Ultvedt

1. TRILLIUM   T. Brown*   Music by (Simone Morris)

2. INDEX   Dunn*, Paxton
   BIRD SOLOS   Reid*

3. HELEN'S DANCE   Gordon*   (Erik Satie)

4. DIAGONAL   Rainer*, Davis, T. Brown, Dunn, Paxton, Reid

5. DUET   Rainer*, T. Brown   (Philip Corner)

intermission

6. RANDOM BREAKFAST Gordon*, Setterfield   (Misc.)

                        1 The Strip
             2 Prefabricated Dance   3   The Seasons
                        4 Lemon Hearts Dance
                        5 Big Girls Don't Cry
                        6 Grand Finale

7. WORD WORDS   Paxton*, Rainer*   (Music from MUSIC FOR WORD WORDS)
   SPEEDLIMIT   Dunn*, Morris

8. SOLO SECTION   Rainer*, Davis, T. Brown, Dunn, Paxton, Reid

intermission: audience please remove chairs from rink

9. PELICAN   Rauschenberg*, C. Brown, Ultvedt   (Rauschenberg)

10. PROXY   Paxton*, Rainer, Tipton

11. MANNEQUIN DANCE Gordon*   (costume: B. Kastle-Brill)
    LIGHTFALL   T. Brown*, Paxton   (Simone Morris)

intermission

12. FIELD   Davis*, Lloyd   (Music: for Davis, Radio Station WRC
                                                for Lloyd, Radio Station WOL)

13. PLAY   Rainer*, T. Brown, Davis, Dunn, Paxton, Reid

                     Slow   Stance
                     Game   Rest
                     Pick-up   Bounce
                     Ball   Stop
                     Fast   Love (Rainer, Davis)

14. BACH   Rainer*, T. Brown, Davis, Dunn, Paxton, Reid

= = = = = =

The choreographers and cast of CONCERT OF DANCE NUMBER FIVE thank Mrs. Alice Denny,
Assistant Director of the Washington Gallery of Modern Art, for her interest and
support, and Billy Kluver for his important role in bringing about this concert.

Jennifer Tipton - stage manager
Robert Rauschenberg - lights
Billy Kluver and Robert Dunn - Technical Assist
John Herbert McDowell - Assembled concert tapes

Postcard 1 (top)

1967, by fluxus

© by Ben, 1965

FLUX POST CARD

Trisha Brown
53 Wooster st.
N. Y. 10012
USA

Postcard 2 (bottom)

La Bertesca
via del Carmine
20121 Milano
telefono 87.43.13

Martedì 20 novembre 1973
alle ore 18

Il postino vi ha scelto
per invitarvi al discorso
e alla presentazione dei
films fluxus di Ben.

1967, by fluxus

© by Ben, 1965

FLUX POST CARD

John Cage
107 Bank st.
N. Y. 10014
USA

MAN WALKING DOWN THE SIDE OF A BUILDING, 1970

In works such as *Planes, Ballet,* and *The Dance with a Duck's Head* (all 1968), Brown had begun to use props that the dancers interacted with in very direct ways: the props literally suspended them above the floor. These works were precursors to the Equipment Pieces of the early 1970s in which Brown used climbing harness and rope, the first of which was *Man Walking Down the Side of a Building.*

"Just what [the title] says, seven stories."[37]
Trisha Brown

A natural activity under the stress of an unnatural setting. Gravity reneged. Vast scale. Clear order. You start at the top, walk straight down, stop at the bottom. All those soupy questions that arise in the process of selecting abstract movement according to the modern dance tradition—what, when, where, and how—are solved in collaboration between choreographer and place. If you eliminate all those eccentric possibilities that the choreographic imagination can conjure and just have a person walk down an aisle, then you see the movement as the activity. The paradox of one action working against another is very interesting to me, and is illustrated by *Man Walking Down the Side of a Building*, where you have gravity working one way on the body and my intention to have a naturally walking person working in another way.[38] Trisha Brown

All the pieces I performed at 80 Wooster had rambled in my head for a long time. My rule was, if an idea doesn't disappear by natural cause, then it has to be done. I wanted to work with the wall but not by building one. I looked at walls in warehouses and as I moved around the streets....
I chose this exterior wall and then thought—why not use mountain climbing equipment?... *Man Walking Down the Side of a Building* was like doing *Planes* but purifying the image. It had no rationale. It was completely art.[39] Trisha Brown

CYCLE Equipment Pieces
LENGTH Unknown (brief)
SOUND Ambient
VISUAL PRESENTATION Developed by Brown with the help of Richard Nonas and Jared Bark
EQUIPMENT Ropes and harness
COSTUME Street clothes
DANCER Joseph Schlichter
FIRST PERFORMANCE In and around 80 Wooster, New York City, April 18, 1970

After Joe walked down, the audience went into the building to see *Floor of the Forest* and then out to the street for *Leaning Duets.*[40] Trisha Brown

FLOOR OF THE FOREST, 1970

(For the first performances of this piece, Brown listed all of the titles under consideration: clothes pipe, the floor of the forest & other miracles, dance for a dirty room, everybody's grandmother's bed, the costume, Adam says checkered sea.)

Two people dressed and undressed their way through [the structure described below]. It was done as naturally as it could be done. A normally vertical activity performed horizontally and reshaped by the vertical pull of gravity. It was strenuous. Great strain and effort to support the body weight while negotiating buttons and zippers. We rested at times, and when we rested hanging down, an article of clothing became a hammock. The audience ducked down to see the performers suspended or climbing below the frame, or stretched upward to see the activity above.[41] Trisha Brown

CYCLE Equipment Pieces
LENGTH 30 min.
SOUND Ambient, environmental
VISUAL PRESENTATION Trisha Brown
SET/EQUIPMENT Trisha Brown; ropes, pipes, and clothes

Floor of the Forest was performed in a twelve-foot by fourteen-foot pipe frame across which were tied ropes densely threaded with clothes—sleeves were woven beneath pant legs forming a solid rectangular surface. The frame was suspended horizontally at eye level in the center of an empty room.[42] Trisha Brown
The audience was free to move around in the periphery of the grid.

COSTUMES Shorts and tank tops
DANCERS Trisha Brown and Carmen Beuchat
FIRST PERFORMANCE In and around 80 Wooster, New York City, April 18, 1970

LEANING DUETS [I], 1970

Five couples, feet together, side of foot touching partner's, leaning out to arm's length, maintaining straight posture. Partners choose a direction, walking in that direction, touching side of foot together with each step. Fallen persons were hauled back up by partner while keeping foot contact. Rope device with handles also employed to achieve greater angle.[43] Trisha Brown

CYCLE Equipment Pieces
LENGTH 10 min.
SOUND "Verbal instructions to partners about balance, give and take of weight, and imminent danger."[44]
VISUAL PRESENTATION Trisha Brown
EQUIPMENT Rope device with handles
COSTUMES Street clothes
DANCERS Trisha Brown, Jared Bark, Carmen Beuchat, Ben Dolphin, Caroline Goodden, Richard Nonas, Patsy Norvell, Lincoln Scott, Kei Takei, and one unrecorded
FIRST PERFORMANCE In and around 80 Wooster, New York City, April 18, 1970

THE STREAM, 1970

CYCLE Equipment Pieces
LENGTH Visitors were free to interact with the structure (see below) throughout the day
SOUND Ambient, environmental
VISUAL PRESENTATION Trisha Brown
SET/EQUIPMENT Trisha Brown

A 24-foot-long U-shaped wooden structure [with walls about four feet high], the inside floor lined with pots and pans filled with water. Participants entered and exited as they wished, some stepping in water, some avoiding water, some racing up and down the sides.[45]
Trisha Brown

COSTUMES Street clothes
DANCERS Anyone interested in exploring the structure
FIRST PERFORMANCE Astrofest, Union Square, New York City, October 3, 1970

WALKING ON THE WALL, 1971

The performers stood, and walked, and ran parallel to the floor along two adjacent walls while suspended in special harnesses rigged on cables to trolleys on industrial tracks along the ceiling.

The illusion is uncanny. Their shirts are brown like the slings, for camouflage, and some of them are excellent wall-walkers (no falling hair, drooping head or legs betray them). For dizzying moments at a time, you seem to be in a tower looking down on the foreshortened bodies of people promenading endlessly on two intersecting white streets.... After a while, wall-walking seems like something that you may once have been able to do. A long time ago.[46] Deborah Jowitt
CYCLE Equipment Pieces
LENGTH 20–30 min.

SOUND Sound of trolleys in tracks and dancers' dialogue to gain passage while aerial
VISUAL PRESENTATION Trisha Brown
EQUIPMENT Harnesses, cables, tracks, and trolleys
COSTUMES Dance work clothes
DANCERS Trisha Brown, Carmen Beuchat, Barbara Dilley, Douglas Dunn, Mark Gabor, Sylvia Palacios,[47] Steve Paxton
FIRST PERFORMANCE Whitney Museum of American Art, New York City, March 30, 1971

That Whitney event of 1971—entitled another fearless dance concert—helped me, and others I think, to acknowledge the presence in dance of a new kind of virtuosity.[48] Deborah Jowitt

LEANING DUETS II, 1971

Ten couples facing each other, toes touching partner's, leaning out with rope extensions, maintaining straight posture. Couples chose directions to travel in and instructed each other on what foot to use, going in what direction and precisely how big of a step to take. Maintained balance through instructions like "Give me some more [weight] or take a little."[49] Trisha Brown

CYCLE Equipment Pieces
LENGTH Variable
SOUND Some dialogue between the pairs of dancers to maintain balance
VISUAL PRESENTATION Trisha Brown
EQUIPMENT Wooden back supports attached to ropes
COSTUMES Street clothes
DANCERS Trisha Brown, Carole Berman, Carmen Beuchat, Victor Brocapas, Ben Dolphin, Mark Gabor, Caroline Goodden, Susan Harris, Mike Howard, Jon Kalina, Ginger Michels, Richard Nonas, Leslie Orr, Darby Ortolano, Fernando Torm, and four unrecorded
FIRST PERFORMANCE Whitney Museum of American Art, New York City, March 30, 1971

FALLING DUET II, 1971

Two dancers, one stands on the shoulders of the other. They fall, alternate roles, and repeat for about three minutes.[50] Trisha Brown

LENGTH Approximately 3 min.
SOUND Some dialogue to maintain balance
COSTUMES Dance work clothes
DANCERS Trisha Brown and Steve Paxton
FIRST PERFORMANCE Whitney Museum of American Art, New York City, March 30, 1971

Previous spread from left: Program for "Concert of Dance Number Five/America on Wheels/Washington, D.C.," at the Washington Gallery of Modern Art, Washington, D.C., May 9, 1963, Photocopy on paper, 11 x 8 1/2 in (27.9 x 21.6 cm). Collection of Trisha Brown.

Invitation card to see Fluxus films by Ben [Vautier], Milan, 1973. Addressed to John Cage on one side and Brown on the other. Delivered to Brown. 6 x 8 1/4 in. (15.2 x 21.0 cm). Collection of Trisha Brown.

Opposite page: Photographs taken of Trisha Brown during the filming of Autobiographical Film, 1969 (an unfinished work). Photograph by Caroline Goodden.

words--
angry, cause, sock, some, plough

ACTIONS:

GIVING THE NECK A KNIFING OR COMING TO GIVE
     A PARALLEL MEAL, BEAUTIFUL AND SHOCKING.

words--
interest, lip, month, sock, I, though, trick.

ACTIONS:

GIVING AN EGG TO SOMEONE LOOSE OR SEEMING TO
               DO SO,

SEEMING TO HAVE A PURPOSE,
MEETING SOMEONE OVER WATER,
GOING ABOUT BEING A UNIT.

GRAND UNION

TRISHA BROWN BARBARA DILLEY DOUG DUNN DAVID GORDON NANCY LEWIS STEVE PAXTON

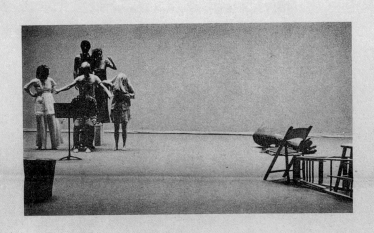

ROOF PIECE, 1971

12 dancers placed on roofs covering a 10-block area. Comprised improvised gestures, more or less stationary, which were initiated at 53 Wooster, copied by next in line, and so on. In this way the movement was transmitted to 381 Lafayette Street in a process that continued for 15 minutes, stopped and reversed direction for 15 minutes.[51]
Trisha Brown

LENGTH **Approximately 30 min.**
SOUND **Ambient, environmental**
VISUAL PRESENTATION **Trisha Brown**

The organization of roofs, roof owners, and dancers was a staggering project. The procedure for getting the locations and permission for use went like this: Go up on roof A with binoculars, spot several possible roof B's which are visible to each other and also to the audience placed anywhere from one to eight blocks away. Go downstairs, around to the first choice of roof B, look to see if I know anyone in the building. If I do—homefree; if I do not … ring the doorbell and say, "Hello, my name is Trisha Brown, I am a dancer and I need your roof on which to place one dancer etc. etc." Bowing, smiling, discussing "avant-garde" dance…. If they said no, I went to choice 2. If choice 2 said no, I started over on roof A with the binoculars. If choice 2 said yes, I got permission to go up on their roof at that moment to verify the roof was usable and if so, to sight for 2 choices of roof C. Up, down…. It took weeks in unknown hallways and rooftops, sliding in hot tar, explaining my presence to alarmed people in adjacent buildings. Exposed to personal revelations by total strangers who burst forth with such statements as, "Try the building across the street but don't tell his wife I suggested it."[52]
Trisha Brown

COSTUMES **Red clothes**
DANCERS **Twelve dance students**
FIRST PERFORMANCE **53 Wooster Street to 381 Lafayette Street, New York City, May 11, 1971**

ACCUMULATION, 1971

Movement one, rotation of the fist with the thumb extended, was begun and repeated seven or eight times. Movement two was added and one and two were repeated eight times. Then movement three was added and one, two, and three were repeated, eventually bringing into play the entire body.[53] Trisha Brown

CYCLE **Mathematical**
LENGTH **4 1/2 min.**

MUSIC **The Grateful Dead, "Uncle John's Band"**
COSTUME **White long-sleeved t-shirt and white and pale red bell-bottom pants**
DANCER **Trisha Brown**
FIRST PERFORMANCE **New York University Gymnasium, October 22, 1971**

RUMMAGE SALE AND THE FLOOR OF THE FOREST, 1971

Two dancers dress and undress their way through the old clothes attached to the grid while a full-scale rummage sale is conducted beneath them.

The first version of this piece in which the structure was hung at eye level [1970] forced the viewers to crouch down or stretch up (depending on where the dancers were) in order to see the action. In this version the rummage sale was conducted so as to force the viewers to choose between looking at the dance or getting a bargain, or backing way out to see both from a distance.[54] Trisha Brown

CYCLE **Equipment Pieces**
LENGTH **Approximately 45 min.**
SOUND **Ambient, environmental**
VISUAL PRESENTATION **Trisha Brown**
SETS/EQUIPMENT **Trisha Brown; 12' x 14' rectangle of pipes. Onto the pipes are tied ropes forming a horizontal grid. Old clothes are threaded on the grid giving the structure the appearance of a tapestry. It is suspended just above the sales-people tending their tables.**[55] Trisha Brown

Hanging upside down in a dress hand-knit by Deborah Hay's mother, looking at some stranger trying on a kimono that my dear friend Suzushi [Hanayagi] had given me before she had to leave this country, watching the woman preen in it, using that gesture of feeling yourself in your new-bought clothes, wondering what was in her mind—it was just an incredible experience for me…. The piece is still continuing, I still see people in the clothes. For them it's a piece of clothing that they liked, a bargain; for me those clothes are artifacts of history.[56]
Trisha Brown

COSTUMES **Shorts and tank tops**
DANCERS **Trisha Brown and Carmen Beuchat**
FIRST PERFORMANCE **New York University Gymnasium, October 22, 1971**

ACCUMULATION 55, 1972

4 ½ minutes of actions from *Accumulation* expanded to 55 minutes. I worked in performance to keep the separateness and clarity of each move against the blurring effect of relentless repetition. What went through my mind was "This is all there is." By then another move would be active and "This is all there is."…Since I did not use music, these delicate changes in time could occur. Both the dance and its structure were visible and bare-bone simple. None of the movements had any significance beyond what they were. And I never felt more alive, more expressive or more exposed in performance.[57] Trisha Brown

CYCLE **Mathematical**
LENGTH **55 min.**
SOUND **Ambient**
COSTUME **White long-sleeved t-shirt and white-and-pale-red bell-bottom pants**
DANCER **Trisha Brown**
FIRST PERFORMANCE **Galleria L'Attico, Rome, Italy, June 2, 1972**

PRIMARY ACCUMULATION, 1972

A supine figure generates 30 moves in 18 minutes. The figure rotates 45 degrees each on the last two moves, making a 90-degree turn with the completion of the phrase. The phrase is repeated until, in the last two minutes of the dance, a 360-degree turn is achieved and all sides of the dance/dancer revealed.[58] Trisha Brown

CYCLE **Mathematical**
LENGTH **18 min.**
SOUND **Sweeping sounds of the actions on the floor**
COSTUME **Trisha Brown; first use of what would become the "regulation" costume: white long-sleeved t-shirt and white cotton drawstring pants**
DANCER **Trisha Brown**
FIRST PERFORMANCE **Wadsworth Athenaeum, Hartford, Connecticut, December 1, 1972**

THEME AND VARIATION, 1972

Duet, dancer A presents and repeats a simple phrase of movement. Dancer B does everything imaginable to interrupt Dancer A.[59] Trisha Brown

LENGTH **5 min.**
SOUND **Ambient**
COSTUMES **Dance work clothes**
DANCERS **Carmen Beuchat and Penelope[60]**
FIRST PERFORMANCE **Wadsworth Athenaeum, Hartford, Connecticut, December 1, 1972**

WOMAN WALKING DOWN A LADDER, 1973

CYCLE **Equipment Pieces**
LENGTH **Variable**
VISUAL PRESENTATION **Trisha Brown**
EQUIPMENT **Rope and harness**
SOUND **Ambient**
COSTUME **Street clothes**
DANCER **Trisha Brown**
FIRST PERFORMANCE **130 Greene Street, New York City, February 25, 1973**

ACCUMULATING PIECES, 1973

Includes *Discs, Sticks, Running-Mistitled, Circles, Theme and Variation, Group Accumulation, Announcement,* and *Spanish Dance.* See also *Structured Pieces I–IV.* Eight events were accumulated: event 1, start over, event 1 and then 2, start over, event 1, 2, and 3, start over, etc.

Discs: a dancer walks naturally across the floor, three other dancers pitch discs in an attempt to get them under her feet, rarely succeed.

Sticks: a 10-foot-long, 3/4" x 3/4" stick was placed with one end against the base of the wall and the other end on the dancer's head. The dancer facing the wall moved forward maintaining the original angle of the stick until the head was wedged in between the stick and the floor. Performed by four dancers placed at equal distances along one wall or in partners—stick against stick—in the center of the gallery.

Running-Mistitled: a starting line was established in adjacent Rooms A and B. All 5 dancers began in Room A. A tape-recording of a wooden stick striking a glass every 5 seconds was played. The dancers took one step across the starting line and returned to starting position within 10 seconds, then 2 steps and return to start in 10 seconds, 3 steps return etc. The piece continued until the number of steps going out was greater than the time allotted for returning to start. Size and speed of each step altered. The dancers were not identical. Each time the piece was repeated through the accumulating format, one dancer moved from room A to B until all 5 were in Room B and none in Room A. The audience could move from A to B but most chose to remain in A and listen to the final editions.

Circles: dancers A and B are partners and travel on parallel circular tracks. Dancers C and D are partners and travel on parallel circular tracks different from A and B. The four dancers carry their heads centered and do not look to the right or left. When no one is in their vision they initiate

Pages 308–309 from left: Jackson Mac Low, two cards from a set entitled "Nuclei for Simone Forti," 1963. Red and black typewritten ink on card stock, 3 x 5 in. (7.6 x 12.7 cm) each. Collection of Trisha Brown.

Cover of leaflet for the Grand Union dance group, c. 1975. 37 x 23 in. (94.0 x 58.4 cm). Collection of Trisha Brown.

Previous spread: Inside of leaflet for the Grand Union dance group, c. 1975. 37 x 23 in. (94.0 x 58.4 cm). Collection of Trisha Brown.

Opposite page from top: Burt Barr, her husband, and Trisha Brown on the top of the World Trade Center, 1976.

Tatyana Grosman, Trisha Brown, Hendel Teicher, and Jane Savitt at Universal Limited Art Editions, West Islip, Long Island, September 10, 1980. Photograph by William Goldston.

Teatro di San Carlo, Naples, December 1986. Pictured: bottom row, Trisha Brown, Lina Wertmüller; top row, Natale Tulipani, Enrico Job, Francesco Canessa. Photograph by Luciano Romano.

movement. When 1, 2, or 3 other dancers are in their vision, focused or peripheral, they copy the movement simultaneously.

Theme and Variation: a five-minute variation; see separate listing above.

Group Accumulation: see separate listing below.

Announcement: a sign was posted stating that three of the five dancers were pregnant.

Spanish Dance: dancer A slowly raises arms like a magnificent Spanish dancer and travels forward, in time to Bob Dylan's "Early Mornin' Rain." When the front of dancer A moves into the back of dancer B, dancer B slowly raises her arms like a magnificent Spanish dancer and the two travel forward, moves into the back of dancer C, etc. until they all reach the wall.[61] Trisha Brown

CYCLE Mathematical
LENGTH 90 min.
MUSIC Bob Dylan's recording of Gordon Lightfoot's "Early Mornin' Rain," and the sound of a wooden stick striking a glass
VISUAL PRESENTATION Trisha Brown
PROPS Discs and sticks
COSTUME White long-sleeved t-shirts and white cotton drawstring pants
DANCERS Trisha Brown, Carmen Beuchat, Caroline Goodden, Sylvia Palacios, Penelope
FIRST PERFORMANCE Sonnabend Gallery (420 West Broadway), New York City, March 27, 1973

GROUP ACCUMULATION, 1973

Each of the four dancers made a 40-count phrase of movement and sound which was accumulated one movement at a time. Dancers stood four abreast in the space and began one at a time with a two-count delay.[62] Trisha Brown

CYCLE Mathematical
LENGTH Variable (approx. 20 min. when premiered)
SOUND Ambient
COSTUMES White long-sleeved t-shirts and white cotton drawstring pants
DANCERS Carmen Beuchat, Caroline Goodden, Sylvia Palacios, Penelope
FIRST PERFORMANCES Sonnabend Gallery, New York City, March 27, 1973; Festival d'Automne, Musée Galliera, Paris, October 6, 1973 (as *Group Accumulation II*, with three dancers: Carmen Beuchat, Caroline Goodden, and Sylvia Palacios). This performance marked Trisha Brown's first appearance in France, on a tour that Ileana Sonnabend helped to initiate, and with the support of Michel Guy, the French minister of culture.

GROUP PRIMARY ACCUMULATION, 1973

Four dancers placed equidistant from each other in a line from downstage to upstage perform the piece in unison. After the 360-degree turn [see *Primary Accumulation,* 1972], the dancers continue to repeat the sequence as two other dancers enter and transport them to new positions that relate to the physical space and also to each other. The movement unavoidably changed in an unconscious theme and variations as the dancers were carried, stacked, stood, and separated.[63] Trisha Brown

CYCLE Mathematical
LENGTH 20–30 min.
SOUND Ambient
COSTUMES White long-sleeved t-shirts and white cotton drawstring pants
DANCERS Trisha Brown, Carmen Beuchat, Caroline Goodden, Sylvia Palacios; carriers: Douglas Dunn and David Gordon
FIRST PERFORMANCE Spring Dance Festival, sunken plaza of McGraw-Hill Building, New York City, May 16, 1973

ROOF AND FIRE PIECE, 1973

A dance initiated by a single dancer on the roof of 420 West Broadway and transmitted downtown to other dancers for 15 minutes, whereupon it stopped and reversed direction for 15 minutes.

The method of transmitting the movement, copying, is a technique used in dance classes and rehearsals for learning steps. The teacher does the steps first, and then the student copies, effecting a transference of physical information.... In the *Roof [and Fire] Piece*, the emphasis was on immediate and exact duplication of the observed dance and the silent passing of this dance to a series of performers on down the line. The intuitive and kinesthetic systems were impaired by the distance between buildings, and details and nuances were lost or incorrectly translated forcing an eventual disintegration or distortion of the original dance. The performers worked diligently to maintain accuracy and the breakdown occurred in fractions of time and gestures and was not necessarily recognizable between any two of the links.[64] Trisha Brown

LENGTH 30 min.
SOUND Ambient
VISUAL PRESENTATION Trisha Brown
COSTUMES Red long-sleeved shirts and red sweat pants
DANCERS Trisha Brown, Carmen Beuchat, Douglas Dunn, Tina Girouard, Caroline Goodden, David Gordon, Nancy Green, Susan Harris,

Elsi Miranda, Emmett Murray, Eve Poling,
Sarah Rudner, Nanette Seivert, Valda Setterfield,
Liz Thompson, Sylvia Palacios
FIRST PERFORMANCE 420 West Broadway to
35 White Street, New York City, June 24, 1973

STRUCTURED PIECES [I], 1973

The Structured Pieces, performed between 1973
and 1976, comprised a fluctuating collection of
experimental ideas in form closely allied with
the Accumulations (1971–73, 1978, 1997). The individual dances within the Structured Pieces were
like one-line ideas that often evolved into larger
sections of later choreographies. The list of dances
at each performance was not always recorded.

Includes *Sticks, Scallops, Discs, Bug, Running-
Mistitled, Leaning Trio, Falling Duets, Circles,* and
Group Primary Accumulation (circle formation).[65]
Trisha Brown

CYCLE Mathematical
LENGTH Approximately 40 min.
SOUND Silent except for dialogue of the dancers
PROPS Discs and sticks
COSTUMES White long-sleeved t-shirts and white cot-
ton drawstring pants
DANCERS Trisha Brown, Carmen Beuchat, Caroline
Goodden, Sylvia Palacios
FIRST PERFORMANCE Festival d'Automne, Musée
Galliera, Paris, France, October 6, 1973

ACCUMULATION WITH TALKING, 1973

A lecture combined with choreography. I spontaneously started dancing while lecturing.[66]
Trisha Brown

CYCLE Mathematical
LENGTH Approximately 45 min.
SOUND Brown talking
COSTUME Street clothes
DANCER Trisha Brown
FIRST PERFORMANCE Centre Americain, Paris, France,
October 12, 1973

FIGURE 8, 1974

Time crossing: (left) 12345678/1234567/123456
/12345/1234/123/12/1; (right) 1/12/123/1234/
12345/123456/1234567/12345678
Spatial arrangement: a row, like stewardesses
demonstrating safety measures on an airplane.
Eyes closed. Right arm arcs from the side of
the body to the top of the head and back again,
marking, enlarging time patterns, while the

left arm arcs from the side of the body to the top
of the head in diminishing time patterns.[67]
Trisha Brown

The audience moved around to face the entrance
to another room where four dancers stood one
behind the other with eyes closed. Until someone
called out, "O.K. stop," they all performed the
same sharp arm movements in unison to the beat
of a metronome. I was amazed that the dancers
managed to stay perfectly together as they blindly
performed these complicated arm movements—
which looked like coordination exercises. *"Figure 8"*
is structurally the opposite of *"Group Primary
Accumulation"* in that the metronome works to pre-
vent the disintegration of form and rhythm. The
latter dance wears away like a delicately shaped
seashell. *"Figure 8"* persists like a pyramid.[68]
Nancy Moore

CYCLE Mathematical
LENGTH Approximately 5 min.
SOUND Metronome and verbal cue to stop
COSTUMES White long-sleeved t-shirts and white
cotton drawstring pants
DANCERS Probably Trisha Brown, Carmen Beuchat,
Caroline Goodden, Sylvia Palacios
FIRST PERFORMANCE Contemporanea Festival, Rome,
January 2, 1974

SPLITS SOLO, 1974

Two dancers [lie] side by side eighteen inches
apart…. All of the movements of *Primary
Accumulation* that occur on the right side of the
body were done by the person on the right and
all the movements on the left side of the body
by the person on the left. The dance went in and
out of looking like one huge fat person or two
people sharing one dance, shifting their roles of
doing and waiting.[69] Trisha Brown
LENGTH Approximately 20 min.
SOUND Ambient
COSTUMES White long-sleeved t-shirts and white
cotton drawstring pants
DANCERS Trisha Brown and one other dancer
(unrecorded)
FIRST PERFORMANCE Contemporanea Festival, Rome,
January 2, 1974

DRIFT, 1974

Five dancers stood side by side, to the right of
center at the rear of a performing area that was
120 feet long and 40 feet wide. The action was
to walk straight forward at a medium pace until

Opposite page from top: Trisha
Brown and Fujiko Nakaya, 1980.
Photograph by Harry Shunk.

Trisha Brown and Nancy Graves,
Long Cove, Fire Island, August
1977.

Donald Judd and Trisha Brown,
Angers, France, 1987.

Trisha Brown, John Cage, and
Robert Rauschenberg after the
premiere of *Astral Converted 55,*
National Gallery of Art,
Washington, D.C., May 14, 1991.

reaching the front edge of the audience. The dancers' feet moved a fraction of an inch to the right with each step. They appeared to be walking straight forward but the image slides to the right of the space at the same time as it loomed into the foreground.[70] Trisha Brown

[The dancers gave] the illusion that they were in fact walking straight ahead. But in actual fact they were drifting ever so slightly, maintaining their straight line, so that they ended up, still perfectly parallel at the right on front of stage—where they stopped, held their positions and looked straight ahead. Since the sunlight was coming in from the Potomac when they reached stage front, the orange-red glow of the sunset hit their faces and it was extremely impressive, as they stood for a full 30 or 45 seconds with the sunlight hitting the left side of the faces. Then they broke and left the stage.[71] Dennis Bark

LENGTH Approximately 4 min.
SOUND Ambient
COSTUMES Black long-sleeved t-shirts and black jeans or pants
DANCERS Trisha Brown, Carmen Beuchat, Douglas Dunn, Caroline Goodden, Sylvia Palacios
FIRST PERFORMANCE Art Now 74 (presented by the Artrend Foundation), The John F. Kennedy Center for the Performing Arts, Washington, D.C., June 2, 1974

SPIRAL, 1974

Carmen Beuchat, Sylvia Palacios and Brown climb ladders in order to strap themselves to ropes which spiral down three pillars. Then, slowly, incredibly, they walk around the pillars—bodies hanging out in space, parallel to the floor. Each winds down a pillar until her head nearly touches the audience's feet. The lower they get, the heavier they seem. Right before they disconnect themselves and stand up on the floor, you get the feeling that you're the one who's hanging.[72] Nancy Moore

CYCLE Equipment Pieces
LENGTH Approximately 15–30 seconds (variable according to height of column or tree)
SOUND Ambient
EQUIPMENT Harnesses, ropes, and carabiners
COSTUMES Street clothes
DANCERS Trisha Brown, Carmen Beuchat, Sylvia Palacios
FIRST PERFORMANCE 383 West Broadway, New York City, June 11, 1974

PAMPLONA STONES, 1974

A careful distribution of words, objects, and gestures in a large square room with an interplay of ambiguity in language and reference—with multiple themes and variations.[73] Trisha Brown

"Pamplona Stones" appeared to be a partially structured improvisation. Trisha Brown and Sylvia Whitman…manipulate props—a king-sized mattress, an armchair and some stones which anchor down the bottom of a wall hanging. Funny, weird correspondences develop between props, movement and verbalizing. Whitman picks up a large rock and drops it as Brown commands, "Stop!" Whitman complains, "It doesn't do what I say." Silence. Then, smiling, "It stopped." There's also a terrific…scene in which both performers suddenly leap up and straddle the sides of the mattress—which they've set up on end—and "ride" it as it slumps to the floor.[74] Nancy Moore

LENGTH 18 min.
SOUND Dialogue, text by Brown
PROPS Trisha Brown; mattress, two armchairs, three stones approximately six inches in diameter
COSTUMES Dance work clothes
DANCERS Trisha Brown and Sylvia Palacios
FIRST PERFORMANCE 383 West Broadway, New York City, June 11, 1974

STRUCTURED PIECES II, 1974

See description at Structured Pieces [I], 1973

Ten-foot-long sticks (1" x 1") are placed end to end in a horizontal line just above the supine bodies of the performers. Keeping contact between sticks, the performers circle or roll in careful motion around their sticks. If contact is lost, they must stop and correct it. The action of rolling is shaped by the second task of holding the sticks in a fixed position and in turn, the balance of the sticks is made more difficult by the large activity of the body maneuvering. The horizontal line of the sticks changes from one long line to several smaller units at angles to each other as the piece progresses.[75] Trisha Brown

CYCLE Mathematical
LENGTH Approximately 40 min.
SOUND Talking between the dancers, sound of props
VISUAL PRESENTATION Trisha Brown
COSTUMES White long-sleeved t-shirts and white cotton drawstring pants
DANCERS Trisha Brown, Carmen Beuchat, Caroline Goodden, Sylvia Palacios
FIRST PERFORMANCE Walker Art Center, Minneapolis, Minnesota, November 7, 1974

LOCUS, 1975

Locus is an eighteen-minute quartet of continuous action. That action is based on an ordered series of movement within a compartmentalized space. I was trying to make a sphere of [movement] in a grid of 4 boxes. 1st [performance] of *Locus* as work in progress.[76] Trisha Brown

I wanted to analyze, graph the immediate space around my body in an attempt to understand my elusive movement style in order to teach it to others.[77] Trisha Brown

Locus is organized around 27 points located on an imaginary cube of space slightly larger than the standing figure in a stride position. The points were correlated to the alphabet and a written statement, 1 being A, 2, B.... I made four sections each three minutes long that move through, touch, look at, jump over, or do something about each point in the series, either one point at a time or clustered. The dance does not observe front, it revolves. The cube base is multiplied to form a grid of five units wide and four deep. There are opportunities to move from one cube base to another without distorting the movement. By exercising these options, we travel.[78] Trisha Brown

CYCLE Mathematical
LENGTH 18 min.
SOUND Ambient
COSTUMES Sleeveless leotards and pants
DANCERS Trisha Brown, Elizabeth Garren, Judith Ragir, Mona Sulzman
FIRST PERFORMANCE 541 Broadway, New York City, April 6, 1975

STRUCTURED PIECES III, 1975

See description at Structured Pieces [I], *1973*

CYCLE Mathematical
LENGTH Approximately 40 min.
SOUND Ambient
COSTUMES White long-sleeved t-shirts and white cotton drawstring pants
DANCERS Trisha Brown, Elizabeth Garren, Judith Ragir (and possibly others)
FIRST PERFORMANCE American Dance Festival, New London, Connecticut, July 18, 1975

PYRAMID, 1975

An accumulation of thirty dance actions. At action number fifteen, action number one is dropped. As the dance progresses through action sixteen, action two is dropped, seventeen drop three, eighteen drop four, and so on.[79] Trisha Brown

CYCLE Mathematical
LENGTH Unknown
SOUND Ambient
COSTUMES White long-sleeved t-shirts and white cotton drawstring pants
DANCERS Trisha Brown, Elizabeth Garren, Wendy Perron, Judith Ragir, Mona Sulzman
FIRST PERFORMANCES Dance Today, Seibu Theater, Tokyo, Japan, December 15, 1975; Lepercq Space, Brooklyn Academy of Music, Brooklyn, New York, January 8, 1976

SOLOLOS, 1976

A natural progression of non-functional movement. By natural progression I mean that movement B is the simplest most obvious next move after A; C after B. At the halfway mark of this piece, a retrograde is initiated.[80] Trisha Brown

LENGTH Approximately 3 min.
SOUND Ambient
COSTUME White long-sleeved t-shirt and white cotton drawstring pants
DANCER Trisha Brown
FIRST PERFORMANCE Lepercq Space, Brooklyn Academy of Music, Brooklyn, New York, January 8, 1976

STRUCTURED PIECES IV, 1976

See description at Structured Pieces [I], *1973*

CYCLE Mathematical
LENGTH Approximately 40 min.
SOUND Ambient
COSTUMES White long-sleeved t-shirts and white jeans
DANCERS Trisha Brown, Elizabeth Garren, Wendy Perron, Judith Ragir, Mona Sulzman
FIRST PERFORMANCE Fort Worth Art Museum, Fort Worth, Texas, April 8, 1976

DUETUDE, 1976

LENGTH 12 min. at time of premiere, 8 min. thereafter
SOUND Ambient
COSTUMES White long-sleeved t-shirts and white cotton drawstring pants
DANCERS Jean Churchill, Lisa Kraus
FIRST PERFORMANCE New England Dinosaur at the First Congregational Church, Cambridge, Massachusetts, May 8, 1976

Opposite page from top:
Trisha Brown and Merce Cunningham, spring 1997. Photograph by Timothy Greenfield-Sanders.

Trisha Brown and Terry Winters following the premiere of *Five Part Weather Invention* at De Singel Theatre, Antwerp, November 11, 1999. Photograph by Laurent Boeki.

Roland Aeschlimann, Trisha Brown, and Bernard Foccroulle during a rehearsal for *Luci mie traditrici*, early 2001. Photograph by Johan Jacobs.

LINE UP, 1976

Organized around the making, remaking, or unmaking of horizontal lines, resulting in clarity, disorder, clarity, disorder, disorder, clarity, order, disorder, and so on. Trisha Brown

a line
a hinged line
nudging a line into straightness
allowing change
being stable and flexible
talking to the others
helping someone else
warning anticipating correcting
disconnecting/reconnecting (activities)
doing 2 incompatible activities at once
circling with the body (activity)
maintaining contact (activity)[81]
Trisha Brown

LENGTH Approximately 45 min.
SOUND Verbal instructions, metronome, and Bob Dylan's recording of "Early Mornin' Rain"
COSTUMES White long-sleeved t-shirts and white cotton drawstring pants
DANCERS Trisha Brown, Elizabeth Garren, Terry O'Reilly, Steve Paxton, Wendy Perron, Judith Ragir, Mona Sulzman
FIRST PERFORMANCES Festival Musicales de la Sainte Baume, Aix-en-Provence, France, August 1, 1976; Lepercq Space, Brooklyn Academy of Music, Brooklyn, New York, March 10, 1977 (with additional dancers Terry O'Reilly and Steve Paxton)

WATERMOTOR, 1978

Watermotor, the 2nd or 3rd time, I danced how I dance. It was a solo—didn't have to pin it down to others. It is unpredictable, personal, articulate, dense, changeful, wild assed. My model was improvisation…difficult to memorize. Don't look directly at what you are doing. Totally physical.[82]
Trisha Brown

LENGTH 2 1/2 min.
SOUND Ambient
COSTUME Tan t-shirt and gray pants (pants designed by Susan Zucker)
LIGHTING Edward Effron
DANCER Trisha Brown
FIRST PERFORMANCE Newman Stage, Public Theater, New York City, May 22, 1978

SPLANG, 1978

Slide 2 with arms flopping in a duration slightly longer than what would be in sync with the feet. Look to where your toes are pointing, step forward with toes at a 90-degree angle to where they were. Do a huge big-bodied move, out of which comes a delicate line being drawn with simultaneous and parallel hand and foot—the hand stops and the foot continues. Reach, round over, flip sides, and extend arms and one leg dead ahead. Have one arm and leg quietly go away.[83]
Trisha Brown

LENGTH 11 min. 20 sec.
SOUND Ambient
COSTUMES Richard Kerry; hand-dyed, tan bell-bottom pants and spaghetti-strap tank tops
DANCERS Elizabeth Garren, Wendy Perron, Mona Sulzman
FIRST PERFORMANCE Newman Stage, Public Theater, New York City, May 22, 1978

ACCUMULATION WITH TALKING PLUS WATERMOTOR, 1979

CYCLE Mathematical
LENGTH 10–15 min.
SOUND Brown talking
COSTUME Tan t-shirts and gray pants (pants designed by Susan Zucker)
LIGHTING Edward Effron
DANCER Trisha Brown
FIRST PERFORMANCES Oberlin College, Oberlin, Ohio, February 24, 1979; Maison de la Culture de Woluwe, Brussels, Belgium, November 1, 1979

NOTES

NOTES TO DANCE AND ART IN DIALOGUE 1979–2001 (PAGES 90–247)

1. Trisha Brown, "Collaboration: Life and Death in the Aesthetic Zone," in *Robert Rauschenberg: A Retrospective* (New York: Guggenheim Museum, 1997), p. 269.
2. Interview of Robert Rauschenberg by Hendel Teicher, 1 August 1996.
3. Ibid.
4. Rauschenberg quoted in T. Brown, "Collaboration: Life and Death in the Aesthetic Zone," p. 269.
5. T. Brown, "Collaboration: Life and Death in the Aesthetic Zone," p. 269.
6. Rauschenberg interview, 1 August 1996.
7. T. Brown, "Collaboration: Life and Death in the Aesthetic Zone," p. 270.
8. Rauschenberg interview, 1 August 1996.
9. Interview of Trisha Brown by Hendel Teicher, 16 December 2001.
10. Interview of Trisha Brown by Hendel Teicher, 16 October 2001.
11. From the original press release for *Opal Loop*, Trisha Brown Dance Company archive.
12. Interview of Fujiko Nakaya by Hendel Teicher, December 1990.
13. Comments by Judith Shea dated 20 November 2001.
14. Comments by T. Brown dated 16 October 2001. Unless otherwise stated, cited comments by Trisha Brown were made to Hendel Teicher.
15. Shea comments, 20 November 2001.
16. Trisha Brown, choreographer's notes, 6 January 2001.
17. Comments by Trisha Brown dated 13 January 2001 based on conversation with Robert Ashley.
18. Comments by Robert Ashley dated 20 October 2001.
19. Adapted from T. Brown, "Collaboration: Life and Death in the Aesthetic Zone," pp. 270, 271.
20. Comments by Laurie Anderson dated 8 November 2001.
21. T. Brown, "Collaboration: Life and Death in the Aesthetic Zone," p. 271.
22. Rauschenberg interview, 1 August 1996.
23. Trisha Brown quoted in Pedro Cuperman, "A Conversation with Trisha Brown," *Point of Contact*, Fall/Winter 2001, p. 32.
24. Adapted from an interview with Nancy Graves by Hendel Teicher, spring 1990.
25. T. Brown, "Collaboration: Life and Death in the Aesthetic Zone," p. 273.
26. T. Brown in Cuperman, "A Conversation with Trisha Brown," p. 32.
27. T. Brown, "Collaboration: Life and Death in the Aesthetic Zone," p. 273.
28. Rauschenberg interview, 1 August 1996.
29. T. Brown interview, 16 December 2001.
30. Comments by T. Brown dated 2 November 2001; see also her remarks on the collaborations with Judd in her "How to Make a Modern Dance When the Sky's the Limit" in this volume.
31. Comments by Ken Tabachnick dated 8 November 2001.
32. Comments by Trisha Brown dated 12 January 2002.
33. Rauschenberg interview, 1 August 1996.
34. T. Brown, "Collaboration: Life and Death in the Aesthetic Zone," pp. 273–74.
35. Ibid., p. 274.
36. Rauschenberg interview, 1 August 1996.
37. T. Brown, "Collaboration: Life and Death in the Aesthetic Zone," p. 274.
38. Comments by Trisha Brown dated 13 January 2002.
39. Comments by Trisha Brown dated 6 January 2002.
40. Comments by Carolyn Lucas dated 15 October 2001.
41. Trisha Brown, letter to Louisa Adams (her sister), September 1990.
42. T. Brown comments, 6 January 2002.
43. Ibid.
44. Comments by Alvin Curran dated 31 October 2001.
45. Comments by Spencer Brown dated 31 October 2001.
46. Quote from a press conference in Paris at the inception of the project.
47. Deborah Jowitt, "Sea Crossings," *The Village Voice*, 14 July 1992, p. 93.
48. Choreographer's notes, 6 January 2002.
49. Comment from 1993 discussion between Trisha Brown and Hendel Teicher, 1 September 1996.
50. Ibid.
51. Rauschenberg interview, 1 August 1996.
52. Ibid.
53. S. Brown comments, 31 October 2001.
54. The Paxton letter to Brown was originally printed in *Contact Quarterly*, no. 1 (Winter/Spring 1995): 94.
55. T. Brown comments, 6 January 2002.
56. "Misha and Trisha Talking Dance," *The New York Times*, 8 August 1999.
57. Comments by T. Brown dated 3 January 2002.
58. Comments by Jennifer Tipton dated 4 November 2001.
59. Choreographer's notes, 6 January 2002.
60. T. Brown comments, 3 January 2002.
61. Choreographer's notes, 6 January 2002.
62. T. Brown comments, 6 January 2002.
63. In *Dance Umbrella News* (London) 6 (Autumn 2000): n.p.
64. Comments by Simon Keenlyside dated 5 November 2001.
65. Aeschlimann interviewed by Marie-Geneviève Pinsart, *La Monnaie Magazine*, May–June 1998, n.p.
66. T. Brown comments, 6 January 2002.
67. Interview of Carolyn Lucas by Hendel Teicher, 15 October 2001.
68. Ibid.
69. Comments by Dave Douglas dated 22 November 2001.
70. Comments by Terry Winters dated 27 November 2001.
71. Interview of Trisha Brown by Hendel Teicher, 27 November 2001.
72. "In conversation with Terry Winters," *The Brooklyn Rail*, October–November 2001, pp. 27–28.
73. T. Brown comments, 6 January 2002.
74. Comments by Salvatore Sciarrino from 7 November 2001.
75. Comments by Annette Stricker dated 16 November 2001. Translated by Karina von Tippelskirch.

NOTES TO CHRONOLOGY OF DANCES 1961–1979 (PAGES 299–318)

1. Penelope Newcomb danced under her first name only.
2. Comments by Trisha Brown dated 12 January 2002.
3. Trisha Brown quoted in Anne Livet, *Contemporary Dance* (New York: Abbeville Press, 1978), p. 46, with edits by Brown of 12 January 2002.
4. Jill Johnston, "Dance Journal: Spring," *The Village Voice*, 1 June 1967, p. 15.
5. Interview of Steve Paxton, 11 April 1980, quoted in Sally Banes, *Democracy's Body: Judson Dance Theater 1962–1964* (Ann Arbor: UMI Research Press, 1983), p. 121.
6. Interview of Elaine Summers, 4 February 1988, quoted in Marianne Goldberg, "Reconstructing Trisha Brown: Dances and Performance Pieces 1960–1975," Ph.D. diss., New York University, 1990, p. 94.
7. Jill Johnston, "Dance: Judson Concerts #3, #4," *The Village Voice*, 28 February 1963, p. 19.
8. Interview of Yvonne Rainer, 29 March 1988, quoted in Goldberg, "Reconstructing Trisha Brown," p. 99.
9. Trisha Brown in Livet, *Contemporary Dance*, p. 48.
10. Interview of Robert Rauschenberg, 15 March 1989, quoted in Goldberg, "Reconstructing Trisha Brown," p. 99.
11. Comments by Brown dated 13 January 2002.
12. Jackson Mac Low, e-mail to Trisha Brown, 26 November 2001.
13. Ibid.
14. Trisha Brown, choreographer's notes, fall 2001.
15. Choreographer's typed and handwritten chronology of 1961–78, date of compilation unknown, unpaginated.
16. Choreographer's notes, not dated.
17. Choreographer's chronology 1961–78.
18. Choreographer's notes, not dated; updated by Brown, 13 January 2001.
19. Choreographer's notes, not dated.
20. Comments by Robert Whitman dated 19 November 2001.
21. Brown in Livet, *Contemporary Dance*, p. 48.
22. Discussion with Brown, fall 2001.
23. Choreographer's notes, fall 2001.
24. Choreographer's chronology 1961–78.
25. Interview of Brown, 21 and 30 July 1987, quoted in Goldberg, "Reconstructing Trisha Brown," p. 183.
26. Jud Yalkut in Film-makers' Cooperative, New York, cat. 7, p. 506.

27. Brown interview, 30 July 1987, quoted in Goldberg, "Reconstructing Trisha Brown," p. 178.

28. Brown interview, 21 and 30 July 1987, quoted in Goldberg, "Reconstructing Trisha Brown," p. 181.

29. Choreographer's notes, not dated.

30. Deborah Jowitt, "Dance," *The Village Voice*, 8 April 1971, p. 37.

31. Choreographer's chronology 1961–78. For a partial reconstruction of the piece, see also Hendel Teicher's "Bird/Woman/Flower/Daredevil: Trisha Brown" in this volume.

32. Choreographer's notes, not dated.

33. Discussion with Brown, fall 2001.

34. Brown in Livet, *Contemporary Dance*, p. 45.

35. Interview of Brown, November 2001.

36. Brown comments, 13 January 2002.

37. Choreographer's notes, not dated.

38. Brown in Livet, *Contemporary Dance*, p. 51.

39. Brown interview, 30 July 1987, quoted in Goldberg, "Reconstructing Trisha Brown," p. 185.

40. Discussion with Brown, October 2001.

41. Brown in Livet, *Contemporary Dance*, p. 51.

42. Ibid.

43. Choreographer's chronology 1961–78.

44. Comments by Brown dated 31 October 2001.

45. Choreographer's chronology 1961–78.

46. Deborah Jowitt, "Dance," *The Village Voice*, 8 April 1971, p. 37

47. At the time, Sylvia Palacios danced under the name Sylvia Whitman.

48. Deborah Jowitt, "Trisha Brown Makes Dances that Talk Back," *The Village Voice*, 12 January 1976, p. 110.

49. Choreographer's notes, fall 2001.

50. Choreographer's notes, not dated.

51. Choreographer's chronology 1961–78.

52. Choreographer's notes, not dated.

53. Brown in Livet, *Contemporary Dance*, p. 45.

54. Choreographer's notes, not dated.

55. Ibid.

56. Trisha Brown quoted in Sally Sommer, "Equipment Dances: Trisha Brown," *The Drama Review* 16, no. 7 (September 1972), p. 139.

57. Brown in Livet, *Contemporary Dance*, p. 45.

58. Adapted from Brown in Livet, *Contemporary Dance*, p. 46.

59. Choreographer's chronology 1961–78.

60. Penelope Newcomb.

61. Choreographer's chronology 1961–78.

62. Choreographer's notes, not dated.

63. Brown in Livet, *Contemporary Dance*, p. 46.

64. Trisha Brown, "Three Pieces," *The Drama Review* (March 1975), pp. 26–27.

65. Choreographer's chronology 1961–78.

66. Discussion with Brown, November 2001.

67. Choreographer's notes, not dated.

68. Nancy Moore, "Reviews," *Dance Magazine* 48, no. 8 (August 1974), p. 62.

69. Brown in Livet, *Contemporary Dance*, p. 46.

70. Choreographer's notes, not dated.

71. Letter from Dennis Bark to his parents after seeing the Trisha Brown Dance Company at the Kennedy Center.

72. Moore, "Reviews," p. 62.

73. Choreographer's notes, not dated.

74. Moore, "Reviews," p. 62.

75. Choreographer's notes, not dated.

76. Ibid.

77. Comments by Brown dated 12 January 2002.

78. Brown in Livet, *Contemporary Dance*, p. 54.

79. Brown comments, 12 January 2002.

80. Choreographer's notes, not dated.

81. Both quotes from choreographer's notes, not dated.

82. Brown comments dated 12 January 2002.

83. Comments by Brown dated 13 January 2001.

DANCERS PICTURED IN DANCE AND ART IN DIALOGUE 1979–2001 (PAGES 88–247)

Dancers are listed left to right.

Glacial Decoy, 1979
pp. 92–93: Trisha Brown, Nina Lundborg. Photograph by Babette Mangolte.
pp. 96–97: Nina Lundborg, Elizabeth Garren, Lisa Kraus. Photograph by Babette Mangolte.
pp. 102–103: Nina Lundborg, Lisa Kraus, Elizabeth Garren. Photograph by Boyd Hagen.

Opal Loop/Cloud Installation #72503, 1980
pp. 104–105: Eva Karczag, Lisa Kraus, Stephen Petronio, Trisha Brown. Photograph by Babette Mangolte.
pp. 106–107. Top left: Trisha Brown, Eva Karczag, Stephen Petronio, Lisa Kraus. Photograph by Babette Mangolte. Top right: Stephen Petronio, Lisa Kraus, Trisha Brown, Eva Karczag. Photograph by Harry Shunk. Bottom left: Trisha Brown, Stephen Petronio, Eva Karczag, Lisa Kraus. Photograph by Harry Shunk. Bottom right: Trisha Brown, Stephen Petronio, Eva Karczag, Lisa Kraus. Photograph by Babette Mangolte.
pp. 108–109: Stephen Petronio, Lisa Kraus, Eva Karczag, Trisha Brown. Photograph by Harry Shunk.

Son of Gone Fishin', 1981
pp. 110–111: Stephen Petronio, Eva Karczag, Diane Madden, Vicky Shick, Lisa Kraus, Randy Warshaw. Photograph by Johan Elbers.
pp. 114–115: Lisa Kraus, Eva Karczag, Stephen Petronio, Vicky Shick, Diane Madden, Randy Warshaw. Photograph by Nathaniel Tileston.

Set and Reset, 1983
pp. 116–117: Iréne Hultman, Eva Karczag, Vicky Shick. Photograph by Beatriz Schiller.
pp. 118–119: Trisha Brown, Wil Swanson. Photograph by Mark Hanauer.
pp. 120–121: Carolyn Lucas, Trisha Brown, Wil Swanson. Photograph by Mark Hanauer.
pp. 122–123: Trish Oesterling, Trisha Brown, Wil Swanson. Photograph by Mark Hanauer.
pp. 128–129: Trish Oesterling, Carolyn Lucas, David Thomson, Gregory Lara. Photograph by Mark Hanauer.

Lateral Pass, 1985
pp. 130–131: Vicky Shick, Randy Warshaw, Diane Madden, Lance Gries. Photograph by Babette Mangolte.
pp. 136–137: Randy Warshaw, Vicky Shick. Photograph by Johan Elbers.
pp. 138–139: Lance Gries, Shelly Sabina Senter, Jeffrey Axelrod, Iréne Hultman. Photograph by Luciano Romano.

Newark (Niweweorce), 1987
pp. 142–143: Diane Madden, Lance Gries. Photograph by Tristan Valès/Agence Enguerand, Paris.
pp. 144–145: Lance Gries, Diane Madden, Jeffrey Axelrod. Photograph by Tristan Valès/Agence Enguerand, Paris.
pp. 150–151: Lance Gries, Diane Madden. Photograph by Tristan Valès/Agence Enguerand, Paris.

Astral Convertible, 1989
pp. 152–153: Carolyn Lucas, Shelly Sabina Senter, Lisa Schmidt. Photograph by Tristan Valès/Agence Enguerand, Paris.
pp. 154–155: Lisa Schmidt, Gregory Lara, Shelly Sabina Senter, Carolyn Lucas, Nicole Juralewicz, David Thomson. Photograph by Agnès Courrault/Agence Enguerand, Paris.
pp. 156–157: Top left: David Thompson, Wil Swanson, Diane Madden, Lisa Schmidt, Shelly Sabina Senter, Carolyn Lucas, Nicole Juralewicz. Photograph by Vincent Pereira. Top right: Photograph by Vincent Pereira. Bottom left: Shelly Sabina Senter, Lance Gries, Gregory Lara. Photograph by Tristan Valès/Agence Enguerand, Paris. Bottom right: Lance Gries, Diane Madden, Wil Swanson. Photograph by Johan Elbers.
pp. 158–159: Diane Madden, Lance Gries, Gregory Lara. Photograph by Vincent Pereira.

Astral Converted 55, 1991
pp. 160–161: Unknown, Diane Madden. Photograph *Christian Science Monitor*.

Foray Forêt, 1990
pp. 162–163: Lisa Schmidt, Diane Madden, Wil Swanson, Lance Gries, Shelly Sabina Senter, Nicole Juralewicz, Gregory Lara, David Thomson. Photograph by Christian Ganet.
pp. 164–165: Top left: Lisa Schmidt, David Thomson, Nicole Juralewicz, Wil Swanson, Shelly Sabina Senter, Gregory Lara, Lance Gries, Diane Madden. Photograph by Will Shively. Top right: Wil Swanson, Lance Gries, Diane Madden. Photograph by Will Shively. Bottom left: Gregory Lara, Lisa Schmidt, Diane Madden, Lance Gries. Photograph by Laurent Philippe. Bottom right: Trisha Brown and members of La Lyre Provençale. Photograph by Elian Bachini.
pp. 166–167: Trisha Brown. Photograph by Christian Ganet.

For M.G.: The Movie, 1991
pp. 168–169: Nicole Juralewicz, Wil Swanson, Gregory Lara, Kevin Kortan. Photograph by Johan Elbers.
p. 171. Top: Liz Carpenter, Wil Swanson, Kevin Kortan, Nicole Juralewicz. Photograph by Michael O'Neill. Bottom: Wil Swanson, Liz Carpenter, David Thompson, Nicole Juralewicz.
pp. 172–173: Trish Oesterling, Lisa Schmidt. Photograph by Tristan Valès/Agence Enguerand, Paris.

One Story as in Falling, 1992
pp. 174–175: Dominique Bagouet Dance Company: Hélène Cathala, Fabrice Ramalingom, Sylvain Prunenec, Dominique Jegou, Matthieu Doze, Juan Manuel Vicente; with Wil Swanson and Gregory Lara from the Trisha Brown Dance Company. Photograph by Tristan Valès/Agence Enguerand, Paris.
pp. 176–177: Dominique Bagouet Dance Company. Photograph by Roland Aeschlimann.

Another Story as in Falling, 1993
pp. 178–179: Unknown, Kelly McDonald, Wil Swanson, unknown, Carolyn Lucas, Kevin Kortan. Photograph by Roland Aeschlimann.

Yet Another Story, 1994
pp. 180–181: Gregory Lara, Diane Madden. Photograph by Roland Aeschlimann.

Long and Dream, 1994
pp. 182–183: All: Trisha Brown, Steve Paxton. Photographs by Joanne Savio.

If you couldn't see me, 1994
pp. 184–185: Trisha Brown. Photograph by Tristan Valès/Agence Enguerand, Paris.
p. 187: Trisha Brown. Photograph by Joanne Savio.

You can see us, 1995/1996
pp. 188–189: Trisha Brown, Bill T. Jones. Photograph by Marc Ginot.
pp. 190–191: Mikhail Baryshnikov, Trisha Brown. Photograph by Joanne Savio.

M.O., 1995
pp. 192–193: Kevin Kortan, Diane Madden, Stanford Makishi, Gena Rho, Kathleen Fisher, Keith Thompson. Photograph by Patrick De Spiegelaere.
pp. 194–195: Kathleen Fisher, Stanford Makishi, Diane Madden, Kevin Kortan. Photograph by Patrick De Spiegelaere.

Twelve Ton Rose, 1996
pp. 196–197: Keith A. Thompson, Diane Madden, Kathleen Fisher, Gena Rho, Stanford Makishi, Abigail Yager. Photograph by Tom Brazil.
pp. 198–199: Diane Madden, Wil Swanson, Stanford Makishi, Ming-Lung Yang, Gena Rho. Photograph by Tom Brazil.

Accumulation with talking plus repertory, 1997
pp. 200–201: Top left: From *Newark (Niweweorce)* (1987), Lance Gries, Diane Madden. Photograph by Tristan Valès/Agence Enguerand, Paris. Top right: From *For M.G.: The Movie* (1991), Nicole Juralewicz, Kevin Kortan, Gregory Lara. Photograph by Michael O'Neill. Bottom left: From *Set and Reset* (1983), Gregory Lara, David Thomson, Carolyn Lucas, Diane Madden, Wil Swanson. Photograph by Mark Hanauer. Bottom right: From *Astral Converted 55* (1991), Lance Gries, Diane Madden, Wil Swanson. Photograph Ph. Coqueux/Specto.

For Merce, 1997
pp. 202–203: Trisha Brown.

Canto/Pianto, 1997
pp. 204–205: Stacy Matthew Spence, Ming-Lung Yang, Keith A. Thompson, Katrina Thompson, Stanford Makishi, Brandi Norton. Photograph by Marcus Lieberenz.

L'Orfeo, 1998
pp. 206–207: Carlo Vicenzo Allemano with chorus and dancers. Photograph by Andre-Paul Jacques.
pp. 208–209: Stanford Makishi, Kathleen Fisher, Simon Keenlyside, Stacy Matthew Spence, Abigail Yager. Photograph by Andre-Paul Jacques.
pp. 210–211: John Bowen, Diane Madden. Photograph by Andre-Paul Jacques.
pp. 212–213: Juanita Lascarro, Simon Keenlyside. Photograph by Andre-Paul Jacques.

El Trilogy, 1999–2000
Five Part Weather Invention, 1999
pp. 216–217: Brandi Norton, Mariah Maloney, Abigail Yager, Katrina Thompson, Todd Lawrence Stone. Photograph by Joanne Savio.
pp. 220–221: Photograph by Joanne Savio.
pp. 222–223: Photograph by Joanne Savio.
pp. 224–225: Abigail Yager, Stacy Matthew Spence, Katrina Thompson, Kathleen Fisher, Todd Lawrence Stone, Mariah Maloney. Photograph by Joanne Savio.

Interlude 1 (Rage), 2000
pp. 226–227: Diane Madden. Photographs by Joanne Savio.

Rapture to Leon James, 2000
p. 215: Katrina Thompson. Photograph by Joanne Savio.
pp. 228–229: Katrina Thompson, Todd Lawrence Stone, Brandi Norton, Seth Parker, Keith A. Thompson, Kathleen Fisher, Mariah Maloney, Stacy Matthew Spence, Abigail Yager. Photograph by Joanne Savio.
pp. 230–231: Kathleen Fisher, Abigail Yager, Todd Lawrence Stone, Stacy Matthew Spence, Keith A. Thompson, Mariah Maloney, Katrina Thompson, Brandi Norton. Photograph by Joanne Savio.
pp. 232–233: Katrina Thompson, Seth Parker. Photograph by Joanne Savio.

Interlude 2 (Ladder), 2000
pp. 234–235: Diane Madden. Photographs by Joanne Savio.

Groove and Countermove, 2000
pp. 236–237: Kathleen Fisher. Photograph by Joanne Savio.
pp. 238–239: Kathleen Fisher, Keith A. Thompson, Todd Lawrence Stone, Abigail Yager, Stacy Matthew Spence, Mariah Maloney. Photograph by Joanne Savio.
pp. 244–245: Lionel Popkin, Kathleen Fisher. Photograph by Joanne Savio.

Luci mie traditrici, 2001
pp. 246–247: Annette Stricker, Lawrence Zazzo. Photograph by Johan Jacobs.

DANCERS

Listed alphabetically; dates indicate period of activity. An asterisk (*) indicates the individual listed was either a guest of the Trisha Brown Dance Company or performed in a work or works by Trisha Brown prior to the founding of her company in 1970.

Jeffrey Axelrod, 1986–87
Jared Bark,* 1970, 1974
James Barth,* 1974
Mikhail Baryshnikov,* 1996
Carmen Beuchat, 1970–74
David Bradshaw,* 1968
Liz Carpenter, 1991–94
Steve Carpenter,* 1968
Jean Churchill,* 1976
Walter de Maria,* 1964
Barbara Dilley,* 1968, 1971, 1973
Ben Dolphin,* 1970
Douglas Dunn,* 1971, 1973, 1974
Kathleen Fisher, 1992–2001
Simone Forti,* 1961, 1968
Mark Gabor, 1971
Elizabeth Garren, 1975–79
Tina Girouard,* 1973
Caroline Goodden, 1970–74
David Gordon,* 1973
Nancy Green,* 1973
Lance Gries, 1985–91
Sandra Grinberg, 2000–
Susan Harris,* 1973
Alex Hay,* 1964
Iréne Hultman, 1983–87
Bill T. Jones,* 1995
Nicole Juralewicz, 1988–95
Eva Karczag, 1979–84
Kevin Kortan, 1990–95
Lisa Kraus, 1976–82
Gregory Lara, 1987–93
Daniel Lepkoff,* 1979
Dick Levine,* 1961
Carolyn Lucas, 1984– (Assistant
    to the Choreographer, 1996–)
Nina Lundborg, 1977–79
Diane Madden, 1980–
Stanford Makishi, 1992–99
Mariah Maloney, 1995–
Kelly McDonald, 1992–95
Elsi Miranda,* 1973
Emmett Murray,* 1973
Richard Nonas,* 1970

Brandi Norton, 1997–
Patsy Norvell,* 1970
Trish Oesterling, 1990–93
Terry O'Reilly,* 1976, 1979
Sylvia Palacios [Whitman],
    1971–74
Seth Parker, 1999–
Steve Paxton,* 1963, 1964, 1971,
    1976, 1994, 1996
Penelope [Newcomb], 1972–73
Wendy Perron, 1975–79
Stephen Petronio, 1979–86
Eve Poling,* 1973
Peter Poole,* 1968
Lionel Popkin, 2000–
Judith Ragir, 1975–77
Yvonne Rainer,* 1963
Robert Rauschenberg,* 1964
Melvin Reichler,* 1968
Gena Rho, 1994–98
Elie Roman,* 1968
Sarah Rudner,* 1973
Joseph Schlichter,* 1964,
    1968, 1970
Lisa Schmidt, 1985–92
Lincoln Scott,* 1970
Nanette Seivert,* 1973
Shelley Sabina Senter, 1986–90
Valda Setterfield,* 1973
Vicky Shick, 1980–85
Stacy Matthew Spence, 1997–
Todd Lawrence Stone, 1998–
Michelle Stowell,* 1968
Mona Sulzman, 1975–79
Wil Swanson, 1988–97
Gail Swerling,* 1973
Kei Takei,* 1970
Katrina Thompson, 1998–
Keith A. Thompson, 1992–2001
Liz Thompson,* 1973
David Thomson, 1987–93
Randy Warshaw, 1980–86
Abigail Yager, 1995–
Ming-Lung Yang, 1992–99

OTHER WORK

Unless otherwise noted, works listed are dance performances. Full information (site of performance, date, participants, and so on) is provided whenever possible.

BURT BARR

The Elevator, 1985 (video).
Trisha and Carmen, 1988 (video).
Aeros, 1990 (video).
Focus II, 2001 (video).

YOKO ONO

Works by Yoko Ono, Carnegie Recital Hall, New York, November 24, 1961 (performance). Performance by Ono, with Ay-O, George Brecht, Philip Corner, Jackson Mac Low, Jonas Mekas, Yvonne Rainer, La Monte Young, Charlotte Moorman, and Patricia [Trisha] Brown.

STEVE PAXTON

Proxy, The Once Festival, Ann Arbor, February 27, 1962. Organized by the Once Group. Performed by Trisha Brown, Lucinda Childs, and Robert Rauschenberg.
Section of a New Unfinished Work (1965) and *Augmented* (1966), Judson Dance Theater, A Dance Concert of Old and New Works, Judson Memorial Church, New York, January 10–12, 1966. Performed, variously, by Trisha Brown, Alex Hay, Deborah Hay, Steve Paxton, and Robert Rauschenberg, depending on the night of performance.

YVONNE RAINER

Satie for Two, Maidman Playhouse, New York, March 5, 1962.
Dance for 3 People and 6 Arms, Master Theater, New York, April 1962.
We Shall Run, Judson Memorial Church, New York, January 29, 1963.

Terrain, Judson Memorial Church, New York, April 28–29, 1963. Set and costumes by Rainer. Lighting by Robert Rauschenberg. Performed by Trisha Brown, William Davis, Judith Dunn, Steve Paxton, Rainer, and Albert Reid.

ROBERT RAUSCHENBERG

Spring Training, First New York Theater Rally, Dance Concert II, held at former CBS studio, Broadway and 81st Street, New York, May 11–13, 1965. Performed by Trisha Brown, Viola Farber, Deborah Hay, Barbara Dilley, Steve Paxton, Christopher Rauschenberg, and Robert Rauschenberg. Subsequent performances at Once Again Festival, Maynard Street Parking Structure, University of Michigan, Ann Arbor, September 18, 1965; and Milwaukee Art Center, September 22, 1965, both performed by Trisha Brown, Lucinda Childs, Alex Hay, Deborah Hay, Steve Paxton, and Robert Rauschenberg.
Map Room II, Expanded Cinema Festival [originally titled New Cinema Festival I], Film Makers' Cinematheque, Forty-first Street Theater, New York, December 1–3 and 16–18, 1965. Performed by Trisha Brown, Alex Hay, Deborah Hay, Steve Paxton, and Robert Rauschenberg. Subsequent performances at Five Choreographers in Three Dance Concerts, Rollerdome, Culver City, California, April 13, 1966.
Canoe, 1966 (film), with Trisha Brown, Lucinda Childs, Alex Hay, Deborah Hay, Barbara Dilley, Yvonne Rainer, and Elaine Sturtevant.

LINA WERTMÜLLER

Carmen, by Georges Bizet, directed by Wertmüller, Teatro di San Carlo, Naples, December 10–30, 1986. Brown choreographed and

performed the role of La Bruja (Maga, Sorceress), and her company performed with the Ballet of the Teatro di San Carlo.

ROBERT WHITMAN

Mouth, 1961 (Happening), with Trisha Brown, Simone Forti, and others (unknown).
Flower, 1963 (Happening), with Trisha Brown, Simone Forti, and others (unknown).

CHOREOGRAPHIES BY TRISHA
BROWN IN THE REPERTORIES OF
OTHER DANCE COMPANIES

Astral Converted, Opéra National de Lyon

Duetude, New England Dinosaur Dance Theater (defunct)

Glacial Decoy, White Oak Dance Project

Homemade, White Oak Dance Project

Newark (Niweweorce), Opéra National de Lyon

One Story as in Falling, Dominique Bagouet Company, Montpellier, France (defunct)

Opal Loop/Cloud Installation #72503, Ballet Rampert, London

SELECTED VIDEOGRAPHY/FILMOGRAPHY

Accumulation with talking plus Watermotor. 12 min. Directed by Jonathan Demme. Produced for *Alive from Off Center.* Coproduced by KCET–TV, KTCA–TV, Trisha Brown Dance Company, Inc., and UCLA. 1986. Videocassette.

Aeros. 28 min. Directed by Burt Barr. Produced by Susan Fait and the Trisha Brown Dance Company, Inc. Coproduced by La Sept. 1990. New Television, Episode 110 (1991). Videocassette.

Aeros. 32 min. Directed by Burt Barr. Produced in association with WGBH–TV Boston. Release of a 1990 television production. New York: DuArt Film and Video, 1999. Videocassette.

Beyond the Mainstream. 59 min. Dance in America Series. New York: WNET; Chicago: Films Incorporated, 1980. Videocassette.

Conversations with Contemporary Masters of American Modern Dance: Trisha Brown and Robert Wilson. Produced by Susan Dowling (draft footage for the New Television Workshop, 1990–93). American Dance Festival Video, 1996. Videocassette.

Dancing on the Edge. Includes *Opal Loop, Watermotor for Dancer and Camera,* and *Locus/Altered.* c. 29 min. Produced by Susan Dowling. Coproduced by WGBY, Springfield, Mass., and New Television Workshop. 1980. Videocassette.

For M.G.: The Movie. 35 min. New York: Video D Studios, 1993. Videocassette.

Foray Fôret (1990). 33 min. New York: Video D Studios, 1993. Videocassette.

Glacial Decoy. 20 min. New York: Video D Studios, 1993. Videocassette.

Grand Union. 110 min. Videotaped in performance on 5 October 1975 at the Tyrone Guthrie Theatre, Minneapolis. Minneapolis: Walker Art Center. Videocassettes (2).

Guggenheim Museum Bilbao: Robert Rauschenberg, The Art of Performance. 43 min. New York: Solomon R. Guggenheim Museum, 1997. Videocassette.

"If you couldn't see me" and "M.O." 68 min. New York: Video D Studios, 1995. Videocassette.

Group Shoot: Trisha Brown, Robert Rauschenberg, Alex Hay. 82 min. The Bennington Judson Project. Bennington, Vt.: Bennington College, 1981. Videocassettes (2).

Just Dancing Around? Trisha Brown. Ovation TV, Alexandria, Va. Broadcast November 2001.

Lament. 9 min. Trisha Brown. Minneapolis: Walker Art Center, 1985. Videocassette.

The Language of Dance: Deciphering the Code Words. 29 min. Recorded on 30 April 1990 at the studios of WNYC-TV, New York. Directed by Richard Sheridan. Produced by Celia Ipiotis and Jeff Bush. Produced by ARC Videodance for *Eye on Dance* Episode 304. Videocassette.

Lateral Pass. Video of performance at Walker Art Center. Set designed by Nancy Graves. 1985.

Line Up. 39 min. New York: Video D Studios, n.d. Videocassette.

Line Up. 14 min. Recorded on 7 May 1979 at Minnesota Zoological Garden. Directed by Helm. Executive production by the Walker Art Center Production Company.

Looking at Dance: Modern Dance, Jazz Music, and American Culture with Ann Daly, Richard Powell, and Gerry Myers. 74 min. American Dance Festival seminar. Recorded 2 July 2000 at Nelson Music Room, Duke University, Durham, N.C., 2000. Videocassettes (2).

L'Orfeo. 120 min. Videotaped on 12 December 1999 in performance at Brooklyn Academy of Music Opera House, New York. Produced by La Monnaie/De Munt in coproduction with Festival d'Aix-en-Provence, Trisha Brown Dance Company, Inc., and kunstenFESTIVALdes-Arts. 1999. Videocassettes (2).

Making Dances: Seven Postmodern Choreographers. 89 min. Directed and produced by Michael Blackwood. Northvale, N.J.: Michael Blackwood Productions, 1980. Videocassette.

The Man Who Envied Women. 125 min. Directed by Yvonne Rainer. New York: Zeitgeist Films, 1985. Videocassette.

Newark (1987). 32 min. New York: Video D Studios, 1990. Videocassette.

"Newark," "Accumulation with talking plus Watermotor," and "Group Primary Accumulation." 46 min. In French. New York: Video D Studios, 1987. Videocassette.

Rally for Disarmament 1982. 195 min. Program of speeches and performances advocating nuclear disarmament; Trisha Brown was a speaker. 1982. Videocassettes (4).

Robert Rauschenberg: Inventive Genius. 57 min. Directed, written, and produced by Karen Thomas. *American Masters* series. New York: Fox Lorber Associates, 1999. Videocassette.

Set and Reset. 4 min. Trisha Brown Dance Company, Inc. Walker Art Center Archive, 1979.

Set and Reset. Version 1. 21 min. Directed and produced by Susan Dowling. Coproduced by New Television Workshop, WGBH, and Trisha Brown Dance Company. 1985. New York: Video D Studios, 1985. Videocassette.

Solos, Duets, and Pizza. 38 min. Compilation includes *Watermotor for Dancer and Camera* (1980). Produced by Susan Dowling. WGBH Educational Foundation, 1984. Broadcast as an *Alive From Off Center* episode. Videocassette.

Theme and Variations. 13 min. July 1975 Recorded at American Dance Festival, Connecticut College, New London, Connecticut. 1975. Videocassette.

Trisha and Carmen. 13 min. Directed by Burt Barr. Produced in association with New Television (New Television, Episode 407 [1988]). New York: Electronic Arts Intermix, 1987. Videocassette.

Trisha Brown at 25: PostModern, and Beyond. 65 min. Trisha Brown. 1996. Videocassette (2).

Trisha Brown Co. at the Whitney Museum: The Rehearsal (1971). 8.5 min. Walter Gutman. New York: ARC Videodance, 1990. Videocassette.

Trisha Brown Dance Company with Dave Douglas in Performance at the American Dance Festival June 29, 30, and 31, 2000. 82 min. 2000. Videocassettes (2).

Trisha Brown Dance Company. 46 min. Directed by Jean-François Jung. Coproduction of F.R.3, La Sept, and Toulouse Television Project. New York: Video D Studios, 1987. Videocassette.

Trisha Brown Dance Company: Five Part Weather Invention. Vienna Festival and Im Puls Tanz Wiener Staatsoper, Wiener Burgtheater, Wiener Volkstheater, Sofiensäle, Emballagenhalle, WUK. 2000.

Trisha Brown. 125 min. Recorded in performance in November 1974 at the Walker Arts Center Auditorium, Minneapolis. Minneapolis: Walker Arts Center, 1974. Videocassette (2).

Trisha Brown: American Dance Festival. 35 min. Outdoor performances of *Spiral, Structured Pieces*, and *Floor of the Forest* on 18 July 1975 at the American Dance Festival, Connecticut College, New London, Connecticut. New London: Connecticut College, 1975. Videocassette.

Trisha Brown: Conversations with Contemporary Masters of American Modern Dance. 66 min. Charles Reinhart, interviewer; recorded 2 July 1993. Produced and directed by Douglas Rosenberg. Executive producers Charles and Stephanie Reinhart. From the American Dance Festival Video series *Speaking of Dance.* [Durham, NC]: American Dance Festival Video, 1996. Videocassette.

Trisha Brown: Mixed Program. Documentary Video. 2001. Videocassette.

Watermotor. 8 min. New York: Rochester University, 1978. Videocassette.

Watermotor for Dancer and Camera. Camera and editing by Peter Campus. Produced by Susan Dowling for *Dancing on the Edge.* Coproduced by WGBY, Springfield, Mass., and New Television Workshop. 1980. Videocassette.

SELECTED BIBLIOGRAPHY

BOOKS

Banes, Sally. *Terpischore in Sneakers*. Boston: Houghton Mifflin, 1980; Middletown, Conn.: Wesleyan University Press, 1987.

———. *Democracy's Body: Judson Dance Theater, 1962–1964*. Ann Arbor: UMI Research Press, 1983; Durham, N.C.: Duke University Press, 1993.

———. *Writing Dancing in the Age of Postmodernism*. Middletown, Conn.: Wesleyan University Press, 1994.

Blue, Nora. "Changing the Dancer's Image: Rainer, Brown, and Paxton." Master's thesis, American University, 1980. Ann Arbor, Mich.: University Microfilms International, 1983.

Brown, Trisha. "Collaboration: Life and Death in the Aesthetic Zone." In *Robert Rauschenberg: A Retrospective*, edited by Walter Hopps and Susan Davidson, 268–74. New York: Solomon R. Guggenheim Museum, 1999.

Brunel, Lise, Guy Delahaye, and Babette Mangolte. *Trisha Brown*. Paris: Editions Bougé, 1987.

Bruni, Ciro. *Danse et pensée, une autre scéne pour la danse*. Sammeron, France: GERMS, 1993.

Cage, John. *Silence*. Middletown, Conn.: Wesleyan University Press, 1961.

Crémézi, Sylvie. *La signature de la danse contemporaine*. Paris: Editions Chiron, 1997.

———. *Writing in the Dark, Dancing in "The New Yorker."* New York: Farrar, Strauss and Giroux, 2000.

Foster, Susan Leigh. *Reading Dancing: Bodies and Subjects in Contemporary American Dance*. Berkeley and Los Angeles: University of California Press, 1986.

Goldberg, Marianne. "Reconstructing Trisha Brown: Dances and Performance Pieces 1960–1975." Ph.D. diss., New York University, New York, 1990.

———. "Trisha Brown." In *Fifty Contemporary Choreographers*, edited by Martha Bremser and Deborah Jowitt, 37–42. London: Routledge, 1999.

Goldberg, Roselee. *Performance: Live Art Since 1960*. New York: Harry N. Abrams, 1998.

Huxley, Mike, and Noel Witts, eds. *The Twentieth Century Performance Reader*. London: Routledge, 1996.

Johnston, Jill. *Marmalade Me*. Expanded edition with introduction by Deborah Jowitt and afterword by Sally Banes. Hanover, N.H.: University Press of New England, 1998.

Jowitt, Deborah. *Dance Beat: Selected Views and Reviews 1967–1976*. New York: M. Dekker, 1977.

———. *The Dance in Mind: Profiles and Reviews 1976–83*. Boston: David R. Godine, 1985.

Kaplan, Peggy Jarrell. *Portraits of Choreographers*. With texts by Jean-Marc Adolphe, Marianne Goldberg, and Chantal Pontbriand. New York: Ronald Feldman Fine Arts; Paris: Editions Bougé, 1988.

Kirby, Michael R., ed. *The New Theater: Performance Documentation*. New York: New York University Press, 1974.

Kraft, Susan. "Alternative virtuosity in postmodern dance: The Proscenium and the Gymnasium." Ph.D. diss., New York University, New York, 1989.

Livet, Anne. *Contemporary Dance*. New York: Abbeville Press, 1978.

Louppe, Laurence. *Trisha Brown rend lisible la musique in "Rendre lisible."* Alés, France: Cratère Théâtre, 1998.

———. *Poétique de la danse contemporaine*. 2d edition. Brussels: Contredanse, 2000.

Louppe, Laurence, ed. *Traces of Dance: Drawings and Notations of Choreographers*. Translated by Brian Holmes and Peter Carrier. Paris: Editions Dis Voir, 1994.

McDonagh, Don. *The Rise and Fall of Modern Dance*. New York: New American Library, 1970.

———. "Trisha Brown." In *The Complete Guide to Modern Dance*, 343–47. Garden City, N.Y.: Doubleday, 1976.

Michel, Marcelle, and Isabelle Ginot. *La danse au XXe siécle*. [Paris]: Bordas, 1995.

Novack, Cynthia Jean. *Sharing the Dance: Contact Improvisation and American Culture*. Madison: University of Wisconsin Press, 1990.

Numerals 1924–1977. Text by Reiner F. Crone. Exhibition circulated by Independent Curators Incorporated. New York: Leo Castelli Gallery, 1978.

Ormond, Mark. *Robert Rauschenberg: Works from the Salvage Series*. Sarasota, Fla.: Ringling Museum of Art, 1985.

Post-Modern Dance: Trisha Brown, Lucinda Childs, Molly Davies, Douglas Dunn, Simone Forti, Andrew de Groat, Yvonne Rainer, Bob Wilson. Paris: Avant-scène, 1980.

Rainer, Yvonne. *Work 1961–73*. Halifax: Press of the Nova Scotia College of Art and Design; New York: New York University Press, 1974.

Scarpetta, Guy. *L'Impureté*. Paris: B. Grasset, 1985.

Siegel, Marcia B. *Watching the Dance Go By*. Boston: Houghton Mifflin, 1977.

———. *The Shapes of Change: Images of American Dance*. Boston: Houghton Mifflin, 1979.

Steinman, Louise. *The Knowing Body: Elements of Contemporary Performance & Dance*. Boston: Shambhala, 1986.

Trisha Brown: Danse, précis de liberté. Exposition du 20 juillet au 27 septembre 1998, Centre de la Vieille Charité, Marseille. Marseille and Paris: Musées de Marseille and Réunion des musées nationaux, 1998.

Vergine, Lea. *Body Art and Performance: The Body as Language*. Milan and New York: Skira Editore, 2000; distributed in North America and Latin America by Abbeville.

JOURNALS AND NEWSPAPERS

Acocella, Joan Ross. "Trisha Brown Dance Company." Review of performance at City Center Theater, New York. *Dance Magazine* 62, no. 1 (1988): 22–23.

———. "A Modern Education: The Joy of Taking Smaller Leaps." Review of performance at Yale Repertory Theatre, New Haven, Conn. *The New Yorker*, May 1999, 104–6.

Adair, Deborah. "Rebellion Against Stereotypes." *Dance Theatre Journal*, 13, no. 2 (autumn/winter 1996): 50–51.

Allen, Robertson. "We Owe It All to Isadora." *Times* (London), 17 January 1998.

Aloff, Mindy. "Trisha Brown Dance Company." Review of performance at Brooklyn Academy of Music, New York. *Dance Magazine* 56, no. 3 (1982): 32–33.

———. "Trisha Brown Dance Company." Review of performance at Brooklyn Academy of Music, New York. *The Nation*, 26 November 1983, 547–48.

Anderson, Jack. "Trisha Brown Transforms *Newark* from a Homonym to a Stage Work." *New York Times*, 14 September 1987.

———. "Trisha Brown Dance Company." Review of performance at City Center Theater, New York. *New York Times*, 17 September 1987.

———. "Trisha Brown Dance Company." Review of performance at City Center Theater, New York. *New York Times*, 17 March 1989.

———. "Creating Theatrical Worlds for Dancers to Inhabit: Robert Rauschenberg and Donald Judd's Stage Design for Trisha Brown's Choreography." *New York Times*, 26 March 1989.

———. "Trisha Brown Dance Company." Review of performance at City Center Theater, New York. *New York Times*, 30 April 1993.

———. "Meredith Monk, Trisha Brown." Review of performance at P.S. 122, New York. *New York Times*, 5 June 1994.

———. "Trisha Brown to Receive Scripps Dance Award." *New York Times*, 6 June 1994.

———. "Trisha Brown Receives $25,000 and Dances." *New York Times*, 21 June 1994.

———. "Islands of Light, of Ghosts, and of the Mind." *New York Times*, 25 December 1994.

———. "American Newsletter, 1935–1996." *Dancing Times*, no. 1035 (1996): 251–55.

———. "Trisha Brown Dance Company." Review of performance at Page Auditorium, Duke University, Durham, N.C. *New York Times*, 28 June 1997.

———. "What Touches the Heart Can Puzzle the Mind." *New York Times*, 10 August 1997.

———. "With Coughs Punctuating the Artful Disorder." Review. *New York Times*, 1 July 2000.

———. "Thinking Aloud About Movement: All the Rest is Talk." Review. *New York Times*, 9 February 2001.

Anderson, Jack, and George E. Dorris. "New York Newsletter: A Busy, Rewarding Month." *Dancing Times*, no. 1006 (1994): 983–85.

"BAM 1996 Next Wave Festival." *New York*, 7 October 1996, S1–10.

Banes, Sally. "Gravity and Levity: Up and Down with Trisha Brown." *Dance Magazine* 53, no. 3 (1978): 59–63.

———. "Feminism and American Postmodern Dance." *Ballett International–Tanz aktuell* (English ed.), June 1996, 34–41.

Berman, Avis. "Nancy Graves' New Age of Bronze." *ARTnews* 85, no. 9 (1986): 56.

Bernard, Holland. "Opera Made Whole with Dance." Review of performance of *L'Orfeo*, Brooklyn Academy of Music, New York. *New York Times*, 12 June 1999.

Bodensteiner, Kirsten. "At Lisner, Highly Charged 'Attractors.'" *Washington Post*, 5 February 2001, Special edition.

Bonis, Bernadette, and Jacky Pailley. "Bande annonce: Avant-premières." *Danser*, no. 194 (2000): 36–37.

Bourdon, David. "Living in the Moment of the Next Move." *New York Times*, 8 September 1996.

Boxberger, Edith. "The Energy of Silence." *Ballett International–Tanz aktuell* (English ed.), November 1994, 30–31.

Broili, Susan. "American Dance Festival." Review of performances at Page Auditorium and Reynolds Industries Theatre, Duke University, Durham, N.C. *Dance Magazine* 71, no. 11 (1997): 96–97.

Bromberg, Craig. "The Words to Say It." *Dance Ink* 5, no. 2 (1994): 14–16.

"Brown, Trisha." *Current Biography* 58, no. 4 (1997): 12–15.

Brown, Trisha. "Three Pieces." *TDR/The Drama Review* 13, no. 1 (March 1975): 26–27.

Brown, Trisha, interviewed by Marianne Goldberg: "All of the Person's Person Arriving." *TDR/The Drama Review*, 30, no. 1 (spring 1986): 149–70.

———, interviewed by Allen Robertson. "Step Bach to the Future." *Times* (London), 16 May 1996.

———, interviewed by Sophie Constanti. "The 360-Degree Dancer." *The Independent*, 17 May 1996.

Brown, Trisha, and Douglas Dunn. "Dialogue: Trisha Brown [and] Douglas Dunn on Dance." *Performing Arts Journal* 1, no. 2 (1976): 76–83.

Brown, Trisha, and Yvonne Rainer. "A Conversation about *Glacial Decoy*." *October* 10 (fall 1979): 29–50.

Brunel, Lise. "Un certain regard: Trisha Brown." *Saisons de la danse* (Paris), no. 258 (1994): 8–9.

———. "Libres propos avec Trisha." *Saisons de la danse* (Paris), no. 261 (1994): 41–42.

Cash, Debra. "The New Wave in Modern Dance: Three Women Dancers and Choreographic Talent." *Saturday Review* 9 (March 1982): 34–36.

Clarke, Marika, and Paul Ben-Itzak. "Brown Solos on NEA Panel." *Dance Magazine* 71, no. 11 (1997): 31.

Constanti, Sophie. "Trisha Brown Dance Company." *Dancing Times*, no. 1030 (1996): 961–63.

Croce, Arlene. "Dancing: Brooklyn Academy of Music." Review of performance of *Set and Reset* at Brooklyn Academy of Music, New York. *The New Yorker*, 14 November 1983, 185–86.

———. "Dancing: Performances at City Center." *The New Yorker*, 14 November 1989, 108.

Cunningham, Francis. "Trisha Brown." Review of performance at Jacob's Pillow Dance Festival, Lee, Mass. *Dance Magazine* 54, no. 12 (1980): 44.

Cuperman, Pedro. "A Conversation with Trisha Brown." *Point of Contact*, Fall/Winter 2001, 32.

Daly, Ann. "Dancing: A Letter from New York City." *TDR/The Drama Review* 42, no. 1 (spring 1998): 15–23.

———. "From Living Treasures, Coins of Artistic Wisdom." *New York Times*, 26 August 2001.

"*Dance Magazine* Awards 1987." Dance Magazine 61, no. 2 (1987): 44–46.

"*Dance Magazine* Names Five Award Winners: Merrill Ashley, Trisha Brown, Liz Thompson, David White, Doris Hering." *New York Times*, 20 January 1987.

Davis, Peter G. "*Luci mie traditrici*." Review of performance at LaGuardia Drama Theater, New York. *New York*, 30 July 2001, 51–52.

Diamonstein, Barbaralee. "Guiding Lights: Women in the Arts." *Ladies' Home Journal*, June 1980, S16–17.

Diénis, Jean-Claude. "Pleins feux: La tournée des festivals." *Danser*, no. 124 (1994): 34–39.

Dohse, Chris. "Presstime News: Dance Critics Take in Lincoln Center Sights." *Dance Magazine* 75, no. 6 (2001): 40–42.

Dunning, Jennifer. "A Rauschenberg Set to Upstage the Dancers." *New York Times*, 14 March 1989.

———. "Trisha Brown Dance Company." Review of performance at City Center Theater, New York. *New York Times*, 8 March 1991.

———. "Trisha Brown Dance Company." Review of performance at Damrosch Park, New York. *New York Times*, 17 August 1992.

———. "Trisha Brown Dance Company." Review of performance at City Center Theater, New York. *New York Times*, 6 May 1993.

———. "Trisha Brown Dance Company." Review of performance at City Center Theater, New York. *New York Times*, 10 May 1993.

———. "*Twelve Ton Rose*." Review of performance at Brooklyn Academy of Music, New York. *New York Times*, 5 October 1996.

———. "Real Wind Breezes in to Bolster Its Image: Three Artists Unite for a Premiere at Jacob's Pillow." Review of performance at Jacob's Pillow Dance Festival, Becket, Mass. *New York Times*, 13 July 1999.

———. "Interpreting Jazz for Ears, Eyes, and Feet." Review of performance of *El Trilogy*, LaGuardia Concert Hall, New York. *New York Times*, 20 July 2001.

Eigo, Jim. "Trisha Brown and Robert Rauschenberg." *Dance Ink* 5, no. 1 (1994): 22–25.

Felciano, Rita. "Trisha Brown." *Dance Now* 5, no. 1 (1996): 7–11.

"Festivals: Montpellier." Reviews of performances at the 1995 Festival International Montpellier Danse. *Saisons de la danse*, no. 272 (1995): 18–21.

Fichter, Nancy Smith. "Oh Dear, What Can the (Subject) Matter Be?" *Arts Education Policy Review* 97, no. 5 (1996): 2–7.

Fleming, Bruce. Review of Performance in Washington, D.C. *Ballet Review* 28, no. 2 (2000): 10–13.

Garafola, Lynn. "Jacob's Pillow: A Sampler." *Ballet Review* 23, no. 4 (1995): 74–80.

Gladstone, Valerie. "Filling the Stage with Her Inventions: Choreographer Trisha Brown Discusses Her Work." *New York Times*, 30 April 2000.

Goldberg, Marianne. "Trisha Brown's Accumulations." *Dance Theatre Journal* (London) 9, no. 2 (1991).

Goldberg, Roselee. "Space as Praxis." *Studio International* 190, no. 977 (1975): 130–35.

Goldman, Phyllis. "Trisha Brown Dance Company." Review of performance at City Center Theater, New York. *Back Stage* 34, no. 20 (1993): 28.

———. *"M.O."* Review of performance at Lincoln Center, New York. Back Stage 36, no. 34 (1995): 44.

———. Trisha Brown Dance Company. *Back Stage* 42, no. 37 (2001): 61.

Goldner, Nancy. "Next Wave Festival." Review of performance at Brooklyn Academy of Music, New York. *Saturday Review* 10 (February 1984): 42–44.

Gomez Paris, Edward M. "Dance: Guy Darmet Thinks Big." *Time* (International ed.), 8 October 1990.

Gradinger, Malve. "Ein optischer Genuss: Europa-Premiere von Trisha Brown *El Trilogy* in Luzern." *Ballett-Journal/Das Tanzarchiv* 48, no. 5 (2000): 26.

Gran, Annette. "Misha and Trisha, Talking Dance: The Dancer and the Choreographer Compare Notes on Their Lives and Work." *New York Times*, 8 August 1999.

———. "Trisha and Mischa." *Ballett International–Tanz aktuell* (English ed.), May 2000, 22–27.

Greskovic, Robert. "Noodle Doodle at Lincoln Center." Review. *Wall Street Journal*, 14 September 2001.

Gruen, John. "Stephen Petronio: Mixing It Up." *Dance Magazine* 68, no. 6 (1994): 44.

Hardy, Camille. "Pushing Postmodernist Art into Orbit: Trisha Brown." *Dance Magazine* 59, no. 3 (1985): 62–66.

———. *"Lateral Pass." Dance Magazine* 59, no. 9 (1985): 14.

———. "Trisha Brown Dance Company." Review of performance at City Center Theater, New York. *Dance Magazine* 63, no. 7 (1989): 54.

———. "Formula for Success: New York's Joyce Theater." *The World and I*, February 1995.

———. "It's One Mo' Time for Serious Fun." *Dance Magazine* 69, no. 7 (1995): 28.

———. "Serious Fun!: Trisha Brown Dance Company." Review of performance at Alice Tully Hall, New York. *Dance Magazine* 69, no. 11 (1995): 98–99.

Harris, Dale. "Trisha Brown." Review of performance at City Center Theater, New York. *Wall Street Journal*, 28 March 1989.

———. "Trisha Brown." Review of performance in New York. *Wall Street Journal*, 10 August 1995. Harris, William. "A Season of Dreams: Thirty Creative Artists Tell What They Would Like to See in the New Arts Season of Their Dreams." *New York Time*s, 11 September 1994.

———. "Trisha Brown Takes Up the Challenge of Bach." *New York Times*, 16 July 1995.

Hering, Doris. "Trisha Brown Dance Company." Review of performance at City Center Theater, New York. *Dance Magazine* 65, no. 7 (1991): 68–69.

———. *"L'Orfeo."* Review. *Dance Magazine* 73, no. 9 (1999): 89–90.

———. "Modern Risk Grows Sturdy Oak." Review of performance at Brooklyn Academy of Music, New York. *Dance Magazine* 74, no. 10 (2000): 89–90.

Howe-Beck, Linde. "Festival international de la nouvelle danse." Review of performance in Montreal. *Dance Magazine* 61, no. 1 (1986): 24–26.

Howell, John. "Trisha Brown." Review of performance at City Center Theater, New York. *Artforum* 26, no. 3 (1987): 136.

———. "Trisha Brown." Review of performance at World Financial Center, New York. *Artforum* 28, no. 3 (1989): 153–54.

Huynh, Emanuelle. "Face à dos: Entretien avec Trisha Brown." *Nouvelles de danse*, no. 23 (1995): 5–12.

Ingalls, Zoe. "Breathtaking, Gravity-Defying Movement: Trisha Brown Dance Company Performs Founder–Artistic Director's Latest Work." *The Chronicle of Higher Education*, 37, no. 43 (10 July 1991): B32.

Jackson, George. "Brown's Form and Function." Review of performance of *El Trilogy. Dance Magazine* 74, no. 5 (2000): 82–83.

Jacobs, Laura A. "Trisha Brown Dance Company." Review of performance at City Center Theater, New York. *The New Leader*, 7 October 1987, 22.

Jefferson, Margo. "Trisha Brown." Review of performance at Alice Tully Hall, New York. *New York Times*, 30 July 1995.

———. "Bowing to the Then but Enhancing It with the Now." *New York Times*, 29 May 2000.

Jennings, Bernadine. "Serious Fun!" *Attitude* 11, no. 3 (1995): 61.

Johnson, Robert. "Taking Fun Seriously." *Ballet Review* 24, no. 1 (1996): 78–85.

Jordan, Stephanie. "Trisha Brown Dance Company." Review of performance at Sadler's Wells, London. *New Statesman*, 20 November 1987, 24–25.

Jowitt, Deborah. "New Spectacles Needed? Or New Eyes?" *Arts-canada* 38, no. 1 (1981): 15–20.

———. "Twist the Opal—What Color Now?" *The Village Voice*, 4–10 November 1981.

———. "Trisha and France: A Love Story." *Dance Magazine* 64, no. 9 (1990): 42–45.

———. "Trisha Brown: Stepping out with Anton Webern." *Dance Magazine* 70, no. 10 (1996): 58–62.

———. "Was von der Mode der 70er Jahre geblieben ist." *Tanz Affiche* (Vienna) 10, no. 78 (1998): 24–26.

Kaufman, Sarah. "Trisha Brown: From Air to Earthbound." *Washington Post*, 19 February 2000, Style section.

Kendall, Elizabeth. "Private Dancer." *Vogue*, September 1985, 128.

———. "Trisha Brown Comes Down to Earth." *Dance Ink* 2, no. 1 (April 1991): 17–22.

———. "Reality Check." *Harper's Bazaar*, May 1993, 58.

———. "Presstime News: Trisha Brown—And All That Jazz." *Dance Magazine* 74, no. 2 (2000): 58–60.

Kertess, Klaus. "Dancing with Carmen." *Art in America* 75, no. 5 (April 1987): 180–85.

———. "Space Travel with Trisha Brown/Raumfahrten mit Trisha Brown," *Parkett* 21 (June 1989): 118–20/121–26.

Kisselgoff, Anna. *"Newark."* Review of performance at City Center Theater, New York. *New York Times*, 16 September 1987.

———. *"Astral Convertible."* Review of performance at City Center Theater, New York. *New York Times*, 16 March 1989.

———. "Trisha Brown Dance Company." Review of performance at American Dance Festival, Page Auditorium, Durham, N.C. *New York Times*, 7 July 1990.

———. "Trisha Brown Dance Company." Review of performance at Theatre National Populaire, Villeurbanne, France. *New York Times*, 27 September 1990.

———. "Trisha Brown Dance Company." Review of performance at City Center Theater, New York. *New York Times*, 3 March 1991.

———. "Trisha Brown Dance Company." Review of performance at City Center Theater, New York. *New York Times*, 9 March 1991.

———. "Trisha Brown Dance Company." Review of performance at City Center Theater, New York. *New York Times*, 13 March 1991.

———. "Trisha Brown Dance Company." Review of performance at City Center Theater, New York. *New York Times*, 29 April 1993.

———. *"Astral Converted."* Review of performance at City Center Theater, New York. *New York Times*, 3 May 1993.

———. "Trisha Brown Dance Company." Review of performance at Joyce Theater, New York. *New York Times*, 5 May 1994.

———. "Trisha Brown Dance Company." Review of performance at Alice Tully Hall, New York. *New York Times*, 21 July 1995.

———. *"Opal Loop."* Review of performance at Brooklyn Academy of Music, New York. *New York Times*, 3 October 1996.

———. "Trisha Brown." Review of performance at Brooklyn Academy of Music, New York. *New York Times*, 8 October 1996.

———. "A Simple Downtown Look." Review of performance of *L'Orfeo* at Brooklyn Academy of Music, New York. *New York Times*, 12 June 1999.

———. "Blithe on the Surface, Cerebral Deep Down." Review of performance at Joyce Theater, New York. *New York Times*, 4 May 2000.

———. "It Takes Two to Jitterbug, Sometimes More." Review of performance at Joyce Theater, New York. *New York Times*, 11 May 2000.

Klooss, Helma. "Reviews, International: Springdance." Review of performance at Winkel Van Sinkel Utrecht, the Netherlands. *Dance Magazine* 73, no. 8 (1999): 87–88.

Kortan, Kevin. "Running and Standing Still: Diane Madden." *Contact Quarterly* 20, no. 2 (1995): 27–32.

Kotz, Liz. "Talk of the Nation." *Women's Review of Books*, 1 July 1998.

Lewis, Jim. "Souvenirs of Creation: Profile on Artist Robert Rauschenberg." *Harper's Bazaar*, September 1997, 454–58.

Lipfert, David. "Two Grand Dames of Modern Dance." *Attitude* 14, no. 3 (1999): 24–25.

Lissner, Stéphane. "J'aime les metteurs en scène de réflexion." *Danser*, no. 168 (1998): 35–36.

Louppe, Laurence, et al. "Dossier: Écrire sur la danse." *Nouvelles de danse*, no. 23 (1995): 14–54.

Mangolte, Babette. "A Portfolio of Photographs of Trisha Brown." *October* 10 (fall 1979): 51–70.

Maskey, Jacqueline. "The Next Wave: New Masters." Review of performance at Brooklyn Academy of Music, New York. *High Fidelity* 32 (February 1982): 11–12.

———. "Trisha Brown Dance Company." Review of performance at Brooklyn Academy of Music, New York. *High Fidelity* 34 (February 1984): 12.

———. Trisha Brown: "Uptown at Last: Her City Center Season Features a Somewhat Grand *Lateral Pass*." *High Fidelity* 36 (January 1986): 6–7.

———. "Trisha Brown and Company." Review of performance at City Center Theater, New York. *Musical America* 108, no. 1 (1988): 9–10.

——— . "*Astral Convertible*." Review of performance at City Center Theater, New York. *Musical America* 109, no. 5 (1989): 18–19.

Mazo, Joseph H. "Dancing on the Rooftops." *Horizon* 28 (September 1985): 22–24.

Merrill, Bruce. "Theatre de la Ville." Review of performance at Theatre de la Ville, Paris. *Dance Magazine* 62, no. 5 (1988): 31–32.

Mitchell, Emily. "Made in America: Barbican Center's Festival of American Arts." *Time* (International ed.), 27 July 1998, 50.

Moore, Nancy. Review of performance at 383 West Broadway, New York City. *Dance Magazine* 48, no. 8 (1974): 62.

Morgenroth, Joyce. "Dressing for the Dance." *The Wilson Quarterly* 22, no. 2 (1998): 88–96.

Newman, Barbara. "Another Opening, Another Show: *Monsters of Grace* and *L'Orfeo*." *Dancing Times*, no. 1055 (1998): 1004–5.

Noisette, Philippe. "Quand l'opéra mène la danse: Des chorégraphes dans l'univers du lyrique." *Danser*, no. 168 (1998): 32–37.

Owens, Craig. "The Proscenic Event." *Art in America* 69, no. 10 (December 1981): 128–33.

"A Pair of Daring Leaps into Classical Territory." *New York Times*, 29 August 1999.

Paxton, Steve. "The Grand Union." *TDR/The Drama Review* 16, no. 1 (September 1972): 128–34.

———. "Letter to Trisha." *Contact Quarterly* 20, no. 1 (1995): 94–95.

Perron, Wendy. "Trisha Brown on Tour." *Dancing Times*, no. 1028 (1996): 749–51.

———. "Mischa's New Passion." *Dance Magazine* 74, no. 11 (2000): 54–59.

———. "Paying Heed to the Mysteries of Trisha Brown: Her New Dance *El Trilogy* Takes On Jazz." *New York Times*, 8 July 2001.

———. "The Airborne Dances of Trisha Brown." *Dance Magazine* 76, no. 3 (2002): 53.

Phelan, Peggy. "Portrait of the Artist." *Women's Review of Books*, 1 February 1998.

Phillips, Ian. "Trisha Leads Opera a Merry Dance: Choreographer Trisha Brown Produces *L'Orfeo*." *The Independent*, 1 June 1998.

Pitt, Freda. "Carmen." Review of performance at San Carlo Opera House, Naples, Italy. *Dance Magazine* 61, no. 5 (1987): 99–100.

Poesio, Giannandrea. "*L'Orfeo*." Review of performance at Barbican, London. *Spectator*, 13 June 1998, 49.

Poletti, Silvia. "Presstime News: Dance Mavericks Converge in Bologna." *Dance Magazine* 74, no. 11 (2000): 49–50.

"Presstime News: Stargazing at the World Trade Center." *Dance Magazine* 74, no. 9 (2000): 36–37.

Reardon, Christopher. "Trisha Brown." Review of performance at Joyce Theater, New York. *Christian Science Monitor*, 9 May 1994.

Regitz, Hartmut. "Exploiting the Remains: *Canto/Pianto* by Trisha Brown in Berlin." *Ballett International–Tanz aktuell* (English ed.), November 1998, 51–52.

Robertson, Allen. "Gravity's Rainbow." *Ballet News*, 7, no. 3 (September 1985): 28–30.

Rockwell, John. "Today's Blank Art Explores the Space Behind the Obvious." *New York Times*, 17 July 1977.

Rosenblum, Joshua. "From Around the World: New York City." Review of performance of *White Raven, Luci Mie Traditrici*. *Opera News* 66, no. 4 (2001): 62.

Saal, H. "Three Sisters of the Dance." *Newsweek*, 7 December 1981, 109–10.

Scarpetta, Guy. "Trisha Brown, le mouvement brownien." *Art Press* (Paris), (1979): 34.

Schmidt, Jochen. "Trisha Brown's First Opera: Monteverdi's *L'Orfeo* in Brussels." *Ballett International–Tanz aktuell* (English ed.), July 1998, 49–50.

Segal, Lewis. "Trisha Brown's Solo Highlights Program." *Los Angeles Times*, 5 May 1997.

———. "Dance Review: This Music Gets Her Jazzed." *Los Angeles Times*, 4 February 2002.

Sevilla-Gonzaga, Marylis. "Operawatch." *Opera News* 64, no. 9 (2000): 6.

Siegel, Marcia B. "*Astral Convertible*." Review of performance at City Center Theater, New York. *Christian Science Monitor*, 27 March 1989.

Sims, Caitlin. "Downtown Diva Moves Uptown." *Dance Magazine* 70, no. 4 (1996): 23.

———. "Trisha Brown Directs Opera Orfeo." *Dance Magazine* 72, no. 5 (1998): 34.

Sloat, Susanna. "Trisha Brown Dance Company." *Attitude* 10, no. 1 (1994): 48–49.

Small, Linda. "*Opal Loop—Cloud Installation #72503*." Review of Performance at 55 Crosby Street, New York City. *Dance Magazine* 54, no. 10 (1980): 96.

Smith, Amanda. "Jacob's Pillow Dance Festival." Review of performance at Ted Shawn Theatre, Studio/Theatre, and Inside/Out Stage, Becket, Mass. *Dance Magazine* 68, no. 12 (1994): 96–97.

Smith, Dinitia. "How Creative Artists Court the Muse: Collaboration between Directors and Actors, Choreographers and Dancers, Playwrights and Authors." *New York Times*, 30 June 1996.

Solomons, Gus, Jr. "Randy Warshaw Dance Company." Review of performance at The Kitchen, New York. *Dance Magazine* 65, no. 8 (1991): 63–64.

———. "Trisha Brown Dance Company." Review of performance at Joyce Theater, New York. *Dance Magazine* 68, no. 9 (1994): 84–86

Sommer, Sally R. "Equipment Dances: Trisha Brown" *The Drama Review* 16, no. 1 (September 1972): 135–41.

———. "Trisha Brown Making Dances." *Dance Scope* 11, no. 2 (spring/summer 1977): 7–18.

———. "The Sound of Movement." *Dance Ink* 4, no. 1 (spring 1993): 4–6.

Sterritt, David. "Expanding the Boundaries of Modern Theater." Review of performance at Performing Garage, New York. *Christian Science Monitor*, 19 March 1999.

Stuchman, Phyllis. "It All Works." Review. *Town and Country*, July 2001, 49.

Sulcas, Roslyn. "Trisha Brown Dance Company." Review of performance at Theatre de la Ville, Paris. *Dance Magazine* 66, no. 4 (1992): 84–85.

———. "Festival International Montpellier Danse." Review of performance in Montpellier, France. *Dance Magazine* 66, no. 11 (1992): 107–8.

———. "Trisha Brown Dance Company." Review of performance at Theatre de la Ville, Paris. *Dance Magazine* 69, no. 2 (1995): 108–9.

———. "Trisha Brown: Choreography That Spans Continents and Oceans." *Dance Magazine* 69, no. 4 (1995): 42–48.

———. "Reviews, International: French Summer Festivals." *Dance Magazine* 69, no. 11 (1995).

———. "Reviews: New York." *Dance International* 24, no. 4 (1996–97): 47–50.

———. "Master of Movement Decides to Tell a Story with an Opera: Trisha Brown Directs *L'Orfeo*." *New York Times*, 28 June 1998.

———. "View: Trisha Brown." Review. *Dance Magazine* 74, no. 8 (2000): 68.

Sulzman, Mona. "Choice/Form in Trisha Brown's *Locus*: A View from Inside the Cube." *Dance Chronicle* 2, no. 2 (1978): 117–30.

"Summer Festivals: In Music the Livin' Is Easy." *American Record Guide*, 1 May 2001.

Sweeney, Louise. "Trisha Brown Dance Company." Review of performance at Washington, D.C., Mall. *Christian Science Monitor*, 6 June 1991.

Teachout, Terry. "Opera and Dance: Siblings Too Often Estranged." *New York Times*, 6 June 1999.

Thom, Rose Anne. "33 Reviews, New York City: Trisha Brown Dance Company." Review of performance at Brooklyn Academy of Music, New York. *Dance Magazine* 71, no.1 (1997): 114–15.

T'Jonck, Pieter. "Entretien avec Trisha Brown par Pieter T'Jonck." *Danse et Architecture*, no. 42–43 (Spring 2000): 134–44.

Tobias, Anne. "The Clock Is Ticking." *DanceView* 11, no. 4 (1994): 68–71.

Tobias, Tobi. "I Am a Camera: Trisha Brown's Choreography and Robert Rauschenberg's Artistry." *New York*, 9 November 1981.

———. "Trisha Brown." Review of performance at Brooklyn Academy of Music, New York. *New York*, 7 November 1983, 94.

———. "Trisha Brown's Permanent Revolution." *New York*, 16 September 1985, 80–81.

———. "Second Sight." Review of performance at City Center Theater, New York. *New York*, 7 October 1985, 73.

———. "Off the Beaten Path." Review of performance at City Center Theater, New York. *New York*, 5 October 1987, 104.

———. "*Astral Convertible*." Review of performance at City Center Theater, New York. *New York*, 3 April 1989, 82.

———. "Trisha Brown Dance Company." Review of performance at City Center Theater, New York. *New York*, 8 April 1991, 99–100.

———. "Trisha Brown." Review of performance at City Center Theater, New York. *New York*, 17 May 1993, 88–89.

———. "Razzle-dazzle." Review of performance of *If you couldn't see me* at Joyce Theater, New York. *New York*, 16 May 1994, 100.

———. "Pointless Fun!" Review of performance of *M.O.* at Lincoln Center, New York. *New York*, 14 August 1995, 48–49.

———. "Woman on Top." Review of performance of *Twelve Ton Rose* at Brooklyn Academy of Music, New York. *New York*, 21 October 1996, 80–81.

———. "Don't Look Back." Review. *New York*, 28 June 1999, 140.

———. "White Oak Dance Project." Review of performance in New York. *New York*, 26 June 2000, 151–52.

Trachtman, Paul. "New American Dance Is Making Everyday Movement into Art." *Smithsonian*, December 1985, 86–89.

Trede, Fiona. "Orpheus-Momente." *Tanz Affiche* (Vienna) 11, no. 84 (1998): 39.

Trescott, Jacqueline. "Clinton Nominates Eight for Arts Council." *Washington Post*, 16 March 1994.

"Trisha Brown." *American Theatre* 17, no. 3 (2000): 12.

Ullman West, Martha. "White Oak Dance Project." Review. *Dance Magazine* 73, no. 8 (1999): 84–85.

Vail, June. "Moving Bodies, Moving Souls: Trisha Brown Dance Company in Stockholm, 1989." In *Proceedings of the Society of Dance History Scholars*, compiled by Christena L. Schlundt, 187–99. [Pennington, N.J.]: Society of Dance History Scholars, 1992.

Veroli, Patrizia. "Das Faszinosum des Theatralischen." *Ballett-Journal/Das Tanzarchiv* 45, no. 5 (1997): 10–11.

Verrièle, Philippe. "Châteauvallon." *Saisons de la danse* (Paris), no. 261 (1994): 10–11.

Vreeland, Nancy. "Trisha Brown." Review of performance at City Center Theater, New York. *Dance Magazine* 60, no. 1 (1986): 40–41.

Waleson, Heidi. "*Luci mie traditrici*." Review. *Wall Street Journal*, 24 July 2001.

"Watching Europe and the Theater." *New York Times*, 12 September 1999.

Weber, Bruce. "Dance Theory: Trisha Brown, Works in Progress." *New York Times Magazine*, 12 March 1989, 110.

Wesemann, Arnd. "Body-Politics: Postmodernism and Political Correctness." *Ballett International–Tanz aktuell* (English ed.), August / September 1995, 44–47.

White, Jack E. "The Beauty of Black Art." *Time*, 10 October 1994, 66–73.

Zimmer, Elizabeth. "Trisha Brown Dance Company." Review of performance at Brooklyn Academy of Music, New York. *Dance Magazine* 58, no. 1 (1984): 20–21.

INDEX

GENEVE
113 - La Rade et le Jet d'Eau (120 m.)

This is a dance!
(if I say it is)

Hommage to Rauschenberg's
Portrait of
Love, Earle

↘ ↓ ↓ ↓
Reproduction interdite

(choreography
(follows: fotography)

Trisha Brown

39 West 71st Street

New York 23,

N.Y.

U.S.A.

PAR AVION